Experiments in Economics

Uncertainty and Expectations in Economics

Series Editors: J. L. Ford, John D. Hey and Mark Machina

Experiments in Economics

John D. Hey

BLACKWELL
Oxford UK & Cambridge USA

Copyright © John D. Hey 1991

First published 1991

Basil Blackwell Ltd
108 Cowley Road, Oxford, OX4 1JF, UK

Basil Blackwell, Inc.
3 Cambridge Center
Cambridge, Massachusetts 02142, USA

British Library Cataloguing in Publication Data

A CIP catalogue record for this book is available from the British Library.

Library of Congress Cataloging in Publication Data

Hey, John Denis.
  Experiments in economics / John D. Hey.
     p.   cm. -- (Uncertainty and expectations in economics)
  Includes bibliographical references and index.
  ISBN 0-631-17989-5
  1. Economics.   2. Uncertainty.   3. Rational expectations (Economic
theory)   4. Negotiation in business.   5. Decision-making.
I. Title.   II. Series.
HB171.5.H457   1991
330–dc20   91-7762   CIP
Typeset in 10 on 12 pt Times
by Times Graphics, Singapore
Printed and Bound in Great Britain by
Hartnolls Limited, Bodmin, Cornwall.

To Rebecca

Contents

Preface

Experimental economics is growing fast in the United States and Britain, and is beginning to take off in Europe and elsewhere. The journal literature on experimental economics is also growing fast, and in reputable places, and there are a number of edited collections of key contributions to the literature (edited by Vernon Smith, one of the pioneers of the subject, amongst others). Soon there will be a *Handbook of Experimental Economics*, currently being edited by John Kagel and Al Roth, two prominent experimentalists. But there is as yet no textbook on experimental economics. This book fills this gap. It is aimed at three groups: the advanced undergraduate, perhaps doing a specialist course in experimental economics; the postgraduate, possibly preparing to do some experimental work as part of his thesis work; and the general economist who wishes to learn something about this important and rapidly growing discipline. The technical level is relatively modest, though it does assume some familiarity with economic theory, with elementary econometrics and with basic economic methodology. It is intended to give an overview of what has already been done and to prepare the reader, if he or she so desires, to do some experimental work themselves. To this end, I would be happy to share my experimental software with other economists or to point them towards other experimentalists who might have more appropriate software and other experimental tools.

As I hope becomes apparent from reading this book, I find experimental economics a most stimulating subject: it combines theory, econometrics, data analysis, program design, programming – and dealing with people. Other experimentalists also seem a happy bunch, and I find great pleasure in mixing with them. Particularly pleasurable is mixing it with Graham Loomes, Co-Director with me of EXEC, the Centre for Experimental Economics at the University of York. Unfortunately, he cannot be blamed for the contents of this book, but he can be blamed for making experiments so exciting over the years. My thanks also, without attached blame, to David Ansic, Michele Bernasconi and Norman Spivey, Research Fellows at EXEC, and Alastair Fischer, of the Australian Centre for Experimental Economics.

I would also like particularly to thank my indefatigable secretary, Jo Hall, who, despite her allergy to modern technology, has gracefully and politely converted my pencilled scrawl into an elegant typescript. This book marks my return to pencil and paper after dabbling unsuccessfully with modern technology – which speaks volumes for the law of comparative advantage.

Finally, my thanks to my wife with whom I've conducted the most exciting experiment of all – having children. This book is dedicated to the product of the third experiment of this type – our darling daughter, Rebecca.

John D. Hey

Acknowledgements

I would like to acknowledge the vital contribution of the Economic and Social Research Council to the running of many of the experiments described in this book and to their support – both financial and moral – for EXEC, the Centre for Experimental Economics at the University of York, co-directed by Graham Loomes and myself. Especial thanks are given to the Nuffield Foundation for the award of a Nuffield Social Science Fellowship during the academic year 1989–90 which released me from my usual duties and enabled me to concentrate on my experimental activities throughout that year. I would also like to acknowledge the financial support of the Leverhulme Trust, which helped to finance the consumption experiments in chapter 8, and the support – both financial, through the Innovation and Research Priming Fund of the University, and moral – of the University of York. It provides an excellent climate in which to conduct experimental economics.

1

Introduction

The casual browser could be excused for finding the title of this book ambiguous: on the one hand it suggests that the book is about the use of experiments in economics; on the other hand it suggests that the book is concerned with experiments in the methodology of economics – hinting at a revolution in the making. The latter interpretation might well appeal to those economists who instinctively feel the same about the phrase 'experiments in economics' as they do about the phrase 'snow in summer' or 'democracy in dictatorships'. Many economists have been brought up to think of economics as a non-experimental subject; the study of econometrics only serves to buttress this belief.

For those economists who believe that economic theory is important, but that it should be subjected to empirical test, there are two main ways to obtain the data that are needed for such tests. The conventional way in economics is to lie in bed and hope that someone else will collect the data for you. The alternative way is to collect it yourself. The latter way can be done in an uncontrolled or a controlled manner. The second of these is the experimental way.

This experimental way constitutes, of course, the prevailing methodology in many of the hard sciences; physics, chemistry and biology all consistently use the experimental approach. For such sciences, experimental tests of theories are crucially important: only by subjecting a theory to test under the same controlled conditions as those under which the theory itself was generated can a theory be properly tested. The same logic should apply also in economics, especially if economists continue to borrow other aspects of the methodology of the hard sciences. And this they do *par excellence* – certainly the mainstream neoclassical core of the profession, which provides well over 90 per cent of the intellectual weight. Note particularly the same use of well-defined and well-structured theories: just like the hard scientist, the economist starts with certain well-defined assumptions (the *ceteris paribus* conditions) and derives some (hopefully well-defined) predictions/ conclusions. In the hard sciences, these predictions/conclusions would be experimentally investigated under the same *ceteris paribus* conditions. Not so in conventional non-experimental economics. In contrast, data which were

1

generated under conditions 'close' to those of the theory are sought by the applied economist, who, recognizing that 'close' is not the same as 'identical', adds in a stochastic error term to the theory. Thus the art of econometrics is born.

The applied econometrician then puts some structure on the stochastic error term appended to the theory, thereby specifying what he or she thinks is meant by 'close'. But note well that the ultimate econometric test is a combined test of the original theory and of the stochastic assumptions made to represent 'closeness'; it is a combined test of whether the theory is correct under the *ceteris paribus* conditions and whether the theory survives the transition from the world of the theory to the (hopefully 'close') real world – the world in which the data were gathered. This combined test may well be unsatisfactory, as it is not clear what can be inferred from it.

Nevertheless, non-experimental econometric tests of theories continue to dominate economics. Many economists are brainwashed, often from birth, to the effect that economics is a non-experimental subject, and that it is impossible to control the generation of economic data in the same way as the experimental hard sciences control the generation of data.

The purpose of this book is to demonstrate that this is not true: that it is indeed possible to generate economic data under controlled conditions, and that by so doing economists are better able to understand existing theories and develop new ones. I hope to convince the reader, by argument and by example, that experimental methods in economics are an excellent way of generating data of a better quality (and possibly of a lower cost) than the data that are currently available; at the very least, experimental methods provide an alternative way of obtaining alternative data. This can only be for the good.

I am tempted to make the bold claim that one can test *any* economic theory experimentally, but I shall settle for the lesser claim that one can test *many* economic theories experimentally. This book bears witness to that – with examples ranging from individual decision-making under risk, through consumption and search theories and models of auctions and bargaining, to theories with a number of interactive asset markets. From a methodological point of view, what is common to all of these is the precise reproduction, in the economic 'laboratory',[1] of the conditions of the theory. With neoclassical theories, with their well-defined structure and well-defined 'rules of the game', this is usually straightforward, though it is less so with non-neoclassical theories such as evolutionary theories. Indeed, neoclassical economics is particularly well adapted to experimentation as there is always a well-defined objective function for each economic agent in the theory; this provides the ideal motivational device for the subjects.[2]

Of course, it is the subjects of experimental investigation – human beings – that distinguish economic (and psychological) experiments from those in, say, physics and chemistry, where the 'subjects of investigation' are inanimate objects. This does require appropriate motivation, and careful thought. However, to a neoclassical economist the answer is simple: one pays the subjects in money, the amounts being determined by the attained values of the theory's objective function. All one now needs to decide is the appropriate scale.

Such methodological concerns and practical details are the concerns of part I of this book. Chapter 2 looks at the methodological arguments underlying non-experimental and experimental approaches in economics, and argues that experiments are not only possible but methodologically desirable. The practical details are examined in chapter 3; there I try to give a practical guide about how experiments should be carried out – the intention being to enable you, the reader, to carry out your own experiments and to avoid the kind of mistakes that might render your results meaningless and useless. I give guidance at various levels – ranging from the running of a simple one-off manual experiment to the setting-up of a networked computerized experimental laboratory for use in a whole series of experiments. Many experiments, including market experiments, can very successfully and instructively[3] be run 'by hand', though certain experiments lend themselves very naturally to being computerized. I discuss the advantages and disadvantages in chapter 3, as well as giving some more practical guidance on relative costs. Much, as you will see, depends on what kinds of experiments are being contemplated.

The rest of the book gives examples and partial surveys of experiments carried out in various areas of economics; the different parts look at different areas. Part II begins 'at the bottom', if you like, by examining various theories of individual decision-making under risk and a number of experimental investigations of such theories. This is an extremely active area of current research, with work extending back to that of the Nobel Prize winner Maurice Allais in the 1950s. His experiments were concerned with what was then (and is still so today, though to an increasingly lesser extent) the prevailing paradigm in that area: subjective expected utility theory (SEUT). His early experiments cast doubt on that theory. Since then his experiments have been replicated and extended by numerous other experimentalists, repeatedly confirming the weakness of SEUT in certain respects under certain conditions. In true scientific tradition, such evidence has led to the creation of a number of new theories that are alternatives to and generalizations of SEUT. These, in turn, have been subjected to experimental test; the process is ongoing. Chapter 4 describes the various theories and discusses how they might be empirically distinguished from each other. Chapter 5 gives an example of an extremely simple experiment which I ran recently to try to discover which theories my experimental evidence supports. A broad survey of other experimental studies addressed to similar issues is contained in chapter 6.

Economic theories 'in the middle ground' are the concern of part III: here I discuss experiments which have taken specific economic theories of individual decision-making (*not* general theories of decision-making) off the shelf and subjected them to experimental investigation. This is a relatively neglected area, but one which I think should and will become less neglected in the future. My own research work has been concentrated in this area, which explains partly why I give it more weight than other experimentalists might; a further explanation and justification is given in chapter 15. I give two main examples (search and consumption) and some subsidiary ones (the competitive firm and expectations formation). Search is the concern of chapter 7; this is an area of economics which has been in vogue recently, with numerous applications. It is relatively straightforward to test experimentally, with interesting conclusions about actual behaviour compared with optimal. Chapter 8 looks at an experimental test of the life-cycle model of optimal consumption under income uncertainty. This is an informative example in that it shows how an apparently untestable theory (you cannot keep subjects in the laboratory for the whole of their life cycle!) can be reproduced exactly in the laboratory, by appropriately changing the interpretation of the model. Chapter 9 looks at a number of other studies of individual economic behaviour under risk.

Economic theories 'towards the top' are the concern of part IV. Here I look at theories which involve (strategic or non-strategic) interaction between a number of economic agents. Chapters 10 and 11 look at games and bargaining; chapters 12 and 13 look at auctions and markets. These are areas in which an immense amount of experimental work has been done. Whilst some of it has been theory-testing, much has been motivated rather differently. On the one hand, many experiments on markets have been designed to investigate situations where theory sheds relatively little light – a good example being the convergence properties of markets under different market organizations. Here the experiments are theory-suggesting. In contrast, some other experiments, particularly those on games and bargaining, have been designed to investigate situations where theory sheds so much light that one is blinded by it – a good example being the multiple Nash equilibria in randomly repeated Prisoner's Dilemmas.

Finally, part V provides, in chapter 14, an overview of experiments that fall outside the taxonomy of parts II, III and IV and, in chapter 15, a rather personal view of what the future might bring. I make various suggestions as to what will happen and what should happen and about the role of experimental work in the future development of economics. I have great confidence that experimental work can contribute constructively and positively to the development of the subject. I hope that this book will inspire others to join in this experimental revolution, so that on the second interpretation of the title of this book it will be a success.

Notes

1 I fear that experimental economics has inherited this rather unfortunate word from the hard sciences – it incorrectly conjures up visions of bubbling test tubes and flickering cathode ray tubes. In practice, the economic 'laboratory' may be an ordinary classroom, a networked computer room or just the world at large.
2 This is another term inherited from another discipline – in this case psychology. Again its use is rather unfortunate – I would prefer something like participants – but I fear that it is now part of the experimental folklore.
3 Experiments are additionally very useful as a teaching tool.

Part I

Methodological Issues

2

Experimental and Non-experimental Methods in Economics

Economic theory, through a formal deductive system, provides the basis for experimental abstraction and the experimental design, but society in most cases carries out the experiment, possibly using its own design . . . . The nonexperimental restriction . . . means that . . . one must . . . use nonsample information . . . . Thus, much of econometrics is concerned with how to . . . use this nonsample information in conjunction with the sample observations.

Judge et al., *The Theory and Practice of Econometrics*, p. 4

2.1   Introduction

To the majority of economists, economics is a non-experimental subject. This view is reinforced by econometricians who typically begin courses in econometric theory with a statement to that effect. Indeed, the allegedly non-experimental nature of economics is usually blamed for many of the contortions indulged in by econometricians.

Consider the typical methodology adopted (in theory if not always in practice) by economists. First, an area of study is defined and delineated, second, a set of assumptions concerning the 'rules of the game' and the objective functions of the players is proposed; third, a set of conclusions is deduced from these assumptions, usually using mathematical logic. This much is the content of economic theory.

The theory may then be subjected to empirical test. This is where the difficulties begin, since the theory was developed in an abstracted world, while the data – if of the conventional form – were collected in the real world. Indeed, the data are usually collected by someone else, often for some quite different purpose. Thus a gap exists between the world of the theory and the world of the data used to test that theory: in economists' jargon, in the world of the theory, *ceteris* is assumed to be *paribus*, but in the real world this is quite clearly not the case; in the world of the theory, the economic theorist holds constant those things that he wants held constant, but in the real world this is usually not the case (at least with non-experimental data).

This gap, between the world of the theory and the world of the data, is usually bridged by the incorporation into the theory of some additional

7

stochastic variables, which represent the additional impact on the dependent variables of those factors that were assumed to be constant in the world of the theory but were not in fact constant in the world of the data. The inclusion of these stochastic variables also brings into the story the econometric theorists, who are experts at exploring the implications of various stories about these stochastic variables for tests of the underlying economic theory. But note what happens at the end of the day: this type of conventional econometric test of some economic theory is not a test of that theory *per se*, but a combined test of that theory *and* some assumptions about the nature of these additional stochastic variables. (Note that these stochastic variables are typically not part of the original economic theory but an *ad hoc* appendage, though this is occasionally not the case.)

Consider then the implications of such a test: typically, one concludes either that 'the theory' and the data are consistent or that they are not; that is, that 'the theory' survives the test or it does not. But recall that 'the theory' being tested is a combination of the original economic theory and some assumptions about the nature of the additional stochastic variables. So, if 'the theory' survives the test, it could be because *both* the original economic theory *and* the asumptions about the stochastic variables are correct, or because *both* the original economic theory *and* the assumptions are incorrect. There is no way of telling which. Similarly, if 'the theory' does not survive the test, there is no way of telling whether this is because the economic theory is correct and the stochastic assumptions incorrect, or because the economic theory is incorrect and the stochastic assumptions correct, or because both are incorrect. Hence, a conventional econometric test of some economic theory is not really a test of that theory at all.

It is clear that the insistence that economics is a non-experimental science (like astronomy) and the implicit corollary that the best way to obtain data is to lie in bed and hope that someone else will collect them for you is fraught with problems. Perhaps it is all part of a plot to keep the sacred art of econometrics revered by the profession. If so, it is a very dangerous plot. Imagine the same arguments being invoked in the natural sciences. Quite rightly, such arguments would be dismissed as arrant nonsense in the physical sciences: how would chemists, physicists, biologists and the like have made the great inroads that they have over the centuries without the use of controlled experiments? The methodology of experiments is central to these disciplines: it enables the scientist carefully to test alternative theories, to control for extraneous factors and to isolate the key determinants of scientific processes. Indeed, it is probably the case that precisely the opposite argument to that used by economists underlies the currently accepted scientific methodology: if a theory has *not* been tested under controlled conditions, then its validity or otherwise is considered as indeterminate by the scientific community.

I see little reason why any area within economics cannot and should not be subject to experimental investigation. There are, within economics, a plethora of different theories in the various sub-branches of the subject. The onus must surely be on the theorist to subject his or her theories to empirical test and, moreover, to empirical tests that are sufficiently discriminating to allow the relative superiority of competing theories to be evaluated. But this is all too rarely done.

There are reasons and excuses why this is so. The usual excuse is that 'the available data are not sufficiently rich'. Some theorists, at best, present some anecdotal evidence – some broad generalizations, some stylized facts, or, as Partha Dasgupta put it recently, 'some rumours reported by applied economists'.

But this is not good enough: there are important policy issues related to the theoretical problems. Governments, for example, whether passively or actively, necessarily employ some kind of economic policy strategy. We, as economists, are surely concerned that such policy is motivated by the best available theory; and how can we discover that without extensive empirical testing of competing theories?

2.2 An Example

Let me now argue by example. I take as an excellent example of modern economic theorizing the important field of technological progress. Here enormous theoretical upheavals have taken place in recent years. In particular, one can think of all the work done by 'bright young things' on research and development (R&D) and patent races. Here there are lots of exciting applications of the new dynamic game theory.

The hallmark of all this new theory is that it is very well and very tightly specified: the 'rules of the game' are tautly drawn. (This is in marked contrast with so-called evolutionary theories, where – of necessity, I will argue later – the 'rules of the game' are more vaguely drawn.) So, for example, we have patent races where the probability distribution of the time to the discovery of the to-be-patented invention is a well-specified function of the volume of resources devoted to R&D by each of the participants or potential participants in the race. The interest in the theory essentially lies in this specification rather than in the solution to the problem, since it is invariably assumed that the participants or potential participants in the race are amazingly clever at solving complicated dynamic games (in contrast with the poor theorist who has probably struggled for several months in order to derive – and explore the implications of – the optimizing conditions!).

Now let me ask the question: what is the purpose of the theory? To be fair to the theorist, one should answer: it hopefully provides an approximation to a real-life phenomenon. The obvious conclusion then is that it should be subject to empirical investigation. Suppose then that some appropriate real-life data were generated under conditions – a specification, to use the term employed above – different from those of the theory. In the terms I used earlier, familiar to all economists, the *ceteris paribus* of the theory will not be satisfied in the data.

Consider then what is being tested. There are two components, equivalent to the 'original economic theory' and the 'assumptions about the additional stochastic variables' of my earlier discussion:

1 that the theory is correct given the appropriate specification (that is, under the given conditions);
2 that the theory survives the transition from the world of the theory to the real world.

All too often, the theorist (implicitly, as judged by his or her subsequent response) assumes that point 1 is true – usually without discussion. Thus attention focuses on point 2. So, effectively, the theorist is arguing that the theory isolates the essential features of the problem in so far as it relates to the real world: 'OK, the theory is an abstraction – but what is being abstracted away is unessential'.

To most economists, then, whether they would explicitly admit it or not, a test of a theory is not a test of that theory *per se* but a test of whether it survives intact the transition from the world of theory to the real world. But consider the implications of this position. The outcome of the test will be either positive or negative (see my earlier argument). If it is positive, what can one conclude: that the theory is correct? Surely not, for that was taken for granted. That the theory survived the transition? Well maybe, if it was indeed correct to take it for granted that the theory was correct. But how do we know that was so? Perhaps both the theory was wrong and its transition to the real world was imperfect – and conveniently so for the two errors to cancel each other out. And what if the outcome of the test is negative: do we conclude that the theory was wrong or that its transition to the real world was imperfect? Usually the latter; and what is the theorist's response?

Experimental methods enable the economist to separate out the first of the two components discussed above. If the theory survives that test, one can then proceed to the second component. One can therefore separately determine whether the theory is indeed correct under the *ceteris paribus* conditions, and, if it is, whether it survives the transition to the non-*ceteris paribus* world.

So what does the experimental economist do in the context of the patent race example? He or she simply creates the theoretical model in the 'laboratory', under controlled conditions, and observes the outcome. So if the theory is a model of a two-firm race to some patentable discovery under well-specified stochastic conditions, then one simply sets up an experiment in which there are two participants, both of whom have been told that they can spend money (either their own, or some given to them by the experimenter at the start of the experiment or some to be deducted from their eventual payment) which will influence the probability of their being the one to gain a prize of a specified sum of money. They are also told the payoff that they would get if the other participant is the one that gains the prize. (Some patent race models have the loser getting nothing; others allow the loser to get some modest consolation prize.) The precise way in which the instructions are expressed will have to depend, of course, upon the sophistication of the participants, but a form of words can usually be chosen for even the most naive of participants. So, one way or another, the participants are told how the probability of their getting the prize at any specified point in time depends on the amount of money they spend, and on the actions of the other participant.

The participants are then left to get on with the game. At the end, the experimenter pays the participants – giving the winner the prize net of expenses and the loser the consolation prize net of expenses – and the experiment for that particular pair of participants is over. The experimental economist has precisely replicated the theory in the laboratory.

In this particular example, the method is clearly operational: those who are familiar with the two-firm R&D patent race literature will realize that all the necessary ingredients are there: there is a well-defined objective, usually conveniently specified in money terms; well-defined inputs, again usually conveniently specified in money terms; and well-defined relationships between objective and inputs. The only vague parts are in the behavioural responses of the firms/participants – but it is precisely this that the solution to the theory itself specifies. If you like, the theory *is* the behavioural response.

2.3 Objections

While this argument appears perfectly clear to me – and a perfect rationale for the use of experiments in economics – it all too often provokes a negative response along one or other of the following lines.

1   'What you suggest is a pointless exercise as it is obvious what the participants will do: they will behave in accordance with the predictions of the theory; if they do not do so immediately, then they will after a little practice. (OK – I admit that it took me several months to work out the solution myself, but real-life players of the game will employ experts, operations research people, management scientists and the like.)'

2   'What you suggest is valueless since the experiment is so unrealistic; the real world is much more complicated.'

For some reason, argument 1, that such experiments are pointless, is more frequently invoked when one reports on experimental investigations into *firm* behaviour than when one reports on experimental investigations into *household* behaviour: many neoclassicist economists have an almost fanatical faith in the ability of the firm to work out the appropriate optimal strategy, though they may grudgingly admit that the man on the Clapham omnibus may be somewhat less than perfect. The idea that one should empirically investigate whether this is in fact the case, and indeed what behaviour other than perfect optimality might be manifested, seems to such economists a pointless act of blasphemy. However, one occasionally encounters the argument that, although the number of people in the real world who are potential suboptimizers may be very large, they are of relatively little importance since the optimizers dominate the economic scene and the suboptimizers (realizing that they are so!) deliberately ape the optimizers; or, even better, evolutionary forces take care of things, with the suboptimizers dying out precisely because they are suboptimizers! I concede this *may* be true, but surely we need to investigate whether it is?

Argument 2, that such experiments are valueless, is a very bizarre response: if the experiment is too simple, then *a fortiori* the theory is too simple. The solution then surely is to make the theory specification more complex ('more realistic') and then provide an experimental test of the more complex specification. Note that this is always possible with modern neoclassical theories as they are always precisely specified. In contrast, the situation is more difficult with evolutionary theories since their specifications are deliberately vague: it is the very essence of the evolutionary school that their models are incompletely specified. Either the environment is incompletely specified or the agents' objective functions are incompletely specified (or both), for if both of these were completely specified then we would be back in a neoclassical world and we would be obliged to use neoclassical methodology.

In this respect, it is instructive to note that experimental investigations of evolutionary theories are conspicuous by their rarity. The problem here for the experimenter is that the experiment, like the theory, must be set up in an incomplete fashion. So the participants should not be told all the rules of the game, or they should be in some doubt about what the objective is. There are some experiments along these lines – which I term ill-defined experiments in chapter 3 – but they are relatively rare. I do not think that this is a good thing; it probably simply reflects the relative numbers of economists in the neoclassical and evolutionary camps, and the predominance of the neoclassical methodology.

There is, of course, an intermediate position which a few economists have tried to take, with varying degrees of success. The intermediate position might be termed the 'it costs to think' position, or, more colourfully, the 'my brain hurts' position. This position recognizes that the calculation of an optimal strategy, particularly in a complex dynamic decision problem under multivariate uncertainty, might not be trivial or costless as is usually assumed. The difficulty with this position, certainly as far as the neoclassical school is concerned, is that it leaves undefined the central notion of optimality. Some neoclassical economists have tried to incorporate a cost of thinking into their stories, but they are inevitably defeated by the infinite regress problem: 'If thinking were costless I would simply work out my optimal strategy, but as it is not I must first decide what my optimal suboptimal strategy is taking into account the thinking costs, but before I do that I need to decide whether it is worth my working out the optimal suboptimal strategy, but before I do that . . .'.

An additional feature of the 'it costs to think' school is that people differ in their ability to solve decision problems: some people are very good; some people are very bad. In contrast, the neoclassical school assumes that everybody is equally perfect, which seems to contradict the situation in the real world. But if people do differ in their ability to solve decision problems, we need to discover the various suboptimal strategies that are used by less-than-perfect decision-makers. This seems to be an entirely appropriate use of experimental methods in economics.

There are several other main objections that one encounters against the use of experiments in economics. I list some below, in no particular order.

First, 'experiments throw the participants (subjects) into a completely alien environment and give them no chance to learn'. Although this argument runs counter to the prevailing neoclassical methodology (that economic agents always act optimally) it may well have some practical truth in it, and it may have implications for the appropriate experimental methodology. To counter this argument, I have made great efforts (as indeed have other experimental economists) to make the instructions clear and accessible, to distribute them in advance and to give numerous 'help' facilities. Moreover, to investigate the learning arguments, I am increasingly getting subjects to do experiments twice, with several days (and possibly a group discussion) intervening. It is quite clear from such repeated experiments that behaviour does improve with repetition, that the magnitude of the improvement varies from subject to subject and that some subjects would never reach the optimal strategy regardless of the number of repetitions.

Second, 'experiments are artificial: people behave differently in the real world'. One counters this by arguing that, in experiments, the subjects (who are undoubtedly real) are tackling a real problem for real money, that their payment depends on their decisions and that everything about it is real. As the experiment is usually identical with some economic theory, one can further argue that if the experiment is 'artificial' then so must the economic theory be 'artificial', whatever that may be.

Third, 'the subjects are motivated by considerations other than the financial'. This may well be true: they might be trying to confuse the experimenter; they might be looking for somewhere warm to sit for an hour or so; they might be lonely. Just as in 'real life'. One then has to consider the possible strengths of the competing sources of motivation, and, if necessary, adjust upwards the financial motivation. We at EXEC, in common with most experimenters, try to fix our reward schedules so that the average outcome is somewhat higher than the marginal wage rate of the subjects, and the good outcome considerably higher. Nevertheless, at the end of the day we have to admit that we cannot be certain that the subjects were motivated solely in the way we intended. But that is surely also true in the 'real world'?

2.4 Main Areas of Experimental Work

The passage from the econometric text by Judge et al. (1980) that I quoted at the beginning of this chapter summarizes the position nicely: since (neoclassical) economic theory employs a formal deductive system (as in the physical sciences), it 'provides the basis for experimental abstraction' (as in the physical sciences). In principle, therefore, if that is what one wants to do, one can employ experimental techniques to investigate any area of (neoclassical) economics and to test any (neoclassical) economic theory. While much of recent experimental work is indeed along such lines, it is useful to note that much of the early experimental work was along somewhat different lines, with slightly different methodological implications.

Much of this early work was concerned with markets, and in particular with the existence and uniqueness properties of equilibria in certain markets. Let me begin with the former.

Much of the literature of markets is concerned with the existence of equilibrium and not with its attainment. So, for example, a typical body of literature would conclude with a statement that a (price-taking) equilibrium existed and that it had certain properties. That conclusion is of interest, but of only limited interest if the equilibrium is not attained. So a secondary question is whether the equilibrium is attained. However, to answer this question on a theoretical level one needs a theory (a meta-theory if you like) at a higher level than the original theory which demonstrated existence. One could think of the original theory as static and the higher level theory as dynamic, though the correspondence is not perfect. However, to produce such a higher level theory is often extremely difficult; economists turned, instead, to experimental investigations. Of necessity, this changed the rules of the original game, since, for example, not all agents could remain price-takers. The rules of the experimental game differed according to which set of agents were to be endowed with the price-setting role. Interest now settled on the question: did these experimental markets converge to the equilibrium and, if so, were some 'rules of the experimental game' more efficient at so doing than others? Many experimental investigations have revealed that oral double auctions are particularly efficient at attaining the equilibrium.

Such experimental investigations are *not* theory-testing experiments, since no theory exists to say that equilibrium is attained – the extant theory merely says that the equilibrium exists. So the experiments are of a different type to those discussed in earlier sections of this chapter: they are descriptive. Of course, they could become theory-testing experiments if a theory of attainment were to be derived, but not until then.

The early experiments associated with the uniqueness of equilibria were also descriptive. Such experiments are particularly associated with theories which suggest (usually a large number of) multiple equilibria, all equally plausible on theoretical grounds. A good example is the infinitely repeated Prisoner's Dilemma – in which both repeated confession and repeated co-operation (and other strategies) are Nash equilibria. Here, recourse was made to experimental methods to try to determine which of such multiple equilibria were the most likely, or which were more likely than others.

In contrast, experimental investigations of finitely repeated (and random horizon) Prisoner's Dilemmas in the recent past have been more akin to theory-testing experiments. In the case of finitely repeated Dilemmas, the theoretical prediction is clear: the only Nash equilibrium is repeated confession, a finding which is in stark contrast with the experimental evidence. This has led to new refinements in theory and to new experimental tests. In this area most crucially we have seen a Popperian-type strategy operating.

This is also the case with experimental investigations into individual decision-making under risk, an area which I shall be discussing in detail in part II of this book. Early experiments were designed to test the implications of subjective expected utility theory. In the light of the findings from these experiments, new theories have been proposed; these are now themselves the subject of test. Genuine scientific progress is apparently being made.

A third area of experimental work is on economic theories of individual decision-making under risk. This is the concern of part III. Here again, a Popperian strategy is being followed.

2.5 Social Experiments

I must also mention social experiments, although they are not the concern of this book. The most famous of such experiments are the four income-maintenance experiments (designed to investigate the effects on households' labour supply decisions of changes that were being contemplated in the structure of income tax) carried out in the United States during the period 1968–80. In essence, these experiments were designed along the lines of agricultural or biomedical experiments in that a randomly chosen group of households was given the proposed new treatment (the new income tax schedule) while a control group was not. The two groups were then studied to see whether there was any significant difference in the labour supplies of the two groups.

This is a different type of experiment from those considered here. First, this type is a social, or field, experiment which operates 'in real life'. Second, control is exercised only through the allocation of households to the treatment and control groups (though it should be noted that *all* participation was voluntary – which, of necessity, distorts the initial random assignment). Third, at least *ab initio*, the experiments were designed as 'random assignment' experiments, rather than as 'theory-testing' experiments (see Neuberg, 1989). Fourth, participants were clearly aware of the ultimate purpose of the experiment and could therefore be motivated by considerations other than those intended. (For example, if they wanted the new income tax schedule to be implemented permanently, they could act in a 'more favourable' fashion.) Quite clearly, such experiments need different considerations, outwith the scope of this book.

2.6 Conclusions

I have put forward two main arguments in this chapter: first that, as currently practised, economics is ideally suited for experimental investigation; second, that correct methodology requires that such experimental investigation be undertaken. We need to know both that the economic theory works in its own environment and that it survives the transition to the real world. Experimental methods allow us to separate out these two stages. As long as neoclassical economics continues to dominate the mainstream of economics, such methods will prove to be invaluable: since all neoclassical theories are, by definition, well structured, it follows that we can in principle reproduce them in the laboratory and subject them to tests on their own terms.

If neoclassical economics loses its stranglehold, however, then we move into more uncharted territory. We move on to ill-defined experiments. This, I feel, is the way forward. We shall see.

3

Practical Details of Laboratory Experimentation in Economics

3.1 Introduction

In the previous chapter we concentrated on broad methodological issues, verging at times on the abstract. In stark contrast, in this chapter we concentrate on broad practical details, verging at times on the mundane. Nevertheless, this chapter is as important, if not more so, than chapter 2 since the success or otherwise of a particular experiment is heavily dependent on painstaking and careful attention to detail. An experimental investigation of some hypothesis can so easily be ruined by some minor defect of the experimental design or of its implementation; I shall give some examples during this chapter. By following the advice given below (built upon the mistakes of myself and others) you should be able to design and carry out experiments, the results of which should amply repay their cost and effort.

The chapter begins with a description of the capital investment you might need to make before carrying out experiments. The size of this investment depends, of course, on the type and scale of the experiment or experiments that you are planning to do, and so not all this advice applies to all would-be experimenters; nevertheless, all should find some part of it useful. I then discuss the preparations you might need to make for a particular experiment; as before, some bits of this will be more relevant to certain experiments than others, but all will be of use somewhere. The next stage (usually) is the carrying out of a pilot experiment. This is done for a variety of reasons, the main one being to check that the experimental design is appropriate (i.e. it does what you want it to do) and robust (i.e. it survives exposure to experimental subjects). At this stage, you proceed to the actual running of one or more large-scale experiments (the 'large'-ness depending upon the aims of the experiment). I discuss the practical issues below. I then discuss the practicalities of data analysis; this is often a major task since one of the virtues of experimentation is that it generates an enormous amount of data, which needs to be carefully analysed. Then comes the writing up of the experiment, and, hopefully, the publication in some good quality journal. Finally, there is the aftermath, the posing of the question: 'Did the experiment do what we wanted it to do?' By anticipating this question before you start, you can improve the experiment, and hence its significance, immeasurably. That is the main intention of this chapter.

3.2   Preparing to Run Experiments in General

Certain investments are necessary before any experiments are run; the extent of the investment depends, of course, on the type and scale of the experiments being planned. If you are planning to set up a Centre for Experimental Economics which will run a series of experiments over a number of years your needs are obviously different from those relevant to a situation where you are simply planning to run a one-off small-scale experiment. So you must be selective in following the suggestions proffered below. However, one decision that you will have to make at some stage is whether your experiment or experiments will be computer based or not. I turn to that question shortly, after first discussing the requirements of each type.

Computer-based Experiments

Many experiments are ideally suited for computerization; I begin by discussing the various hardware options. I start with experiments run on mainframe computer terminals, which is where I started my first computer-based experiments some years ago. Most universities and polytechnics, and indeed many schools, now have classrooms with upwards of 50 video terminals attached to the institution's mainframe computer. Such rooms could conveniently be used for experiments, though much depends on whether the experimenter can effectively prohibit collusion between subjects when it is not permitted; this, of course, depends upon the spacing between the terminals themselves and their arrangement in the classroom. Such classrooms are often also well designed as far as the organization of an experiment is concerned, with the terminals usually focused on a raised platform from where the experimenter can direct the experiment. Sometimes, the classroom will also have some overhead projection facility which is invaluable for use by the experimenter in instructing the subjects by demonstrating the software to them.

One obvious great advantage of using mainframe terminals for experiments is that the output data from the experiment (the subjects' decisions and other responses) can be recorded directly onto files on the mainframe ready for immediate analysis. Unfortunately, there are offsetting disadvantages: first, one is at the mercy of factors definitely outside one's control, which means, at best, that the response time from the mainframe may be slow and erratic and, at worst, that the experiment has to be terminated because the mainframe has crashed (an all-too-familiar experience!); second, but dependent upon the software available on the mainframe, it may be difficult to write interactive software for use in interactive experiments; and third, the graphics and display facilities on the terminals may be poor – monochrome, for example, with almost non-existent facilities for graphics displays. It should be noted that the mainframe's great advantage – massive computing power – is very rarely of much use in experiments, which instead rely much more on input, output and display (the software for which is much better on personal computers (PCs) than on mainframes) and on passing information around rather than processing it. In this respect, the delays involved with time-sharing mainframe computers (where the time is being shared with other users who are not doing the experiment) often imply unacceptable and erratic delays in the transmission of information between subjects. Finally, it is very difficult to program in real time.

The cheapest alternative is stand-alone PCs, the number being determined by your resources. The vast majority of PCs now in use are IBM compatible; as far as I know all experimental software designed to be run on PCs is written for IBM compatible machines, and I shall confine my remarks to such machines. This is not to deny that other machines (most notably the Apricot and the RM Nimbus) may not be just as good, if not better. But, as ever, there is a software problem . . . .

If your experiments are to be run on stand-alone PCs, I would recommend buying one hard-disk machine (20 Mb or more), preferably an AT (a 286-based machine), and as many simple single-disk machines ($3\frac{1}{2}$ inch or $5\frac{1}{4}$ inch drive according to preference, though the smaller disks are now becoming more popular for obvious reasons) as your budget allows. All, I believe, should be colour and VGA so that you can design experiments that are easy on the subject's eye; there is nothing more tiring for subjects than having to stare at a poor display monochrome screen for an hour or so. You may find it helpful to install both a $3\frac{1}{2}$ inch drive and a $5\frac{1}{4}$ inch drive in the hard-disk machine; this will assist the portability of software. The cost of these machines will vary from make to make, from supplier to supplier and from country to country, and you will certainly gain from shopping around. In the UK at the time of writing this chapter (February 1990) the hard-disk machine as described above, with two floppy drives and a maths co-processor, would cost some £1400 including VAT, the single-drive machines around £500 each. So for £3400 you could have a nice five-machine laboratory.

I recommend one fast (AT) machine with hard disk and maths co-processor so that you have a good machine on which the output data from your experiments can be processed; the machines on which the experiments are to be run can be relatively naive – for reasons already discussed – but the analysis of the data often requires quite massive processing. I shall give examples during the course of the book.

The next step up, and a necessary one if you intend to run interactive experiments and have excluded the use of mainframe terminals, is a PC network. In a sense, this is equivalent to your very own mainframe system with your own computer terminals, although in a PC network there is one powerful machine, the network server, and a number of terminals or workstations, effectively very simple PCs. Again, the number of workstations depends on your resources, but it is crucially important that the server is a fast powerful machine (preferably a 386-based machine) with a fast-access large (150 Mb would not be an extravagance) hard disk. The workstations could be diskless or single drive. Once again, all machines should be colour and VGA, and I would recommend installing a maths co-processor in the server and both $3\frac{1}{2}$ inch and $5\frac{1}{4}$ inch drives. Some network software will be necessary; the cost of this depends partly on the make and the number of machines in the network. I would recommend NOVELL netware, and would advise against economizing on this item of expenditure: the network software controls the communication between the various terminals (subjects), and you do not want the software to fall over (crash, stop working) in the middle of an experiment!

Once again, I would recommend shopping around: considerable savings can be made by doing so. The cost will vary from supplier to supplier etc., so it is difficult to give useful information. Suffice it to say that we at EXEC, the Centre for Experimental Economics at the University of York, recently had a 16-machine + server Elonex network with NOVELL software, along the above specifications, installed for some £22,000. Possibly you get the best deal by buying the whole net in a single package.

Non-computer-based Experiments

Some experiments are better run 'by hand'; I shall discuss the advantages and disadvantages shortly. For non-computer-based experiments, the usual medium is the written or the spoken word, with the former being the most common. Questionnaire-type experiments come into this category. So the 'capital requirements' are relatively few – mainly good quality paper appropriately letter-headed. I shall discuss this shortly.

Computer-based or Non-computer-based?

The decision as to whether to run computer-based experiments or non-computer-based experiments (assuming your capital equipment gives you the choice) depends crucially on the nature of your planned experiment. Some experiments, particularly those involving large numbers of subjects in an anonymous interactive experiment (such as a market experiment, or an oligopoly experiment or a public good experiment) are ideally suited to computer operation: as the subjects are acting individually and anonymously, they can each sit at an individual computer terminal or PC with their decisions co-ordinated by the mainframe or server. Individual experiments, where there is a reasonable amount of computation required between responses of the subjects, are also ideally suited. Computers can do the various calculations much faster than any human experimenter; computers are also very good at producing (controlled) sequences of random numbers and hence at playing out the consequences of risky choices. Of course, the success of this depends on whether the subjects believe that the computer is indeed generating the 'random numbers' randomly; if suspicion creeps in, then the subjects' responses may well be biased. For this reason, it may be preferable to play out risky choices 'by hand' – by letting subjects draw balls out of urns themselves, or draw numbered cloakroom tickets out of a box, or spin a roulette wheel or whatever. Similar considerations might suggest that the whole of the experiment be done by hand. (For example, I am somewhat suspicious of the results of certain computerized public good experiments, for the simple reason that subjects could not ascertain for certain that the experimenter actually did what he said he did, namely distribute the public good to all participants.)

The question of trust is an important one: it is an unfortunate fact that experiments in psychology are tainted by distrust. We do not want the same taint to be attached to experiments in economics. For this reason alone one might be wary of computer-based experiments, but the counter-advantages can be large: identical instructions for everyone; comprehensive 'help' facilities; subjects able to proceed at their own pace; good graphics and presentational facilities; immediate data collection of most (relevant) facets of the subjects' responses. Nevertheless, the choice must be experiment specific and you should think hard before making it.

Room

Some kind of room (or 'laboratory' to borrow a rather unfortunate word from the physical sciences) will be necessary to run the experiment. Ideally, if you are going to run a number of experiments this room should be dedicated to that purpose; it will contain your computers. The size of the room will determine how many subjects you can 'process' at a time; the smaller the room, the fewer subjects at a time, and hence the greater the number of sessions you need to process any given number of subjects. The larger the room, the more subjects at a time, and hence the greater the problems of controlling each experimental session and the greater the practical difficulties of paying off the subjects at the end of the experiment. (You might need several assistants to help in these practical details.)

Ideally, the room should be easily accessible, well signposted (depending on where you get your subjects from) and well lit and friendly but professional-looking. It is crucial that your subjects regard the whole operation as thoroughly professional. It should also be flexible in that you should be able to separate off quiet areas for discussion yet at the same time allow all subjects to view the experimenter when necessary. Display facilities (including the ability to project the image of a PC screen onto an overhead projector screen by use of a Kodak DataShow or similar apparatus) would obviously be useful, in addition to a white or black board. A (silent) clock with a second hand would be useful for timed experiments. Finally, the room should be sufficiently spacious to allow the experimenters to 'patrol' the subjects during the running of the experiment.

Register of Potential Participants

At EXEC, we have found it helpful to set up a register of potential participants. At the beginning of each academic year, we send out a letter to all students (undergraduates and graduates) at the University of York inviting them to join our register, indicating the kind of experiments that we are planning for the coming year and hinting at the kinds of financial rewards that might result from their participation (on this, see later). Those that respond positively to this invitation are recorded on our (computerized) register; this address list is then used for subsequent mail shots for some of the experiments that we perform that year. Some other subjects for some experiments are recruited in other ways. The advantage of the register is that we can restrict invitations for particular experiments to particular types of subjects (for example, first-year undergraduates). Moreover, we can in principle (though we have yet to exploit this fully in practice) follow the performance of particular subjects through a series of experiments, or use information gained in one experiment to interpret the results of a second experiment. (For example, one of my experiments – see chapter 5 – gives information about the extent of a subject's aversion to risk; another of my experiments – see chapter 8 – requires knowledge of this aversion to risk to compute the subject's optimal strategy.)

Publicity Material

In running experiments, you need subjects. In early experiments, such subjects were 'volunteers' in the army sense of the word. However, it is now more normal practice to call for genuine volunteers, by putting out publicity material and invitations of various kinds. Some of our subjects come from our register; others come as a result of general mail shots either to all the members of the University (including staff) or to various visitors to the University (conference attendees, Summer School participants, Open University students, day visitors, tourists etc.). To attract reputable and sincere subjects you need high quality publicity material, preferably professionally produced on headed notepaper. We have a distinctive logo which, we think, adds credibility. Sometimes the publicity material needs to give a brief description of the experiment and of the possible rewards. Occasionally, full instructions need to be distributed to potential participants in advance of the experiment.

Library

A small library is an important element of the necessary capital investment. This will include conventional articles and working papers, software (for running the experiments) and other experimental material.

Human Investment

In addition to the usual skills of an economist, experimental work requires the input of programming skills (TURBO PASCAL or C are useful languages) and data analysis skills (conventional statistical and econometric packages, particularly such software as TSP, GAUSS and LIMDEP); experiments typically generate a lot of data which need to be analysed sympathetically.

3.3   Preparing to Run a Particular Experiment

The preparations for different experiments will, of necessity, differ, and so it is not easy to give general guidance that will be relevant to all experiments. The crucial question to ask is whether the experiment can in principle produce results that will be of value to you. Cast yourself forward to a position after you have completed the experiment and consider whether the data you will have will be useful for answering the questions you want answered: are the data sufficiently discriminating? Remember it is the great virtue of experimental work that you can exercise control over the data that are generated: as in the theory, you can keep constant those things that you want kept constant and vary those things that you want to vary. But make sure that the constant things are genuinely constant; and make sure that the variation in the variable things is of the right type and of the right magnitude to observe the consequent variations in behaviour that you expect. Let me give you an example: in a pilot study of the demand for money in a two-asset (money and bonds) experiment carried out at the University of York it was decided to split the subjects into two groups (one facing a low-variance distribution of bond prices and one facing a high-variance distribution) so as to investigate the effect of variance on behaviour. Unfortunately, it was realized only after the pilot had been completed that the difference between the two variances was insufficient to induce any difference between the optimal strategy for the low-variance group and the optimal strategy for the high-variance group. (This optimal strategy was of a reservation form and the price distributions were discrete.) So, as a test of the theoretical comparative statics propositions, the pilot was worthless!

A second example was even more unexpected: in my experiments on the dynamic competitive firm (discussed briefly in chapter 9) I realized fairly early on that I would need to choose seeds (for the random number generator) that would be fair to the subject in the sense of giving him or her a fair sequence of prices. Otherwise, the subject could be on a hiding to nothing. I decided to give different subjects within each group a different seed (so that different price sequences were generated) but I rather foolishly (as it appears in retrospect) decided to give the same set of seeds to each group. This, of course, though it did not occur to me at the time, meant that the price sequences across groups were perfectly correlated, that is, there was no independent variation. You can imagine the effect this had on econometric estimation! More on seeds later.

Let me now turn to the preparation of a particular experiment. I split my comments below into two sections depending upon whether the experiment you are planning to run is well defined or ill defined. I shall try to explain these terms in a moment, after remarking that the vast bulk of experiments so far performed have been well defined; relatively few have been ill defined. This reflects the fact that the vast majority of experiments have been (either explicitly or implicitly) tests or investigations of neoclassical economic theories, which are themselves well defined. In a sense, this is almost tautological: a neoclassical theory posits well-defined economic agents with well-defined objective functions operating in a well-defined world with well-defined constraints. I should note that 'well defined' does not mean deterministic: stochastic processes (as used in neoclassical theories) are well defined in my sense.

In contrast, evolutionary or behavioural theories in economics tend to be ill defined. I think this is almost inevitable: in a well-defined world it is difficult to counter the argument of the neoclassicists that economic agents behave according to neoclassical theories (though this is not to approve of the strong definitions of rationality proposed by some arch-neoclassicists). Indeed, I feel that evolutionary or behavioural economists are largely fighting a losing battle and wasting their powder by fighting on neoclassical soil: instead, they should move into an ill-defined world where much of the neoclassical charm loses its appeal. But it is difficult to construct ill-defined theories, and, as we shall see, to construct ill-defined experiments. Let us start, therefore, with well-defined experiments.

Well-defined Experiments

The structure of a well-defined theory has been outlined above. To transform it into a well-defined experiment we proceed as follows. First, we decide what it is a theory of – usually it is a theory of how one or more economic agents choose the value or values of one or more economic variables in the pursuit of some goal. This then defines the decisions that the subjects in the experiment will be asked to take. Second, we decide what the nature of the goal is – usually the maximization of some objective function. This then defines the payment or incentive mechanism – payment for participating in the experiment should be directly related to the achieved value of the objective function.

Consider, for example, an experiment designed to investigate how people choose between a pair of risky prospects: we present subjects with a sequence of pairs and ask them to say which of the pair they prefer. At the end we select one pair at random and play out the risky prospect that they said they preferred. As a second example, consider my dynamic competitive firm: here we ask the subjects to take output and sales decisions and then we pay them their realized profits. In an R&D experiment – a patent race, for example – we ask them to take R&D decisions and then pay them their realized patent royalties less the cost of their R&D decisions. And so on. I believe it is crucial to link the payment to the value of the realized objective function. This gives economics experiments a natural advantage over psychological ones where there is often no natural incentive.

Third, we need to decide on the constraints on the subjects' behaviour implied by the theory. Then, rather crucially, we need to decide how to communicate the various 'rules of the game' to the subjects. Remember, for many experiments you may deliberately want to use non-economists as subjects, as you might feel that economists are a biased sample. (Recall the famous public goods experiments of Marwell and Ames (1981) which appeared to suggest that economists free-ride much more often than non-economists!) So you need to 'translate' the rules of the game into a form suitable for assimilation by non-experts. This may sometimes be difficult; let me give two examples, both of which were encountered during my firm experiment. How do we communicate the detail of a cost function to the subjects? How do we communicate a probability distribution (of future prices) to the subjects? In neither case can we use equations. We were also reluctant to use diagrams: as far as the cost function was concerned it would suggest to the subjects the range of outputs in which they 'should' be operating; as far as the probability distribution was concerned the possibility of having to explain probability density to naive subjects was a sufficient deterrent! In the end, it was decided to convey the information by computer interrogation: the subject asked the computer how much a particular output would cost and what proportion of future prices would lie between two specified values. But this was clumsy, and some subjects expressed dissatis-faction with it.

Sometimes it may be necessary to 'translate' a whole theory into a totally different, but completely isomorphic, framework. A good example is provided by my consumption experiment which I discuss in detail in chapter 8.

At this stage you need to decide whether to run the experiment on computers or not. It may possibly be the case that the best method is to run it partly 'by hand' and partly on the computer (for example, an oral double auction, in which the bidding and asking is done orally and the various agreed trades are recorded on a computer) but more often an experiment will be either almost totally computerized or almost totally non-computerized. In the former case, the software will have to be written or be obtained from somewhere else. The second option is becoming increasingly possible, and some well-known experimental packages are generally available (for example PLATO and MUDA), but much of the earlier software was designed for specific experiments and cannot be adapted very easily. If you are building your own software, it may be a good long-term strategy to make it as flexible as possible so that it can be adapted at some stage in the future for some other generation of experiments. You may also find it commercially advantageous to do so, particularly if your experiment is in areas which might make it attractive for use in training and educational contexts.

In any case, the writing of software for experiments is an art which cannot be rushed. It is vitally important that your software is clear, easy to use, attractive and robust. As far as possible, use single keystroking so that the effort required by subjects is as small as possible. Use menus for the same reason. Use colours to make the display attractive and clear. And make the whole software completely idiot-proof so that it does not 'fall over' whatever stupid things the subjects try to do. (There will almost always be some smart aleck who will try and crash your program, or try and get inside it (use only compiled versions), or try and change the parameters or perhaps even pollute the output files.)

My personal preference for a programming language for the PC is TURBO PASCAL; it is ideal for screen displays, graphs etc., and for input and output.

The mainframe version, PASCAL, is satisfactory but suffers from poor terminal facilities like all mainframe software. Some afficianados swear by C, but I find it clumsy and unnecessarily opaque: remember that few experiments require massive computational power – most need instead good input, output and display facilities. My early programs (both on the mainframe and the PC) were written in FORTRAN, but this falls down precisely on these facilities.

Your software will have input data files (to input the parameters of the problem) and output data files. I have found it useful to have different output files for different types of output: for example, one file with all the decisions made by the subject and a second file for all the interrogations (requests for information) made by the subject. Of course, if you wanted you could keep a record of every single keystroke and the time at which it was made; however, unless you were particularly interested in the psychological aspects of the experiment, such information would not be useful.

The software should include a complete description of the 'rules of the game' and, if possible, various 'help' screens along the way in case the subject's memory has faded. The software should also include a very clear statement of how the subject's payment is determined.

For non-computer-based experiments, much of the above applies in spirit, if not in detail. Instructions will now be written on paper, distributed either in advance or at the time of the experiment, or provided orally. Equal care must be taken in drawing up the set of instructions whatever the medium, and great efforts should be made to ensure that the instructions are clear, unambiguous and unlikely to influence the subjects' behaviour in ways you do not wish. If you are running an experiment to test for rationality of people, it may be counter-productive to state 'of course, you will want to . . .' when that itself may be part of the test. But this is not always clear cut: whilst it is easy to say 'of course, you will agree that $2 + 2$ is not equal to 5', it is not so easy to say that 'well, you said you were indifferent between this gamble and 10; therefore you should prefer this gamble to 9.50' which is what I tried to do in one of my early experiments. Indeed, if a subject did not agree, I threw them out of the experiment! One learns.

Some experimentalists, in order to avoid possible bias, will try to use the same form of words from experiment to experiment. Indeed, there are certain phrases that are now part of the folklore:

> The instructions are simple, and if you follow them carefully and make good decisions you may earn a CONSIDERABLE AMOUNT OF MONEY which will be paid to you in cash at the end of the experiment . . . .

In any case, it is important, as I have stated before, to prepare any written instructional material in a professional-looking format on high quality (preferably headed) paper. It is vital that subjects think you are doing a worthwhile job professionally.

Ill-defined Experiments

For ill-defined experiments, much of the above applies but there are additional problems. By definition, an ill-defined experiment is one in which some aspects of the experiment are not told to the subjects. They are therefore not acting in a neoclassical world.

Unfortunately, even though your subjects should be made to think that the experiment is ill defined (at least from *their* point of view) it obviously cannot be from your point of view, for otherwise you lose control over the experiment. So the experimental structure must be completely defined but the subjects are only partially informed about the structure. A simple example of such an experiment was one of my early search experiments in which the subjects were told nothing (literally nothing) about the price distribution other than it was bounded below by zero. The actual software, though, in order to generate price quotes, did use a well-defined distribution for this generation, but the subjects were not told what it was. The idea behind this experiment was to try and discover how people solved the search problem in the complete absence of information.

A more interesting example of an ill-defined experiment is provided by Moon and Keasey (1989) in which subjects were asked to imagine themselves in charge of a firm invited to make a competitive tender for some project. The information needed to estimate an appropriate tender was deliberately not made clear to the subjects by the experimenters, the purpose of the experiment being to see how subjects responded in this relatively unstructured environment. The problem, of course, with such a lack of structure is that it is not clear what questions subjects should be allowed to ask. (Could they ask: 'What is the cheapest profitable bid I can make?' No. Could they ask: 'Can we negotiate a discount on one of our raw material inputs?' Yes.) But such difficulties should not stand in the way of the exploration of such crucially important experiments.

3.4 Running a Pilot Experiment

There are several reasons why it is usually fruitful to run a small-scale pilot of some experiment before spending a large amount of money on a large-scale experiment. All, ultimately, should lead to a saving of money in the long run and to an increase in efficiency of the experiment itself.

The primary purpose of a pilot is to check whether your experimental design and software stand up to subjects' responses: to check that your programs do not crash; to ensure that the subjects find the instructions clear and understandable; to discover whether there are any ambiguities in the instructions and procedures. More importantly, and more positively, you can check whether any design improvements are possible. Often they are: you can reword the instructions, present information in improved formats and alter the presentation of the experiment itself.

I find it useful to give a short questionnaire at the end of any experiment, whether a pilot or a full-scale study. That used at the end of a pilot study is a questionnaire designed to shed light on the experimental design, and so I ask questions concerned with the structure of the experiment and invite suggestions for improvement. The responses are sometimes helpful.

If you are running a pilot study purely for the purpose of testing the experimental design, then you need relatively few subjects, and it is more important that these subjects are good at testing your design than actually doing the experiment. However, you might also want your pilot to shed light on the usefulness of your chosen parameter sets, in which case you want your subjects to be properly motivated. Nevertheless, as it is unlikely (but not unknown) that the results of your pilot study will be used for any serious analysis, or submitted to a journal for possible publication, it is usually not important that you use many subjects for your pilot study. Some 10–20 may be adequate, though much depends upon the nature of your experiment.

3.5 Running a Full-scale Experiment

After making the various amendments and improvements suggested by the pilot study, you should be in a position to run a full-scale experiment. You must now decide upon the number of subjects that you will need.

This depends upon the purpose of the experiment and on the number of different parameter sets that you plan to employ. Here, I am using the phrase 'parameter sets' in a rather broad sense, effectively referring to a 'parameter set' as a particular variant of the experimental set-up. So it may genuinely be different parameters of the price distribution in a search problem, or it may be different sets of market demand and supply curves in a market experiment, or it may be different sets of pairwise risky choices in a decision-making under risk experiment.

If you are interested in comparative statics propositions (as I am in my search, consumption and firm experiments, or as David Ansic is in some of his demand for money experiments) then for each parameter you need at least two values. But, if all permutations are used, this can very quickly lead to large numbers of parameter sets: for example, if you have n parameters and m values of each and use all permutations, then you have n^m parameter sets. For $n = 4$, $m = 3$ this is 64; for $n = 5$, $m = 5$ it is 3125. It soon gets out of hand! You can, of course, economize by not having all permutations, but you should choose the subset with care (to avoid multicollinearity).

For each parameter set you will need enough subjects to give you a reasonable amount of statistical power: if you are using the experiment to test the effect of different parameter sets you need enough subjects to give your test sufficient power; if you are using the experiment to estimate the effect of different parameter sets you need enough subjects to give your estimates sufficient accuracy (or precision). This, in turn, depends on how different your parameter sets are and on the amount of 'noise' in the subjects' responses. This could be inter-subject noise (differences in responses between subjects), or it could be intra-subject noise (differences in response or random errors). If you knew the likely magnitude of this noise you could use standard statistical techniques (or Monte Carlo simulations in more complicated problems) to calculate an appropriate sample size (per parameter set) in order to achieve a given level of statistical power. Unfortunately, at least until after a pilot is run, you have relatively little idea of the magnitude of such noise. This is another reason for running a pilot study. As a rough rule of thumb, some 10–20 subjects per parameter set is not unreasonable.

Given your choice of parameters, you then need to tailor your payment structure appropriately, that is, choose the factor of proportionality between objective and payment. You might want to keep the same factor of proportionality for all parameter sets – in which case some parameter sets will be inherently more profitable than others. Or you could adjust the factor of proportionality to make all parameter sets equally profitable. Of course, actual payments will, in general, be unpredictable as they will be determined by any randomness in the experiment as well as the decision rule used by the subject. You should be able to work out an upper bound to the average payment by working out the expected payment under the optimal strategy. You then need to make some evaluation of how far short of this your subjects are likely to fall by using suboptimal strategies. You could indeed simulate the outcome of some likely suboptimal strategies.

Some thought should also be given to the choice of seeds in a computerized experiment in which a random number generator is employed. Some seeds are bad in that they give bad outcomes even under the optimal strategy. Perhaps these should be avoided.

We try to devise our parameters, seeds and factors of proportionality so that the average payment for a reasonably good response is somewhat above the marginal wage rate of our subjects, for a very good response is considerably higher and for a poor response is considerably lower. We thus hope to provide an appropriate incentive structure.

You now need to attract subjects, by advertising in one form or another. As already described, we make use of our register for some of our experiments. In all cases, you need to put out some kind of literature which indicates what the experiment is about (sometimes to the extent of publishing detailed information about the 'rules of the game' some days in advance of the experiment itself) and which hints at the kind of rewards – usually financial – that the subject might reap. (Remember that the financial reward is supposed to be the key incentive.) This issue of 'hinting' is often quite difficult, though it depends upon the experiment. For some experiments (for example, one involving risky choices over the four amounts £0, £10, £20 and £30) you can be quite precise ('You may earn £0, £10, £20 or £30'), but for other experiments where the payment depends on how well the subjects respond (such as the firm experiment) you need to be much more circumspect ('If you perform reasonably well you could earn between £0 and £10, while if you really perform very well you could earn three times as much') for you do not want to indicate to subjects when they are operating on the wrong basis.

It helps to put up booking sheets which subjects can sign and to ask for reserves to cover for non-showers (the reserves being paid a nominal amount if it turns out that they are not needed). Alternatively, you can make booking arrangements through group leaders, who might be given an additional financial incentive to reward their organizational activities.

We thus come to the actual experiment. This may be spread over several days (depending upon the number of subjects, the number of repetitions and the number of subjects you can process at any one time). Sessions may be continuous or they may be at pre-arranged times. This partly depends on whether a group briefing is needed. If so, this should be done in a professional manner by one of the experimenters who should give exactly the same briefing to each group. (A video-recording may be a good way to ensure consistency.) Alternatively, or additionally, written instructions may be given. Unless the experiment requires otherwise, subjects should be allowed to get on with the experiment at their own speed. It is vital that enough experimenters or assistants are on hand to ensure that strict control is exercised over the running of the experiment, and to answer any questions (in a pre-decided fashion) that may be asked. Collusion and talking should not be allowed unless it is part of the experiment.

At the end of an experiment, I have adopted a habit of asking subjects to complete a short questionnaire asking for brief biographical details and for a brief description of how they tackled the experiment. Clearly such a questionnaire is not financially motivated, but nevertheless the responses may give ideas to the experimenters that will prove useful in analysing the data.

Finally, the subjects should be paid. This should be done immediately, in cash, and a receipt obtained.

3.6   Analysing the Data

Typically an experiment will generate a large amount of data, which need to be handled carefully and analysed sympathetically. If the experiment was a computer-based one, then the output data should already be ready for analysis in convenient electronic files. I would exhort you, at this stage, to take copies of these data files, to back them up, transfer them to the mainframe and archive them. It is all too easy to lose files, or corrupt them or generally lose valuable data. I would also urge you to keep a careful record of precisely what each output data file contains and how the output data relate to the input data. (Your software should automatically keep a record of the input parameters, so that the output data are linked with the relevant input data.) Keep a record also of any random number generator seeds used during the running of the program. I also find it helpful to get my software to label the output data and generally annotate the data files; it is all too easy to forget what you did after the event. Remember that you may want to refer back to the data many years after the experiment itself: you should leave things so that other researchers, in years to come, can reproduce and follow up your analysis.

Produce a hard copy of the output data, and spend some time simply looking at the data; often the naked eye can pick things out that even the most sophisticated econometric software overlooks. You may find it helpful also to get a certain amount of graphical output; this too sometimes reveals useful patterns and regularities. Then you might want to produce various simple summary statistics such as average payment, standard deviation of payment and so on.

The next stage of the analysis depends upon the type of experiment that you have performed and the type of hypotheses that you are testing. If you have some specific hypothesis in mind, it might be the case (though this depends on the nature of the experiment) that you can calculate the appropriate decisions of the subjects under the specific hypothesis. You can then compare actual behaviour with optimal behaviour, both in an absolute sense and a relative (comparative statics) sense. To this end, you might need to use various standard statistical and econometric software packages such as SPSS, TSP, LIMDEP, GAUSS, DataFIT (now called MicroFIT) and so on. Which is the 'best' package depends upon what you are doing: for example, I found TSP most helpful when analysing the results of my experiment on expectations, LIMDEP useful for various regression and probit analyses on my search, firm and consumption experiments and GAUSS helpful for fitting rather complicated non-linear maximization models (for various non-expected utility preference functionals) in my 'circles' experiment (described in some detail in chapter 5). Some packages (for example TSP and LIMDEP) are particularly helpful when you want to repeat the same analysis for large numbers of students as they have looping facilities of one form or another. Much depends on whether you plan to analyse the data subject by subject or in groups; that is, on whether you plan to analyse the subjects' behaviour individually or aggregate it.

Make sure that you keep hard copies of the output from these various analyses and that you label the output files in an informative fashion. A typical experiment can easily produce a pile of computer printout some 6–12 inches thick, and it is a very frustrating task trying to search through an unlabelled pile trying to find some specific result! If necessary, archive the output files.

If your experiment was not computer-based you have a choice of options, but my recommendation is to put the results onto a computer as soon as possible. Remember that if each output statistic is processed just *once* then it makes sense to process it into the computer; it is then available for further analyses without any extra effort. Once the data are in electronic format, then all the above applies. This is true even if your data are qualitative. So get the data onto the computer as soon as possible!

3.7 Preparing the Results for Publication

At the moment, there is no *Journal of Experimental Economics*. Most experimental economists want to keep it that way, since most feel very strongly that papers on experimental economics should compete with, and be published with, other papers in economics. More importantly, most experimental economists feel that they are contributing to economics as a whole, and that they should therefore be talking to the profession as a whole. We do not want to end up being regarded by the mainstream as some kind of fringe grouping.

To this end, it is probably best that papers in experimental economics be submitted, as far as possible, to the core mainstream journals. In this respect, it is important to note that the major general journals have all published papers on experimental economics in the recent past. Such journals include the *American Economic Review, Econometrica*, the *Economic Journal*, the *Journal of Political Economy*, the *Review of Economic Studies* and the *Quarterly Journal of Economics*. When writing up the results of an experiment for publication, however, there is a problem in that the editors of such general journals are interested in a rather different type of paper than are experimental economists themselves. The latter group, when reading about someone else's experiment, typically want to know a lot of detail: precisely how the experiment was conducted; the precise form of the experimental instructions and procedures; the precise details of the software etc. Not so the former group, who, conditional on being reassured in rather broad terms that the experiment was carried out in a competent and professional manner, are more interested in reading about the broad structure of the hypotheses being investigated, the general structure of the experimental test and the main thrust of the results. Much of the detail would be lost on them.

In a sense, then, one needs to write two papers describing any particular experiment: one fairly brief one, encapsulating the broad principles, aimed at the general reader of the general journal; and one considerably longer one, containing all the details, aimed at the fellow experimental economist. A possible compromise is to write the fairly brief general paper and a fairly comprehensive appendix containing the detail 'available to the interested reader on request'. This is the strategy that I encourage in my role as editor.

The data should be made available in some form. Given the volume of data generated by an experiment, possibly the best form nowadays is electronic. I am usually happy to provide both software and data on floppy disk to those that request it. For researchers who subsequently use the software (in a non-commercial context!) I usually suggest a joint publication as payment.

Prior to publication, papers can most fruitfully be circulated in working paper format. We are hoping to be able to provide centralized facilities at York to assist in this preliminary circulation. It is important that experimental economists are aware at an early stage of what their fellow experimentalists are doing.

Of course, some papers may not be particularly suitable for a general audience and specialist journals may be more appropriate. There are a number which may particularly welcome contributions from experimental economists; these include the *Journal of Risk and Uncertainty*, the *Journal of Behavioural Decision Making*, the *Journal of Behavioral Economics*, the *Journal of Economic Behavior and Organization* and, possibly, the new *Journal of Evolutionary Economics*. Whatever the outlet, you should endeavour to ensure that your experiment sees the light of day in some form, and that the science of economics is advanced as a consequence. There might be some spin-offs for you too!

3.8   Aftermath

After the dust has settled, you may find it fruitful to spend some time appraising the experiment: asking, and answering, the question 'did the experiment achieve what we wanted it to achieve?' If the answer is yes, well and good. If not, you will learn from discovering the reasons why not. Possibly you chose bad parameter sets; possibly your experimental design was faulty; possibly your incentive mechanism did not work (or did not work strongly enough); possibly the subjects had other motivations.

Whatever the outcome, the experiment should lead onwards: to the postulation of new, or different, or stronger hypotheses – and hence to a new experiment.

3.9   Conclusions

This chapter has been concerned with practical detail – of preparing for running experiments in general, of preparing for running a particular experiment and of running, analysing and writing up a particular experiment. Much practical advice has been given, but two general maxims emerge: 'Be clear about what you are trying to do' and 'Do it professionally'. Following the first will help you plan the experiment efficiently, isolating those factors which are crucial to the successful achievement of your goal and creating an experimental environment in which you can observe the relevant phenomenon.

Following the second maxim will help to ensure that the subjects are clear about what it is that they are meant to be doing, about the payments that they might get from doing it and about the worthwhileness of the whole venture.

Part II

Experiments on Individual Decision-making under Risk

4

The Theories to be Investigated

4.1 Introduction

The general area of individual decision-making under risk and uncertainty provides a splendid illustration of the use and power of experimental methods in testing alternative theories and in suggesting new ones. It is also an area (perhaps one of the very few in economics) which well illustrates the Popperian strategy for scientific progress: first, a theory is proposed; second, it is empirically tested; if it survives the test, fine; if not, third, an alternative theory is proposed (taking into account the exposed failings of the original theory), and this in turn is tested, the process continuing until a theory is found which survives empirical testing.

In the field of economic decision-making under risk and uncertainty, the maintained hypothesis – the conventional wisdom if you like – throughout the late 1940s and through the 1950s, 1960s and part of the 1970s – was without doubt subjective expected utility theory (SEUT). It was accepted almost without thinking by most economists and applied to numerous economic problems, often with enormous success. And yet, throughout these decades, and increasingly so through the 1980s, direct empirical tests of the foundations of SEUT revealed more and more weaknesses with the basic structure. Subsequently, new theories – alternatives to SEUT – were proposed. In turn, they have been subjected to empirical test.

This part of the book is devoted to these various issues. I begin in this chapter with a discussion of the principal characters in the story: the various theories of decision-making under risk (and sometimes uncertainty), including, of course, the leading actor, SEUT itself. For expositional reasons I find it easiest to hang the discussion around the properties of the indifference maps implied by the various theories. I also find it useful to use the Marschak–Machina triangle as an illustrative device. Let me begin with the latter.

4.2 The Marschak–Machina Triangle

The Marschak–Machina triangle, originally used by Marschak (1950) but more recently resurrected by Machina (see Machina, 1989), provides a way of representing the set of all risky gambles involving just three final outcomes. Let us denote these final outcomes by x_1, x_2 and x_3 and let us suppose that these have been numbered so that x_3 is the most preferred final outcome of the three and that x_1 is the least preferred. Let us denote a risky gamble over these three outcomes by (p_1, p_2, p_3) where p_1, p_2 and p_3 respectively represent the probabilities of getting the final outcomes x_1, x_2 and x_3 (and where $p_1 + p_2 + p_3 = 1$, of course). Naturally, it is assumed that the ps are non-negative – though, of course, for particular 'gambles' one or two of them could be zero.

So a 50–50 gamble between x_1 and x_2 is represented by (0.5, 0.5, 0); a 50–50 gamble between x_1 and x_3 is represented by (0.5, 0, 0.5); the certainty of x_2 by (0, 1, 0); a 20–30–50 gamble between x_1, x_2 and x_3 by (0.2, 0.3, 0.5); and so on. Now, since $p_1 + p_2 + p_3 = 1$, it follows that we can describe any gamble (p_1, p_2, p_3) by just a pair of numbers, say p_1 and p_3. It follows that we can represent any such gamble in a two-dimensional diagram, as in figure 4.1. Here, the horizontal axis measures p_1, the vertical axis measure p_3 and the residual from 1 of $p_1 + p_3$ measures p_2. Clearly, the set of all feasible gambles is bounded below by the horizontal axis, is bounded to the left by the vertical axis and is bounded above and to the right by the hypotenuse of the triangle. So point A represents the 50–50 gamble between x_1 and x_2; point B represents a 50–50 gamble between x_1 and x_3; the vertex 0 represents

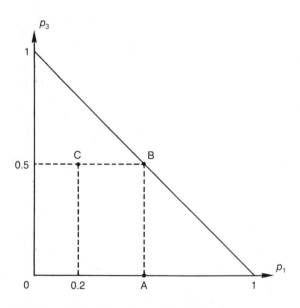

Figure 4.1 The Marschak–Machina triangle.

the certainty of x_2; the point C represents the 20–30–50 gamble between x_1, x_2 and x_3; and so on.

Each point within a particular Marschak–Machina triangle represents a risky gamble. So, if we take any pair of points it seems natural (to economists at least) to ask whether one point (one risky gamble) is preferable to the other point (the other risky gamble), or vice versa. It seems reasonable to say that if one point is to the northwest of the other point then the former is preferable to the latter (it has a higher probability of getting the most preferred outcome, that is, a higher value of p_3, and a lower probability of getting the least preferred outcome, that is, a lower value of p_1; if the probability of getting the intermediate outcome (p_2) is smaller, the decrease is more than compensated by an offsetting increase in the probability p_3 of getting the most preferred outcome – which is, definitionally, more preferred).

That, however, is as far as we can go without considering individual tastes – just as in conventional demand theory, we can argue on *a priori* grounds that points to the northeast in a conventional indifference map are preferred to points in the southwest, but to say more we need information on individual tastes. In this context, taste represents attitude to risk.

Different tastes imply different indifference maps, just as in conventional demand theory. On *a priori* grounds we can argue that indifference curves in the Marschak–Machina triangle must be upward sloping, but the actual shape depends on individual tastes. Let us see whether we can impose any restrictions on these upward-sloping indifference curves.

This is where theory comes in – in the form of axioms of rational behaviour. Let me start with the simplest such axiom, which is termed the betweenness axiom. This is stated as follows. Suppose G_1 and G_2 are two gambles in the Marschak–Machina triangle which a particular individual thinks are equally preferable (that is, he or she is indifferent between them). Let $[G_1, G_2; q, 1 - q]$ denote a risky gamble between G_1 and G_2 that yields G_1 with probability q and G_2 with probability $1 - q$. Then the betweenness axiom says that the individual should be indifferent between $[G_1, G_2; q, 1 - q]$ and G_1 and G_2. In other words, if our individual does not mind whether he or she gets G_1 or G_2 then he or she should not mind if some random device decided the outcome that he or she was to get: if you do not mind whether you get G_1 or G_2 would you mind if I tossed a coin (heads you get G_1, tails you get G_2) or whether I rolled a die ('1' gets you G_1, any other number gets you G_2) to decide?

The betweenness axiom implies that indifference curves in the Marschak–Machina triangle are (upward-sloping) straight lines: see figure 4.2 in which the mixture $[G_1, G_2; q, 1 - q]$ is a point on the straight line joining G_1 to G_2 a proportion $1 - q$ of the way along. It is, of course, an empirical question whether or not a particular individual obeys the betweenness axiom, but it is precisely the purpose of theory to put some such restrictions on behaviour.

So, with the betweenness axiom, we have the restriction that the upward-sloping indifference curves are straight lines. As it is a restriction it implies that it is testable; nevertheless, it is (as we shall see) quite a weak

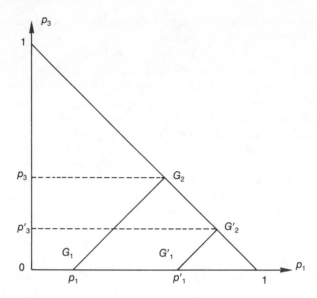

Figure 4.2 The betweenness and independence axioms.

restriction, and so the testable implications are themselves rather weak. Can we impose any stronger restrictions?

One way of doing this is by invoking the independence axiom. In some ways this is the natural extension of the betweenness axiom but it implies the rather remarkable result that the straight indifference lines are parallel straight lines. This is rather a strong restriction – accordingly, the testable implications are rather strong – and, as we shall see, fairly easily refutable.

The independence axiom is as follows: suppose our individual is indifferent between gamble G_1 and gamble G_2; then, if he or she obeys the independence axiom, he or she should also be indifferent between the (compound) gamble $[G_1, G_3; q, 1-q]$ and the (compound) gamble $[G_2, G_3; q, 1-q]$ whatever the gamble G_3 and the probability q. The intuition behind this is straightforward: if the individual is indifferent between G_1 and G_2 then he or she should not mind if, after having been subjected to the compound gamble $[G_1, G_3; q, 1-q]$, his or her outcome is replaced by the outcome G_2 in the cases when he or she got the outcome G_1 (which will happen q of the time). The intuition behind this seems clear enough.

That this implies that the straight line indifference curves are parallel can be illustrated using figure 4.2. Take any two indifference lines in the triangle. For convenience, suppose that they both pass to the right of the origin.[1] Let the p_1 values where they cross the horizontal axis be respectively p_1 and p_1' (note that $p_1 < p_1'$); similarly let the p_3 values where they cross the hypotenuse be p_3 and p_3' (note that $p_3 > p_3'$). So the gambles G_1 and G_2 (at either end of the left-hand indifference line) are respectively $(p_1, 1-p_1, 0)$ and $(1-p_3, 0, p_3)$ while the gambles G_1' and G_2' (at either end of the right-hand indifferenceline) are respectively $(p_1', 1 - p_1', 0)$ and $(1 - p_3', 0, p_3')$. Now note that G_1' can be obtained from G_1 by

$$G_1' \equiv \left[G_1, x_1; \frac{1 - p_1'}{1 - p_1}, 1 - \frac{1 - p_1'}{1 - p_1} \right]$$

That is, G_1' is a compound mixture of G_1 and x_1. Now invoke the independence axiom: since the individual is indifferent between G_1 and G_2 then the individual should also be indifferent between

$$G_1' \equiv \left[G_1, x_1; \frac{1 - p_1'}{1 - p_1}, 1 - \frac{1 - p_1'}{1 - p_1} \right]$$

and

$$\left[G_2, x_1; \frac{1 - p_1'}{1 - p_1}, 1 - \frac{1 - p_1'}{1 - p_1} \right]$$

The latter, being a gamble with final outcome either x_1 or x_3, must be G_2'. It therefore follows that

$$p_3' \equiv p_3 \frac{1 - p_1'}{1 - p_1}$$

and hence that the line joining G_1 to G_2 must be parallel to the line joining G_1' to G_2'. This is the result we wanted.

4.3 Subjective Expected Utility Theory

Betweenness and independence together constitute SEUT (for given probabilities). As we have seen, these axioms seem harmless enough – yet they have the strong implication that the indifference curves in the Marschak–Machina triangle are parallel straight lines. Early experiments seemed to deny this implication. Consider, for example, a variant on a very famous paradox, the Allais paradox, named after the French Nobel Prizewinner Maurice Allais. He asked people (way back in the early 1950s) to say first which of the following two gambles they preferred: G_1, £300 with certainty; or G_2, a gamble between £400 with probability 0.8 and £0 with probability 0.2. He then asked the same people to say which of the following pair of gambles they preferred: G_1', a gamble between £300 with probability 0.25 and £0 with probability 0.75; or G_2', a gamble between £400 with probability 0.2 and £0 with probability 0.8. He found that the majority of people said that they preferred G_1 in the first pair and G_2' in the second. This is a clear violation of the independence axiom and of SEUT, as can be seen as follows. Consider a Marschak–Machina triangle over the three amounts £0, £300 and £400 (figure 4.3). Mark on the triangle the four risky choices described above: G_1 is at the origin, and so on. Finally, note that the line joining G_1 to G_2 is parallel to the line joining G_1' to G_2'; it follows that it is impossible for anyone with parallel straight line indifference curves simultaneously to

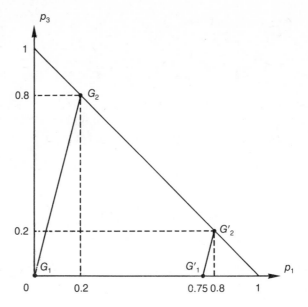

Figure 4.3   An example of the Allais paradox.

prefer G_1 to G_2 and G'_2 to G'_1. (Try and draw such a set!) Hence the contradiction.

Since Allais carried out these first experiments, numerous other economists have carried out similar experiments, with similar conclusions. I shall describe some of these later. Enough experimental evidence has now been accumulated to convince all but the hardest sceptic that the restrictions on behaviour imposed by SEUT are too great for a significant proportion of the human race. The corollary, of course, is that a theory with weaker restrictions is needed to describe the behaviour of this significant proportion. Economic theorists have not been slow in coming up with such weaker (alternative) theories – indeed there is now a frightening plethora of them.

Once again, it will prove helpful to use the Marschak–Machina triangle. Figure 4.4 illustrates some of the various alternatives. Figure 4.4(a) shows a set of linear indifference curves; as we have already demonstrated these are the consequence of invoking just the betweenness axiom. This theory has been proposed by Dekel (1986) under the name implicit expected utility.

Figure 4.4(b) illustrates a set of straight line indifference curves fanning out from a point to the southwest of the origin of the triangle; this requires some other restriction in addition to betweenness. One such restriction (which gives the desired implication) is the weak independence axiom which, not surprisingly, is a weakened version of the independence axiom defined and discussed above. This states that if the individual is indifferent between G_1 and G_2 then for every G_3 and q (> 0) there is some r (> 0) for which the individual is indifferent between $[G_1, G_3; q, 1 - q]$ and $[G_2, G_3; r, 1 - r]$. That this implies (linear) indifference curves fanning out from a point to the southwest of the origin of the triangle can be shown by an argument similar

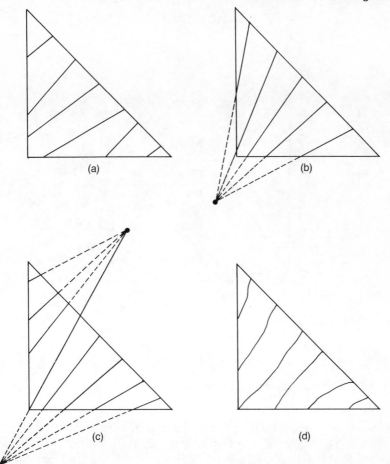

Figure 4.4 Different preference functionals in the Marschak–Machina triangle.

to that used above to demonstrate that the (strong) independence axiom implied parallel indifference curves. Figure 4.5 illlustrates this. Start with gamble $G_1 = (0, 1, 0)$ at the origin and let the point on the hypotenuse that is on the individual's indifference curve passing through G_1 be the gamble $G_2 \equiv (1 - p_3, 0, p_3)$. Now consider the gamble G'_1 defined as $[G_1, x_1; q, 1 - q] = (1 - q, q, 0)$, that is, a gamble leading to final outcome x_1 with probability $1 - q$ and to final outcome x_2 with probability q. Let G'_2 be the gamble on the hypotenuse which is on our individual's indifference curve passing through G'_1. From the weak independence axiom as stated above it must follow that there exist some r for which the individual $G'_2 = [G_2, x_1; r, 1 - r] = (1 - r + rp_3, 0, r(1 - p_3))$. So the p_3 value at G'_1 must be rp_3.

Now let G''_1 be the same mixture of G'_1 and x_1 that G'_1 was of G_1 and x_1; that is, $G''_1 \equiv [G'_1, x_1; q, 1 - q] = (1 - q^2, q^2, 0)$. It follows from the weak independence axiom that G''_2 (the point on the hypotenuse on the indifference

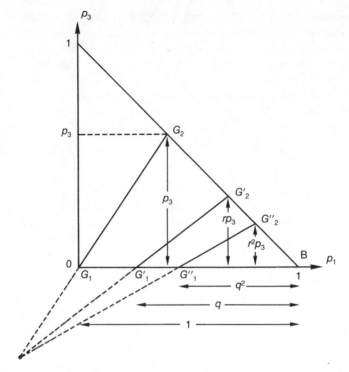

Figure 4.5 The weak independence axiom.

curve through G_1'') must be the same mixture of G_2' and x_1 that G_2' was of G_2 and x_1; so $G_2'' = [G_2', x_1; r, 1 - r] = ((1 - r^2p_3)\ 0,\ r^2p_3)$. So the p_3 value at G_2'' must be r^2p_3. Therefore the ratio of the horizontal distance from apex B to point G_1'' over the horizontal distance from B to G_1' must equal the ratio of the horizontal distance from B to G_1' over the horizontal distance from B to G_1; and at the same time the ratio of the vertical distance from G_2'' to the horizontal axis to the vertical distance of G_2' from the horizontal axis must equal the ratio of the vertical distance of G_2' to the horizontal axis to the vertical distance of G_2 from the horizontal axis. The rest follows from elementary geometry.

4.4 Regret Theory

Interestingly, the same conclusion (about the shape of the indifference curves in the Marschak–Machina triangle) also follows from another (apparently quite different) theory called regret theory (Loomes and Sugden, 1987). A good description can be found in Sugden (1987) were it is shown that the regret theory indifference curves fan out from a point to the southwest of the origin of the triangle. Regret theory simply builds on the notion that when one chooses one option out of a pair of choices then one necessarily rejects the other option; in so doing one might (*ex post*) incur either feelings of regret that one did not choose the other option (if things turn out worse than they would have done under the other option) or feelings of rejoicing that one did choose the chosen option (if things turn out better than they would have done under the other option). If the decision-maker is prone to such feelings of regret and rejoicing (which is not necessarily a rational thing to be[2]) then he or she should rationally take such anticipated feelings into account *ex ante* when taking the decision in the first place. So, under regret theory the decision-maker does not simply work on the basis of the expected utility of the outcomes *per se* (as in SEUT) but on the basis of the expected utility modified by any anticipated feelings of regret and rejoicing.

To see the implications, let me introduce a little extra notation. Let $\psi_{ij} \equiv \psi(x_i, x_j)$ represent the difference between the (modified) utility that our individual gets when the outcome of his or her choice is x_i and the (modified) utility that he or she would have got if he or she had chosen the alternative option and had ended up with the final outcome x_j instead. This $\psi(x_i, x_j)$ measures not only the extra utility obtained from getting x_i *per se* rather than x_j *per se* but also the utility or disutility obtained from rejoicing or regretting the fact of not getting x_j. Clearly $\psi(x, x)$ must be zero for all outcomes x. Now consider the choice between two gambles $G_1 \equiv (p_1, p_2, p_3)$ and $G_2 \equiv (q_1, q_2, q_3)$. According to regret theory, choice G_1 will be chosen in preference to choice G_2 if the expected value of ψ is positive; G_2 will be chosen otherwise. In other words, G_1 is chosen rather than G_2 if the expected difference in (modified) utility in choosing G_1 is positive.

To implement this, we assume that G_1 and G_2 are *independent* gambles. So the various possibilities as far as ψ is concerned are as follows:

choose G_1	ψ_{11}	ψ_{12}	ψ_{13}	ψ_{21}	ψ_{22}	ψ_{23}	ψ_{31}	ψ_{32}	ψ_{33}
choose G_2	ψ_{11}	ψ_{21}	ψ_{31}	ψ_{12}	ψ_{22}	ψ_{32}	ψ_{13}	ψ_{23}	ψ_{33}
probability	$p_1 q_1$	$p_1 q_2$	$p_1 q_3$	$p_2 q_1$	$p_2 q_2$	$p_2 q_3$	$p_3 q_1$	$p_3 q_2$	$p_3 q_3$

The first column represents the situation (which has probability $p_1 q_1$) when the outcome is x_1 under either choice; the second column represents the situation (which has probability $p_1 q_2$) when the outcome under G_1 is x_1 and the outcome under G_2 is x_2; and so on. Of course, $\psi_{11} = \psi_{22} = \psi_{33} = 0$. So the expected difference in (modified) utility from choosing G_1 rather than G_2 is given by:

$$p_1 q_2 \psi_{12} + p_1 q_3 \psi_{13} + p_2 q_1 \psi_{21} + p_2 q_3 \psi_{23} + p_3 q_1 \psi_{31} + p_3 q_2 \psi_{32}$$

Now note that $\psi_{12} = -\psi_{21}$, $\psi_{13} = -\psi_{31}$ and $\psi_{23} = -\psi_{32}$, since the expected difference in utility from getting x_i rather than x_j must be equal to the negative of the expected difference in utility from getting x_j rather than x_i. For convenience let me work with the positive ψ values, which, since x_3 is preferred to x_2 which is preferred to x_1, must be ψ_{21}, ψ_{31} and ψ_{32}. We thus get as the condition for G_1 to be chosen in preference to G_2 that the expression

$$(p_2 q_1 - p_1 q_2)\psi_{21} + (p_3 q_1 - p_1 q_3)\psi_{31} + (p_3 q_2 - p_2 q_3)\psi_{32} \qquad (4.1)$$

be positive. If expression (4.1) is negative then, according to regret theory, G_2 will be chosen in preference to G_1; and if it is zero then the individual will be indifferent between the two. (Note that regret theory reduces to SEUT if the difference between the (modified) utilities is simply equal to the difference between the (unmodified) utilities; that is, if

$$\psi(x_i, x_j) \equiv u(x_i) - u(x_j) \qquad \text{for all } i \text{ and } j$$

where the $u(.)$ function is the utility function of SEUT. This, of course, is the case where the individual gets utility from the final outcome alone, and not additionally from any pleasure at rejoicing or any sorrow at regretting.)

If expression (4.1) is zero, then the individual, according to regret theory, is indifferent between the two prospects. This therefore defines an indifference curve in the Marschak–Machina triangle, namely

$$(p_2 q_1 - p_1 q_2)\psi_{21} + (p_3 q_1 - p_1 q_3)\psi_{31} + (p_3 q_2 - p_2 q_3)\psi_{32} = 0 \qquad (4.2)$$

Take the q values as fixed and trace out the indifference curve passing through the point (q_1, q_2, q_3) by varying the p values. Since (4.2) is an equation linear in the p values for given q values, the indifference curves are quite clearly linear in the triangle. Furthermore, whatever the q values are, the line defined by (4.2) passes through the point

$$(p_1, p_2, p_3) = \left(\frac{-\psi_{32}}{\psi_{31} - \psi_{21} - \psi_{32}}, \frac{\psi_{31}}{\psi_{31} - \psi_{21} - \psi_{32}}, \frac{-\psi_{21}}{\psi_{31} - \psi_{21} - \psi_{32}} \right) \qquad (4.3)$$

since if these values are substituted in the left-hand side of (4.2) the expression is identically zero irrespective of the values of q_1, q_2 and q_3. It immediately follows that all the indifference curves pass through the point defined by (4.3), and as this lies to the southwest of the origin of the triangle (on the assumption that $\psi_{31} - \psi_{21} - \psi_{32} > 0$) it follows that the indifference curves fan out across the triangle from this point, just as in figure 4.4(b).

4.5 Other Theories

Loomes and Sugden, the originators of this version of regret theory (Loomes and Sugden, 1982), have also constructed a further alternative to SEUT based on similar but not identical lines of thought. This they call disappointment theory, and it is more suited to situations where the individual does not know what would have been the outcome under the rejected alternative. So the individual cannot compare the outcome that he or she did get with the outcome he or she would have got under the alternative choice, and therefore cannot experience regret or rejoicing in the sense discussed above. Nevertheless, the individual may experience disappointment if the outcome turns out to be rather worse than had been hoped, or elation if the outcome turns out to be rather better than might have been expected. To implement this intuitively attractive idea, one needs to characterize the outcome that the individual 'hoped', or 'expected', to get (and hence the one to which the actual is to be compared). The procedure adopted by Loomes and Sugden is to posit that the individual experiences disappointment (elation) if the (unmodified) utility of the actual outcome is less (more) than the (unmodified) utility that the individual had expected. One interesting recent characterization along these lines is by Gul (1991) who argues that, in the three-outcome example of the Marschak–Machina triangle, the 'middle' outcome x_2 acts as a kind of reference outcome: an outcome better than x_2, namely x_3, represents elation; while an outcome worse than x_2, namely x_1, represents disappointment. Expected utilities are modified by *ex ante* anticipations of elation and disappointment, as in the regret theory of Loomes and Sugden. This leads to an indifference map of the kind depicted in figure 4.4(c) in which the indifference lines in the upper half of the triangle fan in to a point to the northeast of the hypotenuse of the triangle, while the indifference lines in the bottom right part of the triangle fan out from a point to the southwest of the origin of the triangle, just as in regret theory and weighted utility theory. This seems to accord with some recent experimental evidence.

All the theories discussed so far have straight line indifference maps because of their (implicit or explicit) use of the betweenness axiom. Not all theories invoke this axiom, however. One such theory is the important generalized expected utility theory ('or SEUT without the independence axiom') of Machina (1982). As its subtitle indicates, this theory drops the independence axiom; it also, though rather less explicitly, drops the betweenness axiom. Indeed, in one sense it is a non-axiomatic approach, at least in the first instance, since it simply starts from the assumption that individuals have well-behaved (smooth) preferences over the set of all risky gambles. Let us confine attention, once again, to the Marschak–Machina triangle. This starting assumption of Machina is then simply the assumption that the individual has a well-behaved (smooth) indifference map in the triangle. By using the assumption that x_3 is (strictly) preferred to x_2 which is strictly preferred to x_1, it can be shown that the indifference curves slope smoothly upwards. Smoothness here effectively means continuous and differentiable. This has some predictive content – but not much.

To add further predictive content, Machina adds a further hypothesis: effectively that risk aversion increases as one moves up and to the left across the triangle. Since the slope of the indifference curves indicates the strength of risk aversion (an SEUT indifference curve is given by $p_1u_1 + p_2u_2 + p_3u_3 = $ constant, that is, by $p_3 = p_1[(u_2 - u_1)/(u_3 - u_2)] + $ constant) this effectively means that Machina's indifference curves fan out non-linearly across the triangle. This is illustrated in figure 4.4(d). As should be apparent, this theory includes (independence) regret theory and weighted expected utility theory as special cases.

Chronologically preceding most of the theories I have described above was the rather influential paper by Kahneman and Tversky (1979) on prospect theory, which begins by describing some of the experimental evidence contradicting SEUT (including that briefly described above) before constructing its own alternative. This differs in certain crucial respects from most of the other theories that I have described, most particularly in that it involves two stages, an editing stage and an evaluation stage, while the other theories have just the second stage. Kahneman and Tversky include the first stage in response to experimental evidence which suggests that individuals (when comparing risky prospects) often try and simplify the comparison before actually making it. So, for example, they will eliminate any features common to risky prospects under consideration. Furthermore, individuals appear to shift the reference point from which prospects are evaluated depending upon the way that prospects are presented to them. Consider the following example. First, individuals are asked to suppose that they have been given £1000 and are then asked to say which of the gambles G_1 (£500 with certainty) and G_2 (£1000 with probability 0.5 and £0 with probability 0.5) they would prefer. Then they are asked to suppose that they have been given £2000 and are asked to say which of the two gambles G_1' (– £500 with certainty) and G_2' (– £1000 with probability 0.5 and £0 with probability 0.5) they would prefer. Typically, Kahneman and Tversky found (though I should note that these particular experiments were not financially motivated) that individuals preferred G_1 in the first choice problem and G_2' in the second, even though, relative to the individual's initial wealth, G_1 is identical to G_1' and G_2 is identical to G_2'. This is referred to as the framing effect; it indicates that the framing or presentation of choice problems influences choice – a rather worrying possibility for the economic theorist!

In addition, prospect theory suggests that individuals tend to distort probabilities (even if they are 'objectively'[3] given), tending to overstate small probabilities and understate large ones. So in prospect theory there is an (upward-sloping) mapping from the given 'objective' probabilities to the subjective probabilities used in the valuation function. All these features make prospect theory rather different from the other theories – and make it rather difficult to specify the implied indifference map in the Marschak–Machina triangle (though an attempt has been made by Camerer, 1989).

There are also other theories. References can be found in Camerer (1989) and Machina (1989) and I will refer to them if and when necessary. For the time being, we have what we need for the material of the next chapter: a description of various alternative theories of decision-making under risk and their implied indifference maps in the Marschak–Machina triangle.

Notes

1 The argument goes through in a similar (but obviously not identical) fashion when both lines pass to the left of the origin and when one passes to the left and one to the right of the origin.
2 For a bad outcome *ex post* does not necessarily indicate a bad decision *ex ante*.
3 I do not want to enter into a discussion of what one might mean by this phrase. I hope that the reader reads it in the spirit in which it was written.

5

An Example of a Simple Experiment

5.1 Introduction

There have been a large number of experimental tests of subjective expected utility theory (SEUT), and a rather smaller number of tests of the various generalizations of, and alternatives to, SEUT (see chapter 4). In principle, if a theory is a useful theory in the sense that it has some falsifiable/testable predictions, then experiments can be devised to test such predictions and hence to shed light on the validity or otherwise of that theory. Moreover, if two (competing) theories are actually different in the sense that they have, in certain situations, testably different predictions, then an experiment can be devised to discriminate between these different predictions and hence to shed light on the relative validity of the competing theories.

The early tests of SEUT were straightforward: since SEUT predicts that indifference curves in the Marschak–Machina triangle are parallel straight lines then one asks a series of questions which will reveal whether that is indeed the case. The simplest type of question (which has been used extensively in experiments) is the straightforward preference question between two alternatives: 'This is choice G_1; this is choice G_2; which do you prefer, G_1 or G_2, or are you indifferent between them?' Clearly, given just one such question you cannot refute SEUT, unless, of course, one of the two alternatives dominates the other, that is, in terms of the Marschak–Machina triangle, if one of the Gs lies to the northwest of the other. Suppose G_1 lies to the northwest of G_2; then G_1 dominates G_2 in the sense that, under G_1, there is a higher probability of getting the best outcome x_3, than under G_2, and a lower probability of getting the worst outcome x_1. So all agents should prefer G_1 to G_2, whether they are SEUT agents or not: all theories have upward-sloping indifference curves (see chapter 4) and so if an individual reports that he or she prefers G_2 to G_1 then something rather devastating has occurred to all theories. (Remember that the ordering of the final outcomes – x_3 the most preferred, x_2 intermediate and x_1 the least preferred – is the individual's own ordering, so for him or her to say that he or she prefers x_3 to x_2 to x_1, but at the same time says he or she prefers G_2 to G_1, where the former has a lower probability of getting the best outcome and a higher probability of getting the worst outcome, seems absurd.)

For this reason, experimentalists tend not to use pairs (G_1, G_2) where one gamble dominates the other; they use pairs of points in the Marschak–Machina triangle which lie northeast and southwest of each other. So, depending upon the individual's preferences, he or she may prefer G_1 to G_2 or G_2 to G_1, or be indifferent between them. So one pairwise choice usually tells us nothing.

However, the situation changes with two pairwise choices: start with G_1 and G_2 and select another pair of choices G_1' to G_2' in the triangle so that the line joining G_1' to G_2' is parallel to the line joining G_1 to G_2. Now, for reasons discussed in chapter 4, if the individual obeys SEUT and hence has parallel straight line indifference curves, we can proceed to a test. Suppose G_1 is to the southwest of G_2 and likewise G_1' is to the southwest of G_2' then, according to SEUT, if the individual prefers G_1 to G_2 he or she must prefer G_1' to G_2', while if the individual prefers G_2 to G_1 he or she must prefer G_2' to G_1', and, finally, if he or she is indifferent between G_1 and G_2 he or she must similarly be indifferent between G_1' and G_2' (figure 5.1).

What is often found where such questions are posed is that many experimental subjects say they prefer G_1 to G_2 but that they prefer G_2' to G_1'

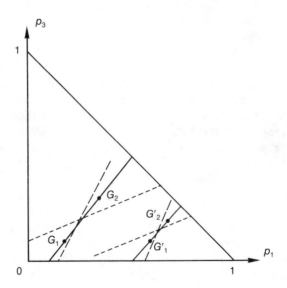

Figure 5.1 A simple test of SEUT: ----------, SEUT indifference curves for G_1 preferred to G_2 and G_1' preferred to G_2'; —————, SEUT indifference curves for G_1 indifferent to G_2 and G_1' indifferent to G_2'; ——————, SEUT indifference curves for G_2 preferred to G_1 and G_2' preferred to G_1'.

(see the example given in chapter 4: G_1, £300 with certainty; G_2, a gamble between £400 and £0 with probabilities 0.8 and 0.2; G'_1, a gamble between £300 and £0 with probabilities 0.25 and 0.75; and G'_2, a gamble between £400 and £0 with probabilities 0.2 and 0.8). Consider also the original Allais paradox: G_1, FF100 million with certainty; G_2, a gamble between FF300 million, FF100 million and nothing with respective probabilities 0.10, 0.89 and 0.01; G'_1, a gamble between FF100 million and nothing with probabilities 0.11 and 0.89; and G'_2, a gamble between FF300 million and nothing with probabilities 0.10 and 0.90. Here, again, many subjects responded that they preferred G_1 to G_2 and G'_2 to G'_1. This violation of the SEUT predictions is much more common than the 'opposite' violation (G_2 preferred to G_1 and G'_1 preferred to G'_2); it suggests that indifference curves in the triangle fan out. These empirical findings are the motivation for many of the new theories discussed in chapter 4.

Pairwise questions of the type discussed above are popular amongst experimental economists for a variety of reasons: first, they are very simple to describe and (apparently) very easy for even naive subjects to understand; second, they are easy to motivate – the experimenter simply tells the subjects that, after answering N questions, one of the N will be selected at random and the choice that the subject said was the most preferred on that question will be played out. This apparently gives the subjects the appropriate incentive to answer truthfully: if they genuinely prefer G_2 to G_1 on question n why should they not say so, for if question n were to be picked at random surely the subject would prefer G_2 to be played out? Unfortunately, the situation is not as clear as might initially appear – as Karni and Safra (1987) point out, this logic really only works when the subjects obey SEUT. Consider, for example, a subject who, in the example from chapter 4 described above, prefers G_1 to G_2 and G'_2 and G'_1 and who is presented with four pairwise choice questions, one of which will be selected at random and the preferred choice played out. Let the first pair be (G_1, G_2) and the other three (D, D) where D is a Dud gamble that always pays out zero (figure 5.2). One could argue that, since the (D, D) pairs are rather trivial, the choice problem boils down to that between G_1 and G_2. If G_1 is chosen, the eventual chance of getting £300 is 0.25 and that of getting £0 is 0.75; if G_2 is chosen, the eventual chance of getting £400 is 0.2 and that of getting £0 is 0.8 (see the right-hand side of figure 5.2). But note that this 'G_1' 'is' G'_1 and that this 'G_2' 'is' G'_2; note further that our individual prefers G'_2 to G'_1. Therefore, he or she will say that he prefers G_2 to G_1 *even though he does not*! It is the payment mechanism coupled with his non-SEUT preferences that are providing this result.

Of course, as a test of SEUT, this is not a problem, for if the individual actually obeys SEUT then he or she will report G_1 preferred to G_2 and G'_1 preferred to G'_2, or vice versa, or will express indifference in both cases. Someone who reports G_1 preferred to G_2 and G'_2 preferred to G'_1 (or G_2 preferred to G_1 and G'_1 preferred to G'_2) cannot obey the axioms of SEUT. So violations of SEUT are genuine violations under this payment mechanism.

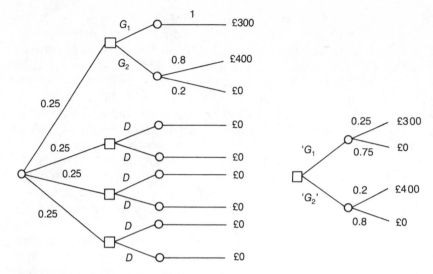

Figure 5.2 The Karni–Safra problem.

The problem, of course, is the other way round: it may be the case that someone whose preferences actually disagree with the axioms of SEUT reports preferences which do agree with SEUT because of the payment mechanism. But, as you can no doubt infer, they would have to have rather strange preferences. As my example shows, an individual whose indifference curves fan out will report preferences (under this payment scheme) which will appear to be even more fanning out than is actually the case. This if anything, will sharpen the test.

There is one final point on this issue that I should make: there are those who would argue that the choice between G_1 and G_2 in the decision problem on the left-hand side of figure 5.2 is not the same as the choice between 'G_1' and 'G_2' on the right-hand side of figure 5.2. Such people would conclude that it would then be prefectly correct for the individual to report G_1 preferred to G_2 in the left-hand side problem and 'G_2' preferred to 'G_1' (i.e. G_2' preferred to G_1') in the right-hand side problem. The payment mechanism I have described above would then induce individuals to reveal their true preferences. This argument is the consequentialist argument (see Hammond, 1988).

Let me now return to my main theme. So far I have discussed simple tests of SEUT, tests relating to the hypothesis of parallel straight line indifference curves. Tests can also be devised for other alleged properties of indifference curves and hence for alternative preference functionals, and also for particular axioms used in the construction of alternative theories. Consider, for example, the betweenness axiom, as defined in chapter 4. You could first discover a pair of gambles G_1 and G_2 about which an individual felt indifferent. You could then check that the individual was also indifferent between G_1, G_2 and any mixture $[G_1, G_2; q, 1 - q]$.

The drawback with this is that it may be difficult to find a pair of gambles G_1 and G_2 about which the individual feels indifferent. The major problem is that human beings (as distinct from economists) have great difficulty understanding the concept of indifference, and even greater difficulty in adjusting probabilities until indifference occurs. Let me be more specific; suppose we take G_1 to be getting x_2 with certainty (this gamble is represented by the origin in the Marschak–Machina triangle), and that we wish to find the point $G_2 = (1 - p_3, 0, p_3)$ on the hypotenuse which lies on the indifference curve through G_1. So we are trying to find the value of p_3 at which the individual is indifferent between $G_1 \equiv (0, 1, 0)$ and $G_2 \equiv (1 - p_3, 0, p_3)$. This is illustrated schematically in figure 5.3. One could, of course, try asking the individual: 'What is the value of p_3 at which you are indifferent between G_1 and G_2?' This is likely to run into difficulties, partly because of the problem concerning human beings' understanding of the term indifference referred to above, but mainly because there is no reason why the subject should reply honestly, even if he or she could. How is the answer to this question financially motivated? Note that you cannot 'play out the most preferred' as you are asking the subject to make them equally preferred. You cannot say that you will play out one chosen at random because the individual then has every incentive to make p_3 as high as possible (almost unity).

There *are* ways to provide an appropriate incentive to reveal the required information truthfully, but they are rather contorted. Consider the following, which is a method I used at the end of my consumption experiment. At the end, the subjects had earned a sum of money – call it x_2. I then gave them the chance to earn more, namely an amount x_3, though at the risk of possibly earning less, namely an amount x_1. What I wanted them to reveal was the p_3 which made them indifferent between G_1 and G_2 as defined above. So I gave them the following (simple?) decision problem: 'You are to choose a number p between 0 and 1, which you will tell the experimenter. You will then spin a "continuous roulette wheel", with the circumference continuously calibrated from 0 to 1, and observe the value q at which the wheel comes to a stop. If q is less than p you will get paid x_2. If q is greater than p, you will spin the wheel again; if on this second spin it comes to rest before q you will get paid x_3; if it comes to rest after q you will get paid x_1. Note that you can guarantee getting x_2 by putting p equal to 1.'

Putting p equal to 1 is what the extreme risk-averter (the minimaxer) would do; less risk-averse people would put p less than 1; a risk-neutral person would put p equal to 0.5 and a risk-lover would put p between 0.5 and 0 (0

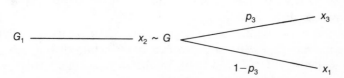

Figure 5.3 Determining the probability at which indifference occurs.

representing extreme risk loving). I assert that the optimal value of p (at least for an individual who obeys SEUT) is the p_3 at which G_1 and G_2 are indifferent. Why? Simply because the individual has no incentive (under SEUT) to do otherwise: putting p greater than p_3 will mean that the individual, when q falls between p_3 and p, will end with the certainty of x_2 when he or she could have had the gamble $(1 - p, 0, p)$ which is clearly preferred to $(1 - p_3, 0, p_3)$ (for p greater than p_3) which is equally as good as the certainty of x_2; putting p less than p_3 will mean that the individual, when q falls between p and p_3, will end up with the gamble $(1 - p, 0, p)$, which is clearly less preferred than $(1 - p_3, 0, p_3)$ (for p less than p_3), rather than the certainty of x_2.

But this is all rather contorted: many subjects found the problem too difficult to understand (even though they had just completed a complicated dynamic decision problem under uncertainty) and simply put p equal to 1; at least that was safe!

An alternative, which gets round the difficulty of the understanding of the indifference concept, but which still runs into motivational difficulties, is to iterate towards indifference. So one starts with some (fairly arbitrary) p_3 and asks whether G_1 or G_2 is preferred, or whether the individual regards them as indifferent. If the latter, all well and good. If G_1 is reported preferred, then p_3 is raised; if G_2 is reported preferred, then p_3 is lowered. Then the question is repeated, and the whole process repeated. After a few iterations, one should get close to the p_3 at which the individual is truly indifferent. (Graham Loomes uses a variant on this technique: after three or four iterations, he then asks the subjects to state a probability, within previously revealed bounds, at which indifference occurs.)

The motivational difficulty arises if the subject is aware that this iterative process is going to occur. Even if the experimenter uses the payment mechanism outlined above ('one of the N questions will be picked out') there is an obvious incentive for the subject to manipulate the mechanism. Suppose my indifference p_3 is 0.8; I still have an incentive to report that I prefer G_1 to G_2 (with $p_3 = 0.8$) so that the p_3 associated with G_2 is raised and I therefore have more attractive gambles in the subsequent choice pairs. Indeed, this argument indicates that I should generally overstate my preference for G_1 (though the fully optimal strategy is not clear cut).

An alternative to the above tests of the strict version of the betweenness axiom is to formulate and test a weaker version. Such a weaker version might be as follows: suppose the individual (strictly) prefers G_1 to G_2; then the individual should strictly prefer G_1 to $[G_1 , G_2; q, 1 - q]$ to G_2 for all q strictly between 0 and 1. A test of this weaker version is much more straightforward, and can be carried out solely using preference questions (and the payment mechanism described above).

Tests of the other axioms can also be carried out, *mutatis mutandis*; by carefully constructing such tests, one can in principle distinguish between the various theories. I give examples in the next chapter, where I discuss the work done by other experimental economists in this area. In the meantime, I turn to my own work (carried out with collaborators Daniela

Di Cagno and Elisabetta Strazzera) which concentrates on estimation rather than testing.

5.2   Estimation

It is by now abundantly clear that people make mistakes when they answer questions or perform experiments, however well motivated these experiments are: it is well documented that an individual may give different answers to the same question asked only moments apart (during which time nothing material has changed). Early experiments tended to ignore such errors or mistakes, effectively assuming them to be unimportant. Randomness in such early experiments (and hence the motivation for any subsequent statistical tests) was normally assumed to originate from randomness between subjects, rather than within subjects. So different subjects had different tastes, but subjects did not make mistakes. So when, in the 'Allais-type' example of the early part of this chapter, 70 per cent of the subjects chose G_1 but 65 per cent chose G'_2, one could conclude that a significant proportion of the subjects in the experiment (and hence a significant proportion of the population at large) displayed preferences that were inconsistent with SEUT.

An alternative explanation (or, rather, partial explanation, as we shall see) is that subjects make mistakes. Unfortunately, none of the various theories includes a 'theory of errors' and so we can get no guidance from theory about how such a 'theory of errors' might be constructed. For illustration, however, let us consider the following rather *ad hoc*, but not implausible, theory of errors. Suppose the individual has a preference function which gives a value to any gamble; suppose further that this valuation is done with error so that the perceived valuation is the actual valuation plus a random error term ε. Suppose, in keeping with tradition, that this error term is white noise: it has zero mean, constant variance and is identically and independently distributed across gambles. You could, I suppose, assume that it is normally distributed, by appeal to the central limit theorem. (You could argue that the final error of valuation is a sum of a large number of independent small errors, but see later.)

For example, suppose that our individual obeys the axioms of SEUT except for this additional error. Then the actual valuation of a gamble $G = (p_1, p_2, p_3)$ is

$$V^A(G) = \sum_{i=1}^{3} p_i u(x) + \varepsilon \qquad (5.1)$$

where $u(.)$ is the individual's (Neumann–Morgenstern) utility function and where ε is identically and independently distributed N $(0, \sigma^2)$. The magnitude of the error variance, σ^2, will depend on the magnitude of the errors made by this individual and on the normalization of $u(.)$ adopted. Suppose the latter takes the form: $u(x_3) = 1$, $u(x_1) = 0$; then (5.1) reduces to

$$V^A(G) = p_3 + p_2 u + \varepsilon \qquad (5.2)$$

where $u = u(x_2)$. Now consider the answer to the question: 'Do you prefer G to G'?'; this will depend on the magnitude of the expression

$$V^A(G) - V^A(G') = (p_3 - p_3') + (p_2 - p_2')u + (\varepsilon - \varepsilon') \tag{5.3}$$

using an obvious notation. Thus, on the assumption that G is reported preferred to G' if and only if $V^A(G) > V^A(G')$ we get that the probability that G is reported preferred to G' is

$$1 - \Phi\left[-\frac{(p_3 - p_3') + (p_2 - p_2')u}{\sqrt{2}\sigma} \right] \tag{5.4}$$

where Φ is the distribution function of the standard normal distribution. Let me give a specific example, the same as that used in the first few pages of this chapter. Let the Marschak–Machina triangle be defined over the three amounts (£0, £300, £400) and define four gambles as follows:

$$G_1 = (0,1,0) \qquad\qquad G_2 = (0.2,0,0.8)$$
$$G_1' = (0.75,0.25,0) \qquad G_2' = (0.8,0,0.2)$$

Adopt the normalization above and suppose that $u \equiv u(£300) = 0.85$ and $\sigma = 0.05/\sqrt{2}$. Then G_1 actually is preferred to G_2 and G_1' to G_2'. But the probability that G_1 is reported as preferred to G_2 is $1 - \Phi(-1) = 0.841$ while the probability that G_1' is reported as preferred to G_2' is $1 - \Phi(-0.25) = 0.587$. So there appears to be a shift in preference from the first of the first pair (G_1, G_2) to the second of the second pair (G_1', G_2'). Admittedly, this is not as strong as the shift observed in experiments, where typically the majority prefer G_1 to G_2 and the majority prefer G_2' to G_1', but the shift is in the observed direction. (Note, in fact, that a 'theory of errors' constructed along the above lines – with a zero mean ε term – can never result in a majority preferring G_1 to G_2 and a majority preferring G_2' to G_1'.)

Virtually no theoretical work has been done to construct a 'theory of errors', and very little empirical work, particularly on the testing side, has paid much attention to the source and structure of such errors. There are good reasons why this is so. A potentially more fruitful route is through estimation, where, in principle at least, one can estimate an error structure along with a preference functional. This is a line of enquiry on which I am currently engaged, and which looks potentially very rewarding.

My present methodology uses the pairwise preference question technique, though I am unsure as to whether this is the most efficient procedure. An earlier technique, based on indifference questions (see Hey and Strazzera, 1989), appeared initially more promising but limitations were discovered as the work proceeded. These indifference questions tried to trace out particular indifference curves by starting with some point (gamble) and then trying to elicit other points on the same indifference curves. A repeat interview technique was used, but there were obviously serious problems with motivation. Accordingly, my subsequent experiment used preference questions. For reasons already discussed, such questions have the advantage of being easily understood, much quicker to answer and easily motivated. At the same time the answers are less informative – all you discover is which is the most preferred gamble, not the magnitude of the preference – and so while you may be able to ask many more questions the information content of each answer is that much lower.

A full description of the experiment can be found in Hey and Di Cagno (1990); here I confine myself to the broad details. The experiment was computerized, and gambles were represented in circle form; figure 5.4(a) shows a typical pair of gambles. Other experimenters use different representations: the representation favoured by Graham Loomes (1991) is portrayed in figure 5.4(b), and that favoured by Colin Camerer (see Camerer, 1989) is portrayed in figure 5.4(c). You will note that the Camerer representation communicates the expected value of each gamble through the total area within the rectangles (labelled with the amounts of the payoffs) and so any subject who responded to a visual stimulus provided by the areas might subconsciously be manipulated into reporting preferences based on expected values. Of course, this type of bias might result from any kind of visual representation: in mine, for example, the shading might distort the impact of the monetary amount in the subject's thought processes. (We did try to make the shading proportional to the amount, so that £0 had no shading, £10 some shading, £20 around twice as much as £10 had and so on, but no such scheme can ever be perfect.) A representation I have used in another context is portrayed in figure 5.4(d).

We used a total of 60 preference questions. We had thought that this was the maximum number that subjects could seriously answer during a typical 30–40 minute session, but it turned out that the vast majority of subjects answered the 60 questions in 15 minutes or so – many were literally 'rattling through' the questions. This could be interpreted in two ways: that they found the experiment easy to understand and easy to do; or that they simply answered at random, with no real thought. The latter seemed to be the case for some half-dozen of the (68) subjects who expressed a preference for the right-hand gamble for virtually all the 60 questions. I should note that this was the 'easiest' preference to express on the experiment: the software allowed the subject to iterate between expressing indifference, expressing preference for the right-hand gamble and expressing preference for the left-hand gamble, in that order. The iteration was implemented by pressing any key on the keyboard and was terminated, when the expressed preference was the one that the subject wanted to express, by pressing the 'F' key (for Fix).

The 60 questions related to four Marschak–Machina triangles: triangle 1 had amounts £0, £10 and £20, triangle 2 had £0, £10 and £30, triangle 3 had £0, £20 and £30 and triangle 4 had £10, £20 and £30. So each of the 60 preference questions involved a pairwise choice between two gambles, the outcomes of both involving at most three of the amounts £0, £10, £20 and £30. We used a slight variant of the payment mechanism described above because the expected winnings from a randomly chosen gamble were around £12.50 – rather more than we wished to pay. We used the following payment mechanism at the end of the experiment: the subject picked one cloakroom

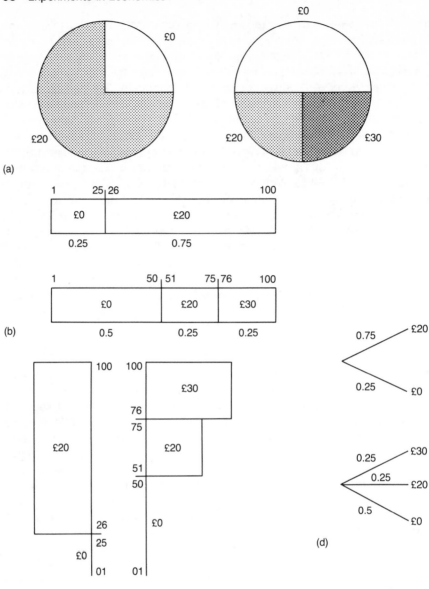

Figure 5.4   Representations of gambles.

ticket at random from a box containing tickets numbered 1 to 100; if this number was greater than 60 the subject went away empty handed; however, if it was between 1 and 60 we played out the subject's preferred gamble on that particular question. The gamble was played out by placing a hard copy of the circle on top of a spinning device (a 'distribution simulator' or continuous roulette wheel) with a freely spinning pointer, and letting the subject set the pointer spinning. So each subject went away with £0 or £10 or £20 or £30.

The question of the choice of the 'best' 60 questions is one to which we gave considerable thought; in principle it is clear that some sets of 60 questions are more informative (and hence statistically more efficient) than other sets, but the efficiency depends partly on the preference functionals that we are trying to estimate. In a sense, therefore, one needs some kind of preliminary study to indicate the rough shape of an individual's function, and then a larger study using a set of questions indicated by the preliminary study. This we plan to do in future experiments, but in this first experiment we rather arbitrarily split the 60 questions equally into 15 in each triangle, and chose the same 15 pairs of points in each triangle. In choosing these 15 pairs, we tried to get a mixture so that the slope of the line joining the pair varied considerably – from 1/7 to 7/1.

A total of 68 subjects performed the experiment, mainly undergraduate students (across the whole range of subjects) on EXEC's register. While these 68 subjects could be regarded as representative of the population from which they were drawn, they should not necessarily be regarded as representative of any wider population; we therefore make no claims regarding the representativeness of our findings.[1] The experiment was performed in EXEC's computerized laboratory.

The data from the experiment consist of the recorded preferences for each of the 68 subjects on each of the 60 questions. Although all subjects were given the opportunity on each question of indicating indifference between the two gambles (in which case *we* would choose the gamble to be played out if that particular question was randomly selected at the payment stage of the experiment), a total of 36 of the 68 subjects *always* expressed a strict preference for one or other of the two gambles; we call these 36 the P subjects. The remaining 32 subjects, whom we call the I subjects, somewhere expressed indifference (possibly on as few as one question, possibly on as many as 12 questions). For reasons we discuss shortly, the responses of these two sets need to be analysed in different ways.

In our paper (Hey and Di Cagno, 1990) we discuss the estimation of three preference functionals: generalized regret, generalized SEUT and difference regret. Here I confine myself, for reasons of space, to just the first two of these. It will be recalled from chapter 4 that the indifference curves under regret theory are straight lines fanning out from some point to the southwest of the origin of the triangle; under SEUT they are parallel straight lines. There are, of course, certain cross-triangle restrictions. So, in essence, we fit fanning-out and parallel indifference lines (with cross-triangle restrictions) to each of the subject's responses. Let me be more specific. Under SEUT the subject's evaluation of the difference between the left-hand gamble and the right-hand gamble is given by

$$\text{val} = (p_1 u_1 + p_2 u_2 + p_3 u_3) - (q_1 u_1 + q_2 u_2 + q_3 u_3)$$

that is,

$$\text{val} = (p_1 - q_1)u_1 + (p_2 - q_2)u_2 + (p_3 - q_3)u_3, \qquad (5.5)$$

where (p_1, p_2, p_3) denotes the left-hand gamble, (q_1, q_2, q_3) denotes the right-hand gamble, and u_1, u_2 and u_3 denote the utilities of the three outcomes in the triangle (x_1, x_2 and x_3 respectively). Under regret, if we assume that the two gambles in any pair are statistically independent, we have that the subject's evaluation of the difference between the left-hand and right-hand gambles is (see equation (4.1))

$$\text{val} = (p_2q_1 - p_1q_2)\psi_{21} + (p_3q_1 - p_1q_3)\psi_{31} + (p_3q_2 - p_2q_3)\psi_{32} \qquad (5.6)$$

where ψ_{21}, ψ_{31} and ψ_{32} respectively represent the modified utility differences (see chapter 4)

$$\psi_{21} = \psi(x_2, x_1) \qquad \psi_{31} = \psi(x_3, x_1) \qquad \psi_{32}(x_3, x_2)$$

We need to extend this to the four Marschak–Machina triangles in our experiment. After some tedious algebra, we get the following: under SEUT

$$\text{val} = \beta_1 V_1 + \beta_2 V_2 + \beta_3 V_3 \qquad (5.7)$$

and under regret

$$\text{val} = \beta_4 V_4 + \beta_5 V_5 + \beta_6 V_6 + \beta_7 V_7 + \beta_8 V_8 + \beta_9 V_9 \qquad (5.8)$$

where β_1 to β_3 are SEUT utilities ($\beta_1 = u(£10)$, $\beta_2 = u(£20)$ and $\beta_3 = u(£30)$) and β_4 to β_9 are ψ values ($\beta_4 = \psi(£10, £0)$, $\beta_5 = \psi(£20, £10)$, $\beta_6 = \psi(£30, £20)$, $\beta_7 = \psi(£20, £0)$, $\beta_8 = \psi(£30, £10)$ and $\beta_9 = \psi(£30, £0)$). (Note that we put $u(£0) = 0$ and $\psi(x, x) = 0$ for all x.) The Vs are variables (over the 60 questions) defined as follows:

$$V_1 = z_1(p_1 - q_1) + (1 - z_2)(p_2 - q_2)$$
$$V_2 = z_2(p_2 - q_2) + (1 - z_3)(p_3 - q_3)$$
$$V_3 = z_3(p_3 - q_3)$$
$$V_4 = (1 - z_2)(p_2q_1 - p_1q_2)$$
$$V_5 = z_1z_2(p_2q_1 - p_1q_2) + (1 - z_3)(p_3q_2 - p_2q_3)$$
$$V_6 = z_2z_3(p_3q_2 - p_2q_3)$$
$$V_7 = (1 - z_1)z_2(p_2q_1 - p_1q_2) + (1 - z_3)(p_3q_1 - p_1q_3)$$
$$V_8 = z_1z_3(p_3q_1 - p_1q_3) + (1 - z_2)z_3(p_3q_2 - p_3q_2 - p_2q_3)$$
$$V_9 = (1 - z_1)z_3(p_2q_1 - p_1q_2)$$

The zs are dummy variables defined as follows:

$$\text{Triangle 1:} z_1 = z_2 = z_3 = 0$$
$$\text{Triangle 2:} z_1 = z_2 = 0 \qquad z_3 = 1$$
$$\text{Triangle 3:} z_1 = 0 \qquad z_2 = z_3 = 1$$
$$\text{Triangle 4:} z_1 = z_2 = z_3 = 1$$

The purpose of this extra notation is simply to get forms ((5.7) and (5.8)) that can be recognized as standard forms for a well-known econometrics package.

As I noted in chapter 4, SEUT is a special case of regret; the latter collapses to the former when

$$\psi(x_i, x_j) = u(x_i) - u(x_j) \qquad \text{for all } i, j$$

In terms of the βs this implies the three restrictions

$$\beta_4 + \beta_5 = \beta_7 \qquad \beta_6 + \beta_7 = \beta_9 \qquad \beta_4 + \beta_8 = \beta_9$$

As these restrictions are linear in the parameters, we can easily test for their validity using standard tests.

It is possible that one or other of these two formulations fits the recorded data for some subject exactly. For example, if some subject worked out the expected winnings from each gamble and expressed his or her preference solely on the basis of this expected value then a perfect fit would be obtained under both formulations. Moreover, it is possible for one set of responses to be consistent with perfect fits of one or more formulations for several (countably infinite) sets of parameters. This is because the data are preference-type data.

'Fortunately', this problem did not arise with any of our subjects: for none of them did either of the formulations fit exactly. The conclusion, then, is either that both formulations are wrong or that the data are recorded with error – that subjects make mistakes. For reasons already discussed, I prefer to subscribe to the latter explanation.

Errors could arise in a number of ways: the subjects could misunderstand the nature of the experiment; they could press the wrong key by accident; they could be in a hurry to finish the experiment; they could be motivated by something other than maximizing the welfare from the experiment *per se*. Some of these are genuine errors; others are quite clearly not. If we confine ourselves to those that are, we are seeking an explanation of why a subject, who is actually endeavouring to behave as regret theory requires or as SEUT requires, gives responses to the questions which do not fit the regret specification or the SEUT specification exactly. If this is the question we are trying to answer then it rules out alternative objectives as a reason for this error. We are thus brought back to 'genuine' error – mistakes, carelessness, slips, inattentiveness etc. One could argue, following good precedent, that such errors would be normally distributed (through the good offices of the central limit theorem) with zero mean (unless there was some inbuilt bias in the experimental design) and with a variance that was independent of the gambles themselves (and hence constant). So we could argue that what the recorded preferences were based on were the values of

$$y_i^* = \text{val}_i + \varepsilon_i \qquad i = 1, \ldots, 60 \qquad (5.9)$$

where the ε_i were identically and independently normally distributed with mean zero and variance σ^2 (i is the question number). In an alternative 'theory of errors' it might be argued that the variance of ε was in some way related to the valuation, val, itself. But recall that val measures the evaluation of the difference between two gambles, so that a large positive value of val indicates that the first gamble is strongly preferred to the second while a small positive value of val indicates that the first gamble is only weakly preferred to the second. It is not clear to us whether the variance of ε in the former case should be larger or smaller than in the latter, but we would be happy to explore the empirical implications of any plausible alternative hypothesis that was suggested to us.

We therefore work with specfication (5.9) and the associated assumption about the error term. We must finally relate this specification to our observations.

For the P group (those 36 subjects who always expressed a strict preference) we assume that preference for the first gamble was expressed whenever y^* was positive and that preference for the second was expressed when y^* was negative. So our observations are on the variable y which takes (by convention) the value 1 when y^* is positive and the value 0 when y^* is negative. We thus get the standard probit model. Note, as usual, that not all the parameters are identified, and so following usual practice we put $\sigma = 1$ and thus get

$$y^* = \text{val} + \varepsilon$$
$$y = 1 \text{ if } y^* > 0 \text{ and } y = 0 \text{ if } y^* \leq 0$$
$$\varepsilon \sim N(0, 1)$$

For the I group of subjects (those 32 subjects who somewhere expressed indifference) we need a slightly different formulation. Here our hypothesis is a simple one: we assume that the subject will express indifference if the value of y^* is 'close' to zero. For obvious reasons, this should be symmetrically defined, and so we operationalize it by assuming that the subject reports indifference if y^* is between $-\tau$ and $+\tau$ where τ is a threshold. We estimate τ along with the other parameters of the model. The full specification is then

$$y^* = \text{val} + \varepsilon$$
$$y = 0 \text{ if } y^* \leq -\tau$$
$$y = 1 \text{ if } -\tau < y^* \leq \tau$$
$$y = 2 \text{ if } \tau < y^*$$
$$\varepsilon \sim N(0, 1)$$

Both specifications were estimated using LIMDEP 5.1. A summary is given in table 5.1 which reports the (negative of) the maximized value of the log likelihood function for both formulations and the Wald test statistic for the test of the restrictions (see above) which reduce regret to SEUT. The critical values for this test statistic ($\chi^2(3)$ under the null) are 6.25 (10 per cent), 7.81 (5 per cent) and 11.3 (1 per cent). For the 68 subjects, no values of the Wald statistic are significant at the 1 per cent level, three are significant at 5 per cent but not at 1 per cent and six are significant at 10 per cent but not at 5 per cent. (The remaining 59 statistics are not significant at 10 per cent.) So the message is clear: regret fits better than SEUT but not significantly better for the vast majority of the subjects. In terms of the Marschak–Machina triangle this suggests that fanning-out indifference lines (the regret model) do not fit significantly better than parallel indifference curves (the SEUT model) for the vast majority of the subjects.

Table 5.1   Summary of main results

| Subject number (type) | Log likelihoods | | Wald test statistic |
	Regret	SEUT	Regret SEUT
1 (I)	46.894	50.685	8.03
2 (I)	34.204	36.190	3.50
3 (I)	33.840	35.586	2.04
4 (P)	26.135	29.064	5.09
5 (I)	39.135	39.528	0.63
6 (P)	32.298	33.669	1.46
7 (P)	16.691	23.462	2.29
8 (I)	28.683	32.685	2.05
9 (I)	40.245	40.904	0.79
10 (I)	38.068	42.541	5.35
11 (I)	28.753	31.422	2.19
12 (I)	30.033	32.187	3.74
13 (P)	31.040	32.778	3.23
14 (I)	31.231	38.104	7.77
15 (P)	22.318	26.017	5.54
16 (P)	28.791	30.718	3.52
17 (P)	28.042	29.618	2.90
18 (P)	20.804	22.784	3.20
19 (P)	31.205	32.066	1.68
20 (P)	27.394	29.874	4.21
21 (P)	29.567	30.515	1.86
22 (I)	30.275	32.658	2.42
23 (P)	20.679	24.419	5.91
24 (P)	15.094	20.038	0.52
25 (P)	10.767	20.329	3.57
26 (I)	43.131	43.624	0.75
27 (I)	28.654	31.151	2.33
28 (I)	40.608	43.087	4.28
29 (I)	45.388	46.568	2.11
30 (P)	25.749	29.623	6.65
31 (I)	31.754	32.508	1.11
32 (P)	25.184	29.172	6.93
33 (P)	25.385	26.747	2.59
34 (P)	22.352	26.052	6.39
35 (I)	34.924	36.552	2.47
36 (P)	19.817	23.661	3.40
37 (I)	34.496	34.741	0.35
38 (I)	35.445	36.134	1.15
39 (P)	17.724	25.647	5.33
40 (P)	13.032	19.126	0.40
41 (I)	29.690	34.343	5.13

continued

Table 5.1   Summary of main results (*continued*)

| Subject number (type) | Log likelihoods | | Wald test statistic |
	Regret	SEUT	Regret SEUT
42 (P)	25.065	29.624	7.51
43 (I)	20.658	29.429	2.14
44 (I)	27.336	32.447	3.83
45 (P)	28.778	29.542	1.38
46 (I)	25.453	30.223	3.06
47 (P)	15.260	16.794	0.91
48 (I)	41.546	44.899	4.62
49 (P)	29.498	31.338	3.36
50 (I)	28.011	29.177	1.11
51 (I)	32.730	33.490	0.63
52 (P)	30.929	31.747	1.53
53 (P)	26.126	28.075	3.54
54 (I)	44.853	50.165	0.48
55 (P)	27.474	28.366	1.74
56 (P)	31.643	33.009	2.46
57 (P)	24.698	24.920	0.44
58 (I)	35.035	37.283	3.76
59 (P)	15.705	25.543	3.84
60 (P)	19.241	30.727	0.49
61 (I)	36.752	38.628	2.29
62 (I)	32.650	34.174	2.55
63 (I)	32.918	34.826	2.22
64 (P)	26.550	28.880	3.87
65 (P)	27.251	33.899	0.58
66 (P)	18.523	23.736	7.29
67 (P)	13.032	19.126	0.40
68 (I)	38.708	40.345	3.27

Table 5.2 gives some further summary information: the incidence of correct parameter values and the numbers of correct predictions under the two formulations. Let us begin with the former. The first most obvious requirement of the various theories is that all the relevant parameters should be positive. Columns a in table 5.2 summarize the situation as far as the estimated parameters are concerned. It will be seen that all parameters are correctly positive for 35 subjects (51 per cent) for the regret formulation and for 64 subjects (94 per cent) for the SEUT formulation. Of these 35 and 64 subjects, all coefficients were significantly positive for 1 and 57 subjects respectively (columns b). Thus on this basis the SEUT formulation does particularly well and the regret formulation particularly badly.

Table 5.2   Summary of correct restrictions and predictions

Subject number	Correct restrictions						Correct predictions	
	Regret			SEUT			Regret	SEUT
	a	b	c	a	b	c		
1	N	N	N	Y	Y	Y	40	40
2	N	N	N	Y	Y	Y	46	44
3	Y	N	N	Y	Y	Y	46	47
4	N	N	N	Y	Y	Y	50	58
5	Y	N	Y	Y	Y	Y	42	44
6	Y	N	Y	Y	Y	Y	43	42
7	Y	N	N	Y	Y	N	51	50
8	Y	N	N	Y	Y	Y	48	48
9	Y	N	Y	Y	Y	Y	44	44
10	N	N	N	Y	Y	Y	46	44
11	N	N	N	Y	Y	N	51	47
12	Y	N	N	Y	Y	N	45	43
13	Y	N	N	Y	Y	Y	43	44
14	N	N	N	Y	Y	Y	46	42
15	N	N	N	Y	Y	N	50	50
16	Y	N	N	Y	Y	Y	46	45
17	Y	N	N	Y	Y	Y	49	46
18*	N	N	N	Y	N	N	53	48
19	Y	N	N	Y	Y	Y	44	46
20	Y	N	N	Y	Y	Y	45	46
21	Y	Y	Y	Y	Y	Y	47	44
22	Y	N	N	Y	Y	Y	47	49
23	N	N	N	Y	Y	Y	54	50
24*	N	N	N	N	N	N	55	51
25*	N	N	N	N	N	N	55	52
26	Y	N	Y	Y	Y	Y	42	45
27	Y	N	N	Y	Y	N	49	47
28	Y	N	Y	Y	Y	Y	43	46
29	Y	N	Y	Y	Y	Y	36	37
30*	N	N	N	Y	Y	Y	49	47
31	Y	N	N	Y	Y	Y	48	46
32*	N	N	N	Y	Y	Y	50	56
33	N	N	N	Y	Y	N	50	47
34	N	N	N	Y	Y	N	52	50
35	N	N	N	Y	Y	Y	47	46
36*	Y	N	N	Y	N	N	51	50
37	Y	N	Y	Y	Y	Y	44	44
38	Y	N	Y	Y	Y	Y	44	44
39*	Y	N	N	Y	Y	N	53	52
40*	N	N	N	N	N	N	56	54

continued

Table 5.2   Summary of correct restrictions and predictions (*continued*)

Subject number	Correct restrictions						Correct predictions	
	Regret			SEUT				
	a	b	c	a	b	c	Regret	SEUT
41	N	N	N	Y	Y	Y	48	45
42	N	N	N	Y	Y	Y	48	49
43*	N	N	N	Y	Y	N	50	46
44	N	N	N	Y	Y	N	50	47
45	Y	N	Y	Y	Y	Y	47	52
46*	N	N	N	Y	N	N	52	53
47*	N	N	N	Y	N	N	55	55
48	Y	N	N	Y	Y	Y	40	41
49	Y	N	N	Y	Y	Y	41	47
50*	N	N	N	Y	N	N	52	50
51	N	N	N	Y	Y	Y	51	47
52	Y	N	Y	Y	Y	Y	45	43
53	N	N	N	Y	Y	Y	43	44
54	Y	N	Y	Y	Y	Y	46	42
55	N	N	N	Y	Y	N	50	50
56	Y	N	N	Y	Y	Y	46	45
57	Y	N	Y	Y	Y	N	49	46
58	N	N	N	Y	Y	Y	53	48
59*	N	N	N	Y	N	N	44	46
60	N	N	N	Y	Y	Y	45	46
61	Y	N	N	Y	Y	Y	47	44
62	Y	N	Y	Y	Y	Y	47	49
63	Y	N	N	Y	Y	Y	54	50
64	Y	N	N	Y	Y	Y	55	51
65	N	N	N	Y	Y	Y	55	52
66	N	N	N	Y	N	N	42	45
67*	N	N	N	N	N	N	49	47
68	Y	N	N	Y	Y	Y	43	46

The asterisks indicate 'rogue subjects' (see text).

The two theories also impose restrictions on the relative values of the parameters. On the assumption that all the subjects (strictly) prefer (strictly) more money to less the restrictions are as follows:

$$\text{Regret: } 0 < \psi(\pounds 10, \pounds 0) < \psi(\pounds 20, \pounds 0) < \psi(\pounds 30, \pounds 0)$$

$$0 < \psi(\pounds 20, \pounds 10) < \psi(\pounds 30, \pounds 10)$$

$$0 < \psi(\pounds 30, \pounds 20)$$

$$\text{SEUT: } \qquad 0 < u(\pounds 10) < u(\pounds 20) < u(\pounds 30)$$

Columns c in table 5.2 test whether the estimated parameters satisfy these restrictions. It will be seen that as far as regret is concerned just 14 subjects (21 per cent) have estimated coefficients which do satisfy the above restrictions, while for generalized SEUT it is 45 subjects (66 per cent). Again, the regret formulation does not perform particularly well.

The final two columns summarize the numbers of correct predictions produced by the fitted models. We should explain what this means. For the P subjects, it is straightforward: $y = 0$ (1) is predicted by the fitted model if the probability of $y = 0$ (1) is greater than 0.5. In the ordered probit cases (the I subjects), $y = 0$ (respectively 1 or 2) is predicted if $y = 0$ (respectively 1 or 2) has the highest probability. As it happened, in no case (i.e. none of the questions for any of the subjects in the I group) was indifference predicted, even though indifference was sometimes expressed. This simply reflects the rather odd operation of the threshold in the ordered probit model.

As will be seen from the final two columns of table 5.2 the regret and the SEUT models do equally well on average in terms of predictions, although for some subjects the regret model does better while for other subjects the SEUT model does better.

Let me now give some flavour of the kinds of estimated functionals that we are obtaining. We give below four examples: two of I subjects and two of P subjects permed with two regret formulations and two SEUT formulations.

We begin with subject 17 who is a good example of an SEUT subject from the P group. Our estimate of equation (5.7) (substituted into equation (5.9)) is

$$y* = 3.6681 V_1 + 4.2199 V_2 + 5.5574 V_3 + \varepsilon \qquad LL = -29.618$$
$$(3.9) \qquad\quad (3.4) \qquad\quad (3.2) \qquad\qquad\qquad [15.7]$$

(the figures in parentheses are t ratios (57 degrees of freedom) and the figure in square brackets is a $\chi^2(2)$). The figure in square brackets tests the significance of the probit as a whole – it is clearly highly significant. As will be seen, all the coefficients are positive, and significantly so. Normalized to $u(£30) = 1$ ($u(£0) = 0$ of course) the estimates yield

$$u(£0) = 0 \qquad u(£10) = 0.660 \qquad u(£20) = 0.759 \qquad u(£30) = 1$$

indicating a moderately risk-averse SEUT subject. Recalling that LIMDEP normalizes the standard deviation of the error term ε to unity, we can appraise the extent of the errors made by subject 17. Suppose that one of the two gambles has an expected utility (unnormalized) of 4.22 (equivalent, to the subject, to the certainty of £20) and that the other gamble has an expected utility (unnormalized) of 3.67 (equivalent to the subject to the certainty of £10), then the difference between the two expected utilities (the val of our discussion above) is $4.22 - 3.67 = 0.55$. Then the subject would (correctly) report that he or she preferred the first gamble with probability 0.709 and would (incorrectly) report that he or she preferred the second gamble with probability 0.291. A similar comparison of a gamble with an expected utility of 4.22 (the certainty equivalent of £20) and a gamble with an expected utility of 0.00 (the certainty equivalent of £0) indicates that the former will (correctly) be indicated as preferred with virtual certainty, while in a comparison of 5.56 (certainty equivalent of £30) with 3.67 (certainty equivalent of £10) the former will (correctly) be indicated as preferred with probability 0.971. In our opinion, these errors are disquietingly large; yet they are not untypical.

A good example of an SEUT subject from the I group is subject 33; the estimated SEUT formulation is

$$y* = 3.9379V_1 + 4.7332V_2 + 6.9908V_3 + \varepsilon \qquad \hat{\tau} = 0.0622 \qquad LL = -32.658$$
$$\quad (6.6) \qquad (6.6) \qquad (7.1) \qquad\qquad (1.4) \qquad\qquad [26.7]$$

(the figures in parentheses are t ratios (57 degrees of freedom) and the figure in square brackets is a $\chi^2(3)$). The τ (threshold) value is estimated at 0.0622, and so this subject reports indifference whenever the valuation (of the difference between the two gambles) lies between -0.0622 and $+0.0622$. This is a relatively small range (compared with the standard deviation of the error term of unity), indicating that indifference would only be reported (when genuine indifference existed) with probability 0.048; the rest of the time one or other of the two gambles would be expressed as preferred (not, of course, that it matters given the incentive structure of this experiment).

The normalized utility values for subject 33 are

$$u(£0) = 0 \qquad u(£10) = 0.563 \qquad u(£20) = 0.677 \qquad u(£30) = 1$$

indicating a subject who is risk averse for small amounts but risk loving for larger amounts. The frequency of errors for this subject is slightly less than for subject 17 (witness the generally larger value of the estimated coefficients) but it is still considerable.

A good example of a regret subject from the P group is subject 45. For this subject, our estimate of equation (5.8) (substituted into equation (5.9)) is

$$y* = 1.5916V_4 + 1.3584V_5 + 2.9415V_6 + 3.6673V_7 + 6.7310V_8 + 7.4714V_9$$
$$\quad (1.6) \qquad (1.5) \qquad (2.9) \qquad (2.7) \qquad (2.8) \qquad (2.0)$$

$$LL = -28.778$$
$$[18.82]$$

(the figures in parentheses are t ratios (54 degrees of freedom) and the figure in square brackets is a $\chi^2(5)$). Normalized to $\psi(£30, £0) = 1$ these estimates (four of which are significant at the 5 per cent level and the remaining two almost so) yield the following $\psi(., .)$ values:

$$\psi(£0, £0) = 0 \qquad \psi(£10, £0) = 0.213 \qquad \psi(£20, £0) = 0.492 \qquad \psi(£30, £0) = 1.0$$

$$\psi(£10, £10) = 0 \qquad \psi(£20, £10) = 0.182 \qquad \psi(£30, £10) = 0.901$$

$$\psi(£20, £20) = 0 \qquad \psi(£30, £20) = 0.394$$

The general shape of these is satisfactory and they imply that this subject's indifference curves are fanning out in triangles 1, 3 and 4, though fanning in in triangle 2. The frequency of error is slightly less than that of the two SEUT subjects discussed above.

Finally we give an example of a generalized regret estimation for a subject from the I group. This is subject 26, and the estimation is

$$y* = 3.3662 V_4 + 1.4346 V_5 + 1.4938 V_6 + 4.52805 V_7 + 4.5264 V_8 + 6.3113 V_9$$
$$\quad\ (2.5) \qquad (1.8) \qquad\ \ (2.2) \qquad\ \ (4.4) \qquad\quad (2.3) \qquad\quad (1.3)$$

$$\tau = 0.2873 \qquad LL = -43.131$$
$$\ \ \ (2.3) \qquad\qquad\ [24.40]$$

(the figures in parentheses are t ratios (53 degrees of freedom) and the figure in square brackets is a $\chi^2(6)$). Normalized to $\psi(£30, £0) = 1$ these estimates (five of which are significant at the 5 per cent level and the remaining one almost so) yield the following $\psi(., .)$ values:

$\psi(£0, £0) = 0 \qquad \psi(£10, £0) = 0.533 \qquad \psi(£20, £0) = 0.717 \qquad \psi(£30, £0) = 1.0$

$\psi(£10, £10) = 0 \qquad \psi(£20, £10) = 0.227 \qquad \psi(£30, £10) = 0.717$

$\psi(£20, £20) = 0 \qquad \psi(£30, £20) = 0.237$

These imply that the indifference curves are fanning out in triangles 3 and 4 and fanning in in triangles 1 and 2. The estimated threshold value (0.287) is considerably larger than the estimate for the SEUT formulation discussed above, and indicates that the subject would report indifference if his or her valuation (including the error term) was between -0.287 and 0.287. For a case of genuine indifference this would happen with probability 0.226. The frequency of errors generally is slightly greater than that for subject 45 above.

5.3   Conclusions

So what can we conclude from all this? First, the experimental design appears to be a good one, although there is a slight difficulty with a few suspected 'rogue subjects' (those marked with an asterisk in table 5.2 who indicated a preference for the right-hand gamble in virtually all the 60 questions). We shall be amending the software to reduce the chance of this happening again in the future, although there may be other ways of achieving this: for example, increasing the magnitude of the monetary outcomes and/or introducing losses as outcomes; these may help to focus the minds of the rather less patient subjects.

As far as the actual results themselves are concerned, the most prominent feature is the importance of the error term. The examples cited above, if anything, err on the conservative side: most subjects had larger errors. This is rather worrying, but it is something that economic theorists will have to consider seriously in the future. In the past, the question of errors has been rather swept under the carpet, but it is clear that the subjects in our experiments were making substantial errors. Our characterization of these errors as an independent normal process with zero mean may not be satisfactory, but we have very little useful theory to guide us. Otherwise, the results suggest that regret does fit better than SEUT, but this is hardly surprising given that it contains SEUT as a special case. But the superiority, in general, is not significant. One might be tempted to conclude that these results show that regret is not significantly better than SEUT, and therefore that indifference lines, while they may fan out across the triangle, do not fan out to any significant extent. But caution should be exercised. The power of these tests does not appear to be particularly great, and the amount of information contained in the data (even with 'as many as' 60 questions) is not as large as might appear. So our results might simply be telling us that we do not have enough information to discriminate between regret and SEUT rather than that the former is not significantly better than the latter. To determine whether this is in fact the case we need to discover the statistical properties of our estimation methodology; this we are now doing through simulation studies.

Finally, you might like to argue that we have excluded the correct formulation by our restriction to the estimation of particular sets of linear indifference sets. This may well be the case. Other possibilities were discussed in chapter 4; one of particular interest is that proposed by Gul (1990) with his disappointment theory. In this, indifference lines fan out (from a point to the southwest of the origin of the triangle) in the bottom right of the triangle and fan in (from a point to the northeast of the hypotenuse of the triangle) in the top left of the triangle. Since the fanning-in and fanning-out points are on a ray through the origin, this implies an extra degree of freedom in fitting a set of indifference lines compared with regret theory. The question once again remains: will the improved goodness of fit be sufficiently large to compensate for this extra degree of freedom? We shall see.

Of course, the indifference curves might not be linear. Moving to non-linear indifference maps introduces further parameters to estimate, thereby further reducing the power and efficiency of the exercise. But this is something we need to do (once again, given an appropriate parameterization) perhaps after we have carried out some Monte Carlo studies illuminating the properties of the present estimation procedures. I wonder, however, whether the noise in the data (the apparent inaccuracies in the subjects' answers) will drown out such refinements.

Note

1 This raises an important issue connected with this type of experiment, and indeed with all experiments concerned with testing various theories of decision-making under risk. While these experiments often unearth a significant proportion of subjects who behave in a manner inconsistent with SEUT, and while there is often an implicit presumption by the authors of such work that their results are not untypical, it could be a mistake to infer that they were. This suggests that more attention should be paid in future to the running of representative experiments – particularly if the experiments are supposed to be descriptions of the extent of differing types of behaviour in the populace at large, rather than demonstrations of the range of types of behaviour that exist in the world at large.

6

A Broad Survey of Other Experimental Studies

6.1 Introduction

Experiments into (economic) decision-making under risk and uncertainty have a long and distinguished history; more than in any other area of economics, experiments have had a profound influence on the development of theory. Indeed, with only a slight exaggeration, one could argue that the development of modern (subjective) expected utility theory was a direct response to the 'experimental' evidence concerning reactions to the famous St Petersburg paradox. (This paradox relates to the observation that an individual typically would never contribute more than a very modest amount of money to enter the gamble which led to outcome 2^{i-1} with probability 2^{-i} for $i = 1, 2, \ldots$, even though the expected winnings from this gamble are infinite.)

SEUT became firmly established in economics as an immediate consequence of the classic book by Neumann and Morgenstern (1944), *Theory of Games and Economic Behavior*, and enjoyed a virtually uncontested reign, despite the early experimental work of Allais in the 1950s, until increasing numbers of economists repeating and duplicating this early work accumulated sufficient experimental evidence against SEUT to cast doubt over its general and universal applicability in economics. In the first part of this chapter I overview the experimental work and the first attempts, by Kahneman and Tversky, to provide a serious alternative to SEUT. After discussing some apparently unrelated experimental work on preference reversals and the Ellsberg paradox, I then move on to the experimental work of the 1980s which tests not only SEUT itself but also the crop of new alternative theories that I discussed in chapter 4. This process of testing is not yet complete, but more evidence is being accumulated daily. Nor is it clear what the conclusion might ultimately be, since no single theory seems, at present, capable of explaining all the evidence. Only time will tell.

6.2   The Early 'Anti-SEUT' Experiments

The Allais Experiment of 1952, the associated Allais paradox and the celebrated episode of Savage's violation of SEUT at the 1952 Colloquium (and his subsequent change of heart) are all part of the folklore of economics. Yet, even now, the full findings of the 1952 experiment have not been published, and their early and partial dissemination was hindered by their being published in French.

The Allais paradox was just part of the experiment. Allais had a more fundamental aim: to show that the (Neumann–Morgenstern or SEUT) utility function of an individual often differed from the same individual's cardinal utility function (termed by Allais 'the index of psychological value') and hence to conclude that the SEUT theory was invalid. I do not want to rehearse his argument here, as my main concern is with his experiment which is of particular interest as it illustrates what can be achieved through the experimental method.

The experiment was administered by questionnaire; it was not financially motivated (which was probably a good thing in view of the amounts of money involved!) and so respondents were presumed to have other reasons for wanting to answer honestly (if indeed that was the case). Let me concentrate first on those questions designed to elicit the individual's SEUT (or Neumann–Morgenstern) cardinal utility function, and let me give an example of one question and one subject's answer to it. This example is given on page 621 of the splendid volume edited by Allais and Hagen (1979), which is a must for anyone wishing to follow up these early experiments. It is de Finetti's (a subject picked at random presumably!) reply to question 96. I have reproduced it in table 6.1 in the format used by Allais and Hagen (1979). The units of currency are ancient French francs (£1 in 1990 is worth about 1000 ancient French francs). The primary purpose of the question is to find the certainty equivalent (the amount of money to be received with certainty) of a 50–50 gamble between 100 million and nothing. de Finetti's answer was 28 million, and so the conclusion drawn is that, for de Finetti, he is indifferent between getting 28 millions for sure and taking part in a 50–50 gamble which yields either 100 million or nothing. You should note the way that the question is constructed, with its tacit suggestion that there should be some value (presumably between 5 and 70 millions) at which the individual would be indifferent, and the even more tacit suggestion that the individual should prefer the gamble at certainty amounts less than that value and prefer the certainty for certainty amounts greater than that value. It is not clear whether all subjects were happy with these tacit suggestions. Nor is it clear what incentives they had to answer honestly – other than that of avoiding ridicule when Allais subsequently published their answers! You will also note the rather nice device of recording the 'degree of conviction' with which the various answers were given. Although this too suffers from the lack of an appropriate incentive, if the answers were honestly given this would provide invaluable information – particularly for any 'theory of errors' (see chapter 5).

Table 6.1   de Finetti's answers to question 96

Question 96	Answer	Degree of conviction with which given[a]
Would you prefer		
– an even chance of winning 100		
millions or nothing		
– or the immediate cash sum of:		
5 millions	No[c]	PAH
10 millions	No	H
20 millions	No	BH
25 millions	No	BH
30 millions	Yes	BH
35 millions	Yes	BH
40 millions	Yes	H
50 millions	Yes	AH
70 millions	Yes	AH
At what approximate level X' does your preference change?		28 millions

[a] BH, much hesitation; H, hesitation; PAH, almost without [b] hesitation; AH, without hesitation.
[[b] See page 616 of Allais and Hagen (1979), where for PAH it is written 'almost with hesitation' which must surely be a misprint.]
[c] No, prefer gamble; yes, prefer cash sum.

The answers obtained from question 96 and questions of a similar type (see below) enable the experimenter to build up a picture of the subject's SEUT (Neumann–Morgenstern) utility function – assuming one exists. For example, if we calibrate the utility function by putting $u(0) = 0$ and $u(100) = 1$ (all monetary amounts in millions of French francs) then de Finetti's answer to question 96 allows us to conclude that, for him,

$$u(28) = 0.5$$

since the expected utility of a 50–50 gamble over 100 and nothing is 0.5 ($= \frac{1}{2} \times 1 + \frac{1}{2} \times 0$) and de Finetti revealed that he was indifferent between that and 28 with certainty. Thus we have one point on de Finetti's utility function (in addition to the two calibration points). Allais then asked two further questions to get two additional points. In essence, these were where $u(x) = 0.25$ and $u(y) = 0.75$. To discover x, Allais effectively asked for the subject's certainty equivalence of a 50–50 gamble between 28 and 0 (expected utility $= \frac{1}{2} \times 0.5 + \frac{1}{2} \times 0 = 0.25$); and to discover y, Allais asked for the subject's certainty equivalence of a 50–50 gamble between 100 and 28 (expected utility $= \frac{1}{2} \times 1 + \frac{1}{2} \times 0.5 = 0.75$). So we now have three points on de Finetti's utility function (in addition to the two calibration points).

Allais now compared this SEUT utility function with the same individual's cardinal utility function ('the index of psychological value'), which, to Allais, is a more primitive yet well-defined concept. To discover this, Allais asked questions of the type illustrated in table 6.2, which portrays de Finetti's response to question 651 (again reproduced in the form given in Allais and Hagen, 1979, p. 616).

This is where I run into difficulties. Although Allais remarks (p. 627) that the 'respondents were able to reply consistently to questions designed to allow their index of cardinal utility to be constructed' (that is, questions of the form of question 651), I would be unable to answer such a question. To me it is simply meaningless, like 'How big is yellow?' I know what he wants to discover: the amount of money which (relative to no money) gives twice as much utility as 10 millions. In effect, he is trying to discover this by the following argument: 'Going from nothing to 10 millions increases your happiness by a certain amount, OK? Now suppose x is bigger than 10; then going from 10 millions to x millions increases your happiness by a certain amount, OK? Now tell me what x must be so that the increase in your happiness going from 10 millions to that x equals the increase in your happiness going from nothing to 10 millions.'

I must admit that I find this meaningless. I would not be able to answer Allais' question 651, nor others like it. I realize that my brain may well have been warped by constant exposure to modern economics (in which cardinal utility functions are SEUT-type utility functions), and I am happy to be reassured by Allais that all his subjects managed to answer such questions. Nevertheless, I am worried about motivation: even if his subjects understood what the questions meant, what incentive did they have for answering honestly?

Table 6.2 de Finetti's answers to question 651

Question 651	Answer	Degree of conviction with which given[a]
Is your preference for an inheritance of 10 millions rather than no inheritance stronger than your preference for an inheritance of		
– 150 millions rather than 10 millions	No	AH
– 100 millions rather than 10 millions	No	PAH
– 60 millions rather than 10 millions	No	H
– 40 millions rather than 10 millions	Yes	BH
– 30 millions rather than 10 millions	Yes	H
– 25 millions rather than 10 millions	Yes	PAH
At what approximate level X′ does your preference change? 45 millions		

[a] For key, see table 6.1.

Be all that as it may, Allais used such questions to build up a picture of the subject's cardinal utility function. de Finetti's answer to question 651 reveals that (relative to a calibration with $v(0) = 0$ and $v(10) = 1$) $v(45) = 2$. We thus have one point on de Finetti's cardinal utility function (in addition to the two calibration points) and additional points can be elicited in a similar fashion.

The main conclusion from Allais' experiment was that, for the majority of the subjects, these two utility functions were clearly different. To my mind, this is hardly surprising. To Allais, this is evidence against SEUT. There is additional evidence, however, of a more convincing type. In essence, this relates to attempts to build up a picture of an individual's SEUT utility function in several different ways. One way I have already described, that is, starting with two calibration points and then discovering, through questions like question 96, which all involve 50–50 gambles, the money amounts which correspond to utilities of 0.25, 0.5 and 0.75. But one does not need to use 50–50 gambles. For example, to find the money amount which yields utility 0.25 one could ask (using the technique of quesion 96) for the certainty equivalent of a 25–75 gamble between the money amounts which yield utility 1 and 0 respectively. Although this is not precisely what Allais did, he effectively accumulated sufficient evidence to suggest that the SEUT utility function derived from the answers varied significantly depending upon the probabilities used in the questions. This, of course, should not be the case if the subjects obey SEUT. The independence axiom, in essence, asserts that such utility functions are indeed independent of the particular probabilities used in the questions. Hence the Allais paradox.

There is some confusion in the literature about the precise definition of the Allais paradox. To avoid such confusion, and to concentrate on the essential point – that the paradox suggests that actual indifference curves in the Marschak–Machina triangle are not parallel – two new terms have been introduced: the common ratio effect and the common consequence effect.[1] The common ratio effect refers to pairs of gambles of one of the following forms:

$$
\begin{array}{ll}
& G_1 = (1 - p, p, 0) \qquad\qquad G_2 = (1 - q, 0, q) \\
\text{(I)} & \\
& G_1' = (1 - pr, pr, 0) \qquad\quad G_2' = (1 - qr, 0, qr)
\end{array}
$$

$$
\begin{array}{ll}
& G_1 = (0, p, 1 - p) \qquad\qquad G_2 = (q, 0, 1 - q) \\
\text{(II)} & \\
& G_1' = (0, pr, 1 - pr) \qquad\quad G_2' = (qr, 0, 1 - qr)
\end{array}
$$

where $p > q$ and $0 < q, r < 1$, $0 < p \le 1$.

In (I) G_1 and G_1' both lie on the horizontal axis, while in (II) both G_1 and G_1' lie on the vertical axis. In both (I) and (II), G_2 and G_2' lie on the hypotenuse and the lines $G_1 G_2$, $G_1' G_2'$ are parallel. Further, note that in (I) (a similar feature holds for (II)) in moving from G_1 to G_1' the probability of getting x_2 is scaled down by a factor r (and the probability of getting x_1 is adjusted appropriately) while in moving from G_2 to G_2' the probability of getting x_3 is scaled down by the same factor r (with the probability of getting x_1 adjusted appropriately): hence the term 'common ratio'. The 'effect' is simply the observation that in many experiments the majority of subjects prefer G_1 to G_2 and G_2' to G_1', a combination not consistent with SEUT.

In contrast, the common consequence effect refers to pairs of gambles of one of the following forms:

(I)
$$G_1 = (1 - p, p, 0) \qquad G_2 = (1 - q, s, q - s)$$
$$G_1' = (1 - p + r, p - r, 0) \qquad G_2' = (1 - q + r, s - r, q - s)$$

(II)
$$G_1 = (0, p, 1 - p) \qquad G_2 = (q - s, s, 1 - q)$$
$$G_1' = (0, p - r, 1 - p + r) \qquad G_2' = (q - s, s - r, 1 - q + r)$$

where $r < p$ and $0 < q, r, s, < 1, 0 < p \leq 1$.

In (I) G_1 and G_1' both lie on the horizontal axis, while in (II) both G_1 and G_1' lie on the vertical axis. In both (I) and (II), the lines $G_1 G_2$ and $G_1' G_2'$ are the same length and are parallel to one another. Further, note that in (I) (a similar feature holds for (II)) in moving from G_1 to G_1' the probability of getting x_2 is scaled down by an amount r (and the probability of getting x_1 is adjusted appropriately) while in moving from G_2 to G_2' the probability of getting x_2 is scaled down by the same amount (with the probability of getting x_1 adjusted appropriately), yet keeping unchanged the probability of getting x_3: hence the term 'common consequence'. The 'effect' is once again the observation that in many experiments the majority of subjects prefer G_1 to G_2 and G_2' to G_1', a combination not consistent with SEUT.

Hagen (1979) presented one of the early post Allais investigations of the common ratio effect. Rather unusually, he asked the first of a pair of questions (designed to investigate the common ratio effect) to one half of his subjects and the second of the pair to the other half. His subjects were randomly assigned to the two halves. Thus none of his subjects actually answered both of the pair. Obviously this procedure loses any information about a particular subject's consistency or otherwise with SEUT; as a test of SEUT it therefore relies on the two halves being similar in their adherence or otherwise to SEUT and indeed on their attitudes to risk. (For if, say, the second half was more risk loving than the first half then more of them would choose the more risky option G_2' in the second pair than those of the first half that would choose the more risky option G_2 in the first pair. Hagen tested for such differences.) Hagen defended this procedure as follows:

> Such investigations are frequently commented on in a way that is very impolite to the respondents, and intellectuals tend to be sensitive about their intellects. I therefore wanted to be able to assure the respondents that no revelation of intellectual shortcomings was logically possible. Since no individual can give vNM[von Neumann–Morgenstern]-inconsister⁺ answers when the questions are put to different groups, the truth of this statement is above discussion. A further advantage is of course that undue pro-vNM influence through knowledge of a theory of allegedly rational behaviour, is barred.
>
> (Hagen, 1979, p. 288)

There are some interesting and useful remarks in this extract!

Hagen reports on two tests, the first in Bergen in 1971 using 106 subjects (all high school teachers), and the second in Oslo in 1975 using 69 subjects. In the first test, he asked two questions to each half, in matched pairs as discussed above. Both were common ratio questions. The first used the amounts 0, 5 million and 25 million (all in Norwegian kroner), and the pairs (using my notation)

$$G_1 = (0.01, 0.99, 0) \qquad G_2 = (0.1, 0, 0.9)$$
$$G_1' = (0.89, 0.11, 0) \qquad G_2' = (0.9, 0, 0.1)$$

These correspond to my type (I) with $p = 0.99$, $q = 0.9$ and $r = 1/9$. The second question used the amounts 0, 10,000 and 20,000 and the pairs

$$G_1 = (0, 1, 0) \qquad G_2 = (0.5, 0, 0.5)$$
$$G_1' = (0.98, 0.02, 0) \qquad G_2' = (0.99, 0, 0.01)$$

These correspond again to my type (I) with $p = 1$, $q = 0.5$ and $r = 0.2$. The principal question set in the second test was similar to question 2 on this first test; it involved the amounts 0, 10,000 and 24,000 and the pairs

$$G_1 = (0, 1, 0) \qquad G_2 = (0.5, 0, 0.5)$$
$$G_1' = (0.5, 0.5, 0) \qquad G_2' = (0.75, 0, 0.25)$$

Again this corresponds with my type (I) with $p = 1$, $q = 0.5$ and $r = 0.5$. In both tests, Hagen found strong evidence of the common ratio effect described earlier: for example, in question 1 of test 1, 70 per cent chose G_1 and 71 per cent chose G_2'; in question 2 of test 1 the respective figures were 89 per cent and 44 per cent, and in the principal question of test 2 the figures were 92.3 per cent and 36.7 per cent.

MacCrimmon and Larsson (1979) followed up this rather primitive experiment with a considerably more sophisticated experimental investigation. I will concentrate here on those parts of the investigation of particular relevance to the common ratio and common consequence effects. I shall begin with the former. They asked common-ratio-type pairs of questions (to all 19 subjects in their experiment) related to a total of 11 Marschak–Machina triangles. The outcomes in the triangles were given by

$$x_1 = 0 \qquad x_2 = x \qquad x_3 = 5x$$

for $x = \$1,000,000$, $\$100,000$, $\$10,000$, $\$1000$, $\$100$; $\$10$ and $\$1$ (the positive expected value sets) and for $x = -\$1000$, $-\$100$, $-\$10$ and $-\$1$ (the negative expected value sets). The questions were all of my type (I) with

$$G_1 = (1 - p, p, 0) \qquad G_2 = (1 - 4p/5, 0, 4p/5)$$

and with p taking the values 1.00, 0.75, 0.50, 0.25, 0.10 and 0.05 (for the positive expected value sets) and 1.00, 0.80, 0.20 and 0.04 (for the negative expected value sets). To quote MacCrimmon and Larsson (1979, p. 354):

Twenty-one different positive expected value sets were presented, with four sets repeated to check for consistency. Eight different negative expected value sets were presented with two sets repeated to check for consistency. Not all combinations were presented since a pilot study had ascertained that some combinations (e.g. a low positive payoff and a low probability level) led to almost all subjects choosing the same alternative.

(Note that, for example, putting $p = 1$ to give G_1 and G_2 and $p = 0.75$ to give G_1' and G_2' generates a pair identical to my common ratio type (I) with $r = 0.75$. Note further that in all cases $q = 4/5p$.)

The main result that emerges from this part of MacCrimmon and Larsson's study is that common ratio effects are observed (i.e. inconsistencies with SEUT are observed) but that their frequency seems to depend crucially on the probabilities: for extreme values (putting $p = 1$ to define G_1 and G_2 and putting $p = 0.05$ to define G_1' and G_2') the 'violation level reached about 65 per cent. However, for smaller values, those more likely to be actually encountered by subjects, the choices were quite consistent.' In other words, indifference curves around the edges of the Marschak–Machina triangle might fan out significantly, but in the middle they are roughly parallel.

A similar conclusion emerges also from the section of MacCrimmon and Larsson's study concerned with the common consequence effect. The questions asked here were of my common consequence type (I) defined over triangles with outcomes

$$x_1 = 0 \qquad x_2 = x \qquad x_3 = \$5,000,000$$

for $x = \$1,000,000$, $\$100,000$, $\$10,000$ and $\$1000$. The pairs were formed from

$$G_1 = (1 - p, p, 0) \qquad G_2 = (1.01 - p, p - 0.11, 0.10)$$

with p values 1.00 0.99, 0.50 and 0.11. Eleven different combinations of these parameters were presented plus two check points. (Note that, for example, putting $p = 1$ to give G_1 and G_2 and $p = 0.99$ to give G_1' and G_2' generates a pair identical to my common consequence type (I) with $r = 0.01$. Note further that in all cases $q - s = 0.10$.) Again MacCrimmon and Larsson confirm common consequence effects for Allais type values but a lower rate of SEUT violation for less extreme values. Indeed, they remark that the incidence of common consequence effects was somewhat lower than the incidence of common ratio effects. I should note in conclusion, however, that MacCrimmon and Larsson's experiments were not financially motivated. Nevertheless, it is a good example of its type, and demonstrates neatly how experimental work can fill in the gaps left by earlier work.

6.3   The Prospect Theory Experiments

Prospect theory was proposed by Kahneman and Tversky (1979) in one of the last papers in *Econometrica* that I understood. I single this paper out for special consideration not only because it is widely quoted but also because it provides an important example of a body of experimental evidence being used both to test SEUT and to motivate a new theory of decision-making under risk as an alternative to SEUT. The experimental evidence presented in the paper consists of 'selected illustrations' of certain effects, so it should not be regarded in any way as being representative. Moreover, none of the experiments was financially motivated. They were all 'presented in questionnaire form with at most a dozen problems per booklet. Several forms of each questionnaire were constructed so that subjects were exposed to the problems in different orders. In addition, two versions of each problem were used in which the left–right position of the prospects was reversed' (Kahneman and Tversky, 1979, p. 264). These experimental procedures were designed to eliminate any possible effects introduced by the ordering of the questions or the ordering of the choices; this is good experimental practice.

The selected illustrations used by Kahneman and Tversky are grouped under four main headings: three effects, named by them the certainty effect, the reflection effect and the isolation effect, and probabilistic insurance. Some, but not all, of these are illustrations of observed behaviour which appears inconsistent with SEUT. The first, the certainty effect, is in essence a subset of the common ratio or common consequence effect, and is an illustration of the Allais paradox. Kahneman and Tversky's problems 1 and 2 are a classic Allais-type test between two pairs in the Marschak–Machina triangle with outcomes 0, 2400 and 2500 (all amounts are in Israeli pounds); in my notation

$$G_1 = (0, 1, 0) \qquad\qquad G_2 = (0.01, 0.66, 0.33)$$
$$G_1' = (0.66, 0.34, 0) \qquad G_2' = (0.67, 0, 0.33)$$

(You should note that in moving from G_1 to G_1' an 0.66 chance of winning x_2 has been changed into an 0.66 chance of winning x_1; similarly in moving from G_2 to G_2' an 0.66 chance of winning x_2 has been changed into an 0.66 chance of winning x_1.) These problems are an example of my common consequence type (I) with $p = 1$, $q = 0.99$, $r = s = 0.66$. Kahneman and Tversky report that in their experiments (administered to students and university faculty in Israel) 82 per cent of the respondents chose G_1 in preference to G_2 while 83 per cent (not necessarily containing the 82 per cent) chose G_2' in preference to G_1'. Further examples are presented.

Problem 3: $G_1 = (0, 1, 0)$ $\qquad\qquad G_2 = (0.2, 0, 0.8)$

Problem 4: $G_1' = (0.75, 0.25, 0)$ $\qquad G_2' = (0.8, 0, 0.2)$

in a Marschak–Machina triangle with outcomes 0, 3000 and 4000. You may recognize this from earlier chapters! It is an example of my common ratio type (I) (with $p = 1$, $q = 0.8$ and $r = 0.25$). Of Kahneman and Tversky's subjects, 80 per cent chose G_1 in problem 3 and 65 per cent chose G_2' in problem 4.

Problem 5: $G_1 = (0, 1, 0)$ $\qquad\qquad G_2 = (0.5, 0, 0.5)$

Problem 6: $G_1' = (0.9, 0.1, 0)$ $\qquad G_2' = (0.95, 0, 0.05)$

in a Marschak–Machina triangle with outcomes nothing, a one-week tour of England, a three-week tour of England, France and Italy. This is another example of a type (I) common ratio (with $p = 1$, $q = 0.5$ and $r = 0.1$); 78 per cent of Kahneman and Tversky's subjects chose G_1 in problem 5 while 67 per cent chose G'_2 in problem 6.

Problem 7: $G_1 = (0.1, 0.9, 0)$ $G_2 = (0.55, 0, 0.45)$

Problem 8: $G'_1 = (0.998, 0.002, 0)$ $G'_2 = (0.999, 0, 0.001)$

in a Marschak–Machina triangle with outcomes 0, 3000 and 6000. This is again an example of a type (I) common ratio (with $p = 0.9$, $q = 0.45$ and $r = 0.001/0.45$); here 86 per cent chose G_1 while 73 per cent chose G'_2.

Kahneman and Tversky use these illustrations of common ratio and common consequence effects to deny the validity of the axioms of SEUT, particularly the independence axiom.

Their reflection effect, however, is not necessarily evidence against SEUT. Rather, it is evidence that preferences are reversed when gains (positive outcomes) are replaced by losses (negative outcomes) or vice versa. So, for example, when problems 3 and 4 are played out with respect to a Marschak–Machina triangle with outcomes – 4000, – 3000 and 0 (note the minus signs, indicating losses), then 92 per cent prefer G_2 and 58 per cent prefer G'_1. Similarly, when problems 7 and 8 are played out with respect to a Marschak–Machina triangle with outcomes – 4000, – 3000 and 0 (again note the minus signs), then 92 per cent prefer G_2 and 70 per cent prefer G'_1. Once again, the common ratio effects – the violations of the independence axiom of SEUT – are being observed, but now in the reverse direction. So, for example, in problem 3 in the domain of gains the modal preference was for the less risky prospect, whereas in problem 3 in the domain of losses the modal preference was for the more risky prospect. Kahneman and Tversky interpret this evidence as suggesting that people are risk averse for gains but risk loving for losses. This, in itself, is not evidence against SEUT; rather it is a repetition of the common ratio effect.

The isolation effect might or might not indicate a violation of SEUT; to quote Kahneman and Tversky (1979, p. 271): 'In order to simplify the choice between alternatives, people often disregard components that the alternatives share, and focus on the components that distinguish them.' Consider the following illustration, based on Kahneman and Tversky's problem 10:

> Consider the following two-stage game. In the first stage, there is a probability of 0.75 to end the game without winning anything, and a probability of 0.25 to move into the second stage. If you reach the second stage you have a choice between G''_1 (3000 with certainty) and G''_2 (a gamble between 4000 and 0 with respective probabilities 0.8 and 0.2). Your choice must be made before the game starts, that is, before the outcome of the first stage is known.

Kahneman and Tversky report that 78 per cent of their subjects precommit themselves to G''_1. Now note that the second stage of problem 10 is precisely the same as problem 3 in which 80 per cent chose G_1. However, problem 10 as a whole is precisely the same in terms of probabilities of the final outcomes as problem 4, in which just 35 per cent chose the first option G_1'. This example therefore suggests that the subjects ignored the first stage of problem 10 when making their choice.

The SEUT prediction is that subjects should either choose G_1 in problem 3, G_1' in problem 4 and (precommit themselves to) G_1'' in problem 10, or choose G_2, G_2' and G_2'' respectively (or be indifferent in all three problems). The modal pattern of choices made by Kahneman and Tversky's subject was G_1, G_2' and G_1''. The isolation effect links G_1 and G_1'' (or G_2 and G_2'') which, in this example, is not inconsistent with SEUT.

However, in another example, it is. Consider problems 11 and 12.

Problem 11:   In addition to whatever you own, you have been given 1000. You are now asked to choose between G_1 (a 50–50 gamble between 1000 and 0) and G_2 (500 with certainty).

Problem 12:   In addition to whatever you own, you have been given 2000. You are now asked to choose between G_1' (a 50–50 gamble between -1000 and 0) and G_2' (-500 with certainty). (Note the minus signs.)

Kahneman and Tversky found that 84 per cent of their subjects chose G_2 in problem 11 while 69 per cent chose G_1' in problem 12. This observation creates serious difficulties, not only for SEUT, but also for virtually any theory of preferences based on final outcomes, since G_1 and G_1' are precisely the same, and G_2 and G_2' are precisely the same, in terms of final outcomes relative to the initial starting position: under G_1 or G_1' you have a 50–50 chance of ending up 1000 or 2000 better than you were initially; under G_2 and G_2' you are bound to end up 1500 better off than you were initially. Yet the modal preference was for G_1 and G_2'.

Here, it is precisely the isolation effect which is creating the problem: since the subjects are isolating the second stage (i.e. the choices between G_1 and G_2 and between G_1' and G_2') from the first stage, they do not perceive the two problems as being essentially the same.

Kahneman and Tversky used this observed isolation effect to argue that people may move the reference point, relative to which they make their decisions, during a preliminary editing phase of their decision process. Indeed, it is precisely this editing phase which crucially distinguishes prospect theory from other alternatives to SEUT.

One final observation is contained in Kahneman and Tversky's paper; it relates to probabilistic insurance. In essence, this relates to a prediction of SEUT that, if an individual is indifferent between not being insured against some risk and being completely insured against the risk, then he or she should prefer partial insurance to either of the two extreme possibilities. Kahneman and Tversky found that 80 per cent of their subjects contradicted this prediction.

Taken together, these various experimental illustrations suggest to Kahneman and Tversky that SEUT is flawed. As a positive alternative, they propose prospect theory which tries to incorporate these illustrations. The crucial features of prospect theory are, first, the editing phase, in which prospects get simplified, and second, the evaluation phase, which has some features in common with SEUT except that probabilities do not enter linearly but through some weighting function. The net result is that prospect theory indifference curves in the Marschak–Machina triangle are rather difficult to define because of the probability function. A possible illustration is given by Camerer (1989, pp. 75–6). Nevertheless, prospect theory presents a nice example of a theory motivated by experiments.

6.4 The Ellsberg Paradox and Preference Reversals

The Ellsberg paradox (Ellsberg, 1961) is a somewhat different phenomenon from those considered hitherto, but it is, once again, a phenomenon on which experimental work has shed some light. Consider the problem as stated in MacCrimmon and Larssen (1979, p. 369):

> Consider an urn containing 100 balls. You know there are 33 red balls but you do not know the composition of the remaining 67 black and yellow balls. One ball is to be drawn at random from the urn. Which do you prefer: G_1 or G_2?
>
> G_1: Receive $1000 if a red ball is drawn.
>
> G_2: Receive $1000 if a black ball is drawn.
>
> Which do you prefer: G_1' or G_2'?
>
> G_1': Receive $1000 if a red or yellow ball is drawn.
>
> G_2' Receive $1000 if a black or yellow ball is drawn.

The conventional wisdom states that G_1 should be preferred to G_2 if and only if G_1' is preferred to G_2'. This can be seen most simply from the matrix representation of the two choice problems in table 6.3. From this matrix, it should be clear that if a yellow ball is drawn it does not matter whether you choose G_1 or G_2 in the first choice problem nor whether you choose G_1' or G_2' in the second choice problem. Therefore, one can ignore the final column in coming to a decision between G_1 and G_2 or between G_1' and G_2'; hence the choice between G_1 and G_2 is the same as the choice between G_1' and G_2'. Hence the conventional wisdom.

Table 6.3   Matrix representation of the Ellsberg problem

Outcome choice	Red ball drawn ($)	Black ball drawn ($)	Yellow ball drawn ($)
G_1	1000	0	0
G_2	0	1000	0
G_1'	1000	0	1000
G_2'	0	1000	1000

In a sense, this is the same argument as that underlying the independence axiom, but it is usually referred to as Savage's sure-thing principle. Either way, it is crucial for SEUT. Unfortunately, experimental evidence suggests that many subjects make what are termed Ellsberg-type violations of SEUT, that is, they prefer G_1 to G_2 and G_2' to G_1'. Relatively few make the other violation (G_2 preferred to G_1 and G_1' preferred to G_2'), indicating some systematic pattern of behaviour violating SEUT. Ellsberg's rationalization is that subjects dislike ambiguity; therefore they prefer G_1 (because they know the proportion of red balls) to G_2 (because they do not know the proportion of black balls); similarly they prefer G_2' (because they know the proportion of black and yellow balls) to G_1' (because they do not know the proportion of red and yellow balls).

MacCrimmon and Larsson (1979) carried out a more detailed investigation with values of p (the proportion of red balls) of 0.20, 0.25, 0.30, 0.33, 0.34, 0.40 and 0.50. They used (notional) payoffs of $1,000,000 in addition to the $1000. They found evidence of Ellsberg-type violations, reaching as high as 70 per cent of the subjects for $p = 0.33$, but also falling to 15 per cent for $p = 0.2$ and to 0 per cent for $p = 0.50$. Once again, they found that the frequency of SEUT violations is sensitive to the parameters of the problem.

A number of explanations of the Ellsberg paradox have been proposed, many of them relying on a distinction between risk and uncertainty. This distinction is unfortunately not recognized by SEUT which imputes subjective probabilities, manipulated linearly, to the various events. However, some of the recent new theories, which involve the relaxation of one or other of the axioms of SEUT, allow non-linear manipulations of subjective probabilities, and hence allow for an explanation of the Ellsberg paradox which does not rest on a distinction between risk and uncertainty. One such explanation is provided by Segal (1987); this rests on a failure of the reduction principle which is something which I have rather taken for granted so far. The reduction principle states that people can reduce compound gambles to simple gambles through the use of elementary probability calculus. It has been implicitly invoked in most of the previous material in this book.

A rather clever experimental investigation into the Segal explanation of the Ellsberg paradox has recently been carried out by Bernasconi and Loomes (1990). Their experiment consisted of a very simple design which focused on the two-stage nature of Segal's explanation (the first stage being the distribution of the balls between black and yellow, and the second stage the drawing of the ball determining the payoff). They asked the subjects to imagine a table with three bags on it, all made of an opaque material. Each bag contains two balls: one bag contains two black balls; one bag contains one black and one yellow ball; and one bag contains two yellow balls. The subjects could not tell which was which. Now one bag is chosen at random and a red ball is placed inside it. The bag is shaken and one ball is drawn out at random. The subjects then have to choose between

G_1: Receive £10 if a red ball is drawn.

G_2: Receive £10 if a black ball is drawn.

G_3: Receive £10 if a yellow ball is drawn.

Then the subjects were asked to imagine exactly the same procedure except that two balls are drawn at random. They are asked to choose between

G_1': Receive £5 if a red or a black ball is drawn.

G_2': Receive £5 if a red or a yellow ball is drawn.

G_3': Receive £5 if a black or a yellow ball is drawn.

Bernasconi and Loomes, like Ellsberg, found that significantly more subjects chose G_1 in preference to either G_2 or G_3, indicating a preference for certainty (they know that a red ball is in the bag) over ambiguity (they are not sure that both a black ball and a yellow ball are in the bag), while significantly more subjects chose G_3' in preference to either G_1' or G_2', indicating once again a preference for certainty (they know that either a black or a yellow ball is in the bag) over ambiguity (they are not sure that both a black ball and a yellow ball are in the bag). But Bernasconi and Loomes delved further: by asking supplementary questions they were able to test the Segal hypothesis. Interestingly, they discovered that while 'at least 60% of subjects did violate the reduction principle' the Segal explanation did not account for all the observed behaviour. An additional factor appeared to be 'the structure of the problem as perceived by the decision-maker'.

This takes us back to framing effects, which we encountered rather briefly during our discussion of the isolation effect and its relationship to prospect theory. Rather worryingly, it does appear to be the case that framing is important, and that the way that problems are presented does affect the subsequent decision. To an economist, this is worrying indeed. Perhaps an extreme manifestation is the preference reversal phenomenon, which has been intensively investigated using experimental methods.

The preference reversal phenomenon is as follows: subjects are asked to choose between two prospects, a P-bet, which has a high probability of winning a small amount, and a $-bet, which has a smaller probability of winning a larger amount. Then the subjects are asked to value each of these prospects by placing reservation prices on them, r_P and $r_\$$ respectively, which represent the lowest price at which they would be willing to sell the gambles. What has been repeatedly discovered in many experimental studies is that a significant number of subjects choose the P-bet in the first stage, but then report an $r_\$$ greater than r_P. In other words, they value the $-bet higher than the P-bet, yet choose the P-bet in preference to the $-bet. A clear case (apparently!) of preference reversals.

Useful discussions of this phenomenon can be found in Machina (1989) and Appleby and Starmer (1987). Of the various explanations proffered, some of the most interesting revolve around the experimental procedures used, particularly those relating to the incentive mechanism. When financial incentives are used, the usual elicitation mechanism for the valuations is the

Becker, DeGroot and Marschak (BDM) procedure. This is described by Loomes et al. (1990) as follows:

> A subject is told that he has been given a particular gamble, which he may keep and play out. Alternatively, he may try to sell the gamble back to the experimenters. He is asked to state his minimum selling price, i.e. the lowest sum of money that is prepared to accept in exchange for the gamble. Then an 'offer' is generated by random device. If the offer is greater than or equal to the minimum selling price, the subject is paid the full amount of the offer; otherwise he plays out the gamble.

It is clear that an individual who obeys the axioms of SEUT will optimize by truly announcing his valuation (his certainty equivalent) of the gamble: he has no incentive to overstate it for otherwise he would end up playing out a gamble rather than getting an amount of money which he regarded as worth more; he has no incentive to understate it for otherwise he might end up with an amount of money which he regarded as less desirable than playing out the gamble. The logic is similar to that used elsewhere (chapter 8) to construct an appropriate elicitation mechanism for probability equivalents.

Unfortunately, this logic does not necessarily work for someone who does not obey the axioms of SEUT: it is relatively straightforward to show that the BDM mechanism may induce apparent preference reversals in a subject who has a well-defined preference functional that is not a SEUT functional (see Karni and Safra, 1987). A response to this criticism is to try a different experimental procedure. One alternative is to present a sequence of pairwise choices, between the $-bet, the P-bet and various certain amounts, 'hoping' to trap subjects into displaying preference reversals. This can be financially motivated by the random gamble-selection procedure discussed earlier. One of the pairwise choices is chosen at random, and the preferred gamble of that pair is played out. But this comes up against the Holt objection, discussed and illustrated in chapter 5.

Loomes et al. (1990) present an ingenious experimental procedure that gets round both these difficulties. They asked 20 pairwise choice questions (thus getting round problems involved with the BDM procedure) carefully chosen so that if the Holt objection was a valid one then a certain pattern of choice over the 20 questions would be observed, whereas if the authors' preferred story (regret theory) was true then an alternative pattern of choice would be observed. The experiment was, of course, financially motivated. It was administered in questionnaire format with the 20 questions in a booklet additionally containing some explanatory notes. A total of 200 subjects took part.

It is instructive to examine the design. In essence, the 20 pairwise choices were built around five triples – choices between A and B, between B and C and between C and A, where A, B and C are risky prospects described in table 6.4. The outcomes are the a, b and c which can, of course, be chosen so that B is a certainty.

In the three pairwise choice problems (A and B, B and C, and C and A) there are eight different possible responses:

Table 6.4 The Loomes et al. design

	Probability					
Action	p_1	p_2	p_3			
A	a_1	a_2	a_3	(i) $a_1 \geq b_1 \geq c_1$	with strict inequality	
B	b_1	b_2	b_3	(ii) $b_2 \geq c_2 \geq a_2$	for one of (i), (ii) or (iii)	
C	c_1	c_2	c_3	(iii) $c_3 \geq a_3 \geq b_3$		

[a] $p_i > 0$ for all i.

(1)	A	B	A	consistent with	A > B > C
(2)	A	C	A	consistent with	A > C > B
(3)	B	B	A	consistent with	B > A > C
(4)	B	B	C	consistent with	B > C > A
(5)	A	C	C	consistent with	C > A > B
(6)	B	C	C	consistent with	C > B > A
(7)	A	B	C	unpredicted cycle	
(8)	B	C	A	predicted cycle	

The expressed preferences (1) to (6) are each consistent with SEUT, and hence with theories which include SEUT as a special case. Preferences (7) and (8) could be reported if the subject was truly indifferent between A, B and C: in such (rare?) instances we would expect to observe (7) and (8) recorded equally often. Regret theory, however, predicts (7) to occur with particular $\psi(.)$ functions, but not (8). So regret theory predicts that (7) will occur more frequently than (8).

The Holt objection is defused because reporting either (7) or (8) is equally preferable if the subject is expressing his or her preferences in terms of the implied overall distribution of final outcomes (see again my discussion of Holt's argument in chapter 5). So, under Holt, we would observe equal frequencies of (7) and (8).

In fact, Loomes et al. observed significantly more instances of (7) than of (8). Indeed, of the 200 subjects who took part in the experiment, 72 recorded no cycles, 98 recorded the predicted cycle (7), 19 recorded the unpredicted cycle (8) and 11 recorded both types of cycle. This is strong evidence in support of regret theory, and hence of intransitivities in behaviour. The preference reversal phenomenon seems more than an experimental artefact.

6.5 Experimental Tests of Various New Alternative Theories

In the final section of this chapter I briefly survey a number of key papers which have used experimental methods in order to test between SEUT and its various rivals. In addition to the papers specifically cited in this section, reference could be made to section 4.3 of Weber and Camerer (1987) which provides a useful overview of the various alternatives to SEUT and gives a brief survey of the early experimental work testing these alternatives. In particular, reference is made to Currim and Sarin (1986) who report on two experiments designed to test prospect theory. They concluded that SEUT and prospect theory predicted the observed choices equally well, though further work needed to be done. Weber and Camerer (1987) also refer to Chew and Waller (1986) and to Loomes (1989). The former is a test of weighted expected utility which predicts (see chapter 4) that indifference curves in the Marschak–Machina triangle fan out linearly from a point to the southwest of the origin of the triangle. This also is a prediction of regret theory when the prospects are statistically independent, but regret theory has further predictions for when the prospects are dependent, which is not the case with most of the other theories. Most other theories are holistic, in the sense that they imply some preference functional defined over the prospects themselves, so that the value of a particular gamble is independent of the available alternative gambles. This is not the case with regret theory, which specifically takes into account what the decision-maker would have got under the alternative choice. This gives regret theory certain important testable implications which are not shared by most of the other theories, a feature which is exploited by Loomes (1989) and by Starmer and Sugden (1989). Let me consider the latter.

Starmer and Sugden (1989) construct their experiment around the following choice problem. There are four states of the world, with probabilities as specified in the table below. Subjects are asked to choose between two actions G_1 and G_2. The payoffs are specified in table 6.5, where x_1, x_2 and x_3 are monetary amounts ($x_3 > x_2 > x_1$).

If action G_1 is chosen,[2] then the outcome is x_2 with probability p and x_1 with probability $1 - p$; if action G_2 is chosen, then the outcome is x_3 with probability q and x_1 with probability $1 - q$. In terms of a Marschak–Machina triangle defined over the three amounts x_1, x_2 and x_3, we have $G_1 = (1 - p, p, 0)$ and $G_2 = (1 - q, 0, q)$. Note crucially that the parameter ω does not enter into the description of either G_1 or G_2. Instead, the parameter ω determines the extent of the dependence between G_1 and G_2: it is a conditional probability – the probability that G_1 yields x_2 conditional on G_2 yielding x_3. If $\omega = p$ then G_1 and G_2 are statistically independent.

My notation (which differs from that used by Starmer and Sugden) has been deliberately chosen to emphasize the connection of this problem with that used to describe the (type I) common ratio effect: in terms of my discussion of section 6.2, if p and q are scaled down to pr and qr ($0 < r < 1$)

Table 6.5   The Starmer and Sugden design

Action	Probability of state of the world			
	ωq	$(1 - \omega)q$	$p - \omega q$	$1 - p - (1 - \omega)q$
G_1	x_2	x_1	x_2	x_1
G_2	x_3	x_3	x_1	x_1

then G_1 and G_2 become respectively G_1' and G_2'. According to SEUT this scaling down should not change preference, but experimental evidence suggests that it does. The purpose of Starmer and Sugden's work is to test whether the regret theory explanation of this experimentally observed common ratio effect is better than alternative explanations.

Regret theory (see chapter 4) implies that $G_1 \gtreqless G_2$ if and only if

$$- \omega q \psi_{32} - (1 - \omega)q_{31} + (p - \omega q)\psi_{21} \gtreqless 0$$

that is, if and only if

$$(p/q - \omega)\psi_{21} - \omega \psi_{32} - (1 - \omega)\psi_{31} \gtreqless 0$$

From this it is clear that, for fixed ω and p/q, preferences between G_1 and G_2 are independent of p; however, with p/q fixed, preferences may be affected by changes in ω. The latter prediction is in marked contrast with holistic theories for which the valuation of G_1 depends on p, x_1 and x_2 and the valuation of G_2 depends on q, x_1 and x_3, which implies that the choice between G_1 and G_2 can depend only on p, q, x_1, x_2 and x_3 – and crucially not on ω. Thus regret theory predicts possible changes in preferences as ω changes while other theories do not. Specifically, regret theory predicts a tendency for switches in preference from $G_1 > G_2$ to $G_2 > G_1$ as ω falls (see Starmer and Sugden, 1989, p. 162). This is what they term the juxtaposition effect.

The experiment was a large one, split into two stages (separated by an interval of several days). There were 283 subjects in stage 1, of which 120 (the target number) went on to complete stage 2. The latter stage, unlike the former, involved possible losses for the subjects. Real money was used at each stage, with the random gamble procedure invoked. At each stage 20 questions were asked. One interesting feature of the experiment was that it included a consistency check: in each stage two of the 20 questions were identical. All theories predict that identical questions should be answered identically, so any change in recorded preferences would indicate either indifference or inconsistency (error). Rather worryingly, Starmer and Sugden found a large incidence of changes in recorded preferences – a little under 30 per cent. I shall have more to say on this later.

As far as the main hypotheses were concerned, Starmer and Sugden found clear evidence in support of the regret theory hypotheses: first, as p was varied with ω and p/q held fixed, there were relatively few changes in preferences; second, as ω was varied with p/q fixed there were highly significant changes in preferences, in the direction predicted by regret theory. For full details, and a comprehensive discussion, see Starmer and Sugden (1989).

The same experimental procedure was employed by Harless (1989) in an interesting follow-up study. This study was designed to investigate the effect of the problem presentation on the subjects' responses. He employed three problem presentations: that of Starmer and Sugden, illustrated in

	1 10	11 95	96 100
G₁	win $8000	get $0	get $0
G₂	get $0	get $0	win $20,000
	10	85	5

(a)

(b)

G₁		G₂
10 in 100 chance to win $8000	‖	95 in 100 chance to get $0
90 in 100 chance to get $0		5 in 100 chance to win $20,000

(c)

G₁		G₂
Ticket 1 to 10 drawn win $8 000	‖	Ticket 1 to 95 drawn get $0
Ticket 11 to 100 drawn get $0		Ticket 96 to 100 drawn win $20,000

Figure 6.1 Harless's problem presentations: (a) the Starmer and Sugden presentation; (b) the 'chances in 100' presentation; (c) the 'tickets' presentation.

figure 6.1(a); a statement of the 'chances in 100' of each outcome, illustrated in figure 6.1(b); and a statement of the specific ticket numbers yielding each outcome, illustrated in figure 6.1(c). I should emphasize that, even though Harless used a total of 493 subjects (322 on a first questionnaire involving 12 pairwise choices and 171 on a second questionnaire involving six pairwise choices) in all cases a flat-rate payment scheme was used ($3 per subject on the first questionnaire and $2 per subject on the second), so some doubt might be expressed about subjects' incentives. Nevertheless, Harless's findings are of interest: using the Starmer and Sugden problem presentation he found regret effects on the same scale as Starmer and Sugden did; however, in the other problem presentations regret effects were not observed. He concludes that 'regret has a substantial impact on choice, but only when the decision is framed in a way that sharply directs the decision maker to compare acts and states rather than prospects'. Once again, framing effects are important.

I conclude with two rather more general papers concerned with testing between the various alternative theories by concentrating on the implied properties of indifference curves in the Marschak–Machina triangle. These two papers are Battalio et al. (1988) and Camerer (1989). Their problem presentations are similar in one respect and different in another. Battalio et al. (1988, p. 4) describe their procedure with an example:

> Example 1:
> A: Losing $14 if 1–100   B: Losing $20 if 1–70
>   Losing $0 if 71–100
> Answer: (1) I prefer A   (2) I prefer B   (3) Indifference. The numbers following each dollar amount referred to 100 numbered poker chips in a bowl, sitting in front of the room, one of which would be drawn to determine payoffs. Thus, if a subject chose A, he/she would lose $14 with certainty as any numbered poker chip gave this result. If however the subject chose B, and a chip numbered 1–70 was drawn, he/she would lose $20, but if a chip numbered 71–100 was drawn they would lose $0.

Camerer (1989) used the presentation illustrated in figure 5.4(c) with the payoff determined by numbered lottery tickets. Note that both presentations explicitly state the dependence between the two lotteries, though their presentation is not quite identical with that of Starmer and Sugden (1989); if Harless is correct, this could be quite important.

In some respects, Camerer's (1989) experimental design is similar to mine discussed in chapter 5, although he used his data to test hypotheses about competing theories whilst I used mine to estimate competing preference functionals. Camerer used three Marschak–Machina triangles: a large gain triangle, with outcomes $0, $10,000 and $25,000 (never used for actual payoffs!); a small gain triangle, with outcomes $0, $5 and $10; and a small loss triangle, with outcomes – $10, – $5 and $0. If a subject was presented with choices over this third triangle, he or she was first given $10 so that no actual loss was ever incurred by a subject.[3] This leaves open the issue of whether the subjects did indeed regard the small loss triangle as leading to losses; this depends on whether the isolation effect operates – on this see later.

In each of the three triangles, 14 pairs of risky gambles were used, the same 14 for each triangle (table 6.6). These pairs are distributed evenly through the triangle. In each instance, the more risky gamble is a transformation of the less risky gamble with some of the probability shifted from x_2 to x_1 and x_3. More specifically, if the less risky gamble is (p_1, p_2, p_3), then the more risky gamble is $(p_1 + \alpha, p_2 - 2\alpha, p_3 + \alpha)$ where α is either 0.1 or 0.2. It will be noted, therefore, that the slope of the line joining the two gambles in each pair is always unity – in contrast with my design where the slope varied from 1/7 to 7/1.

Every subject made choices for four pairs of gambles in each of the three triangles and a single repetition of one of the 12 pairs, giving a total of 13 choices. The repetition was designed to test reliability or consistency: if subjects never make mistakes then they would never reverse their stated preference (unless they were truly indifferent). Rather alarmingly, Camerer found that 31.6 per cent of the subjects reversed their stated preference. This emphasizes the need to develop a 'theory of errors'.

Camerer used three payment conditions: (a) 179 subjects did not play out any of the gambles and were simply paid a flat rate of $2 for participating; (b) 80 subjects played out one of the small gain gambles; (c) 96 subjects were

Table 6.6 Camerer's risky pairs

Pair no.	Less risky gamble			More risky gamble		
	p_1	p_2	p_3	p_1	p_2	p_3
1	0.0	0.2	0.8	0.1	0.0	0.9
2	0.0	0.6	0.4	0.1	0.4	0.5
3	0.0	0.6	0.4	0.2	0.2	0.6
4	0.1	0.4	0.5	0.3	0.0	0.7
5	0.0	1.0	0.0	0.1	0.8	0.1
6	0.0	1.0	0.0	0.2	0.6	0.2
7	0.3	0.4	0.3	0.5	0.0	0.5
8	0.4	0.2	0.4	0.5	0.0	0.5
9	0.4	0.6	0.0	0.5	0.4	0.1
10	0.4	0.6	0.0	0.6	0.2	0.2
11	0.5	0.4	0.1	0.7	0.0	0.3
12	0.8	0.2	0.0	0.9	0.0	0.1
13	0.2	0.2	0.6	0.3	0.0	0.7
14	0.6	0.2	0.2	0.7	0.0	0.3

given $10 and then played out one of the small loss gambles. These differences enable a test to be made as to whether incentives matter (it appears they do not) and whether attitudes to risk are different for gains than for losses (it appears that they are, but not strongly so).

I do not have space here to do much more than give a glimpse of Camerer's results. A sample is illustrated in figure 6.2 which is Camerer's figure 10. This portrays the fraction of subjects choosing the less risky gamble in each pair in the small gain triangle. The thin lines connect the two gambles in a pair; in figure 6.2 they are also iso-expected value lines. The thick line represents the fraction of subjects who chose the less risky gamble in each pair: the fraction is written next to the thick line, and the slope is a linear function of the fraction. SEUT predicts that the thick lines will be parallel. It is clear that they are not. It is also clear that there is no obvious overall pattern: there are signs of fanning out in most parts of the triangles, but there are also signs of fanning in in other parts. Camerer concludes (1989, p. 95): 'there are substantial violations of SEUT, but no single theory can explain the pattern of violations'.

An almost identical conclusion is reached by Battalio et al. (1988, p. 27), 'none of the alternatives to expected utility theory considered consistently organizes the data ...', after studying a set of responses from (I think) 31 subjects, all 'undergraduate students enrolled in introductory or intermediate economics classes at Texas A&M University'. All subjects answered two sets of questions: a first set of 41 hypothetical pairwise choice questions and, several days later, a second set of 15 pairwise choice questions motivated by the random gamble-selection mechanism. Once again, this experimental design allows a test of whether financial incentives matter. Battalio et al. conclude that 'there are systematic and significant quantitative differences

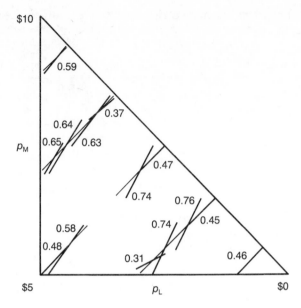

Figure 6.2 Fraction of subjects choosing the less risky gamble in each pair, small gains.

over real and hypothetical choice questions, but the qualitative conclusions reached regarding the substantive behavioral issues in question do not differ between hypothetical and real choices'.

Battalio et al., like Camerer, also presented some gambles involving gains and others involving losses: subjects who were to play out a gamble involving gains were given an initial endowment of $5; subjects who were to play out a gamble involving losses were given an initial endowment of $30. My earlier comments still apply. Nevertheless the authors conclude that the isolation effect operates, and that risk loving was displayed in loss space and risk aversion in gain space, although some of their results do cast some doubt on other predictions of prospect theory. Battalio et al. also remark that they 'do not observe regret effects in our data' (which could result from the Harless phenomenon noted earlier); 'we identify conditions generating large systematic violations of hypothesis II [of Machina] in previously unexplored areas of the [Marschak–Machina] triangle, and we observe common ratio effect violations of expected utility theory under conditions where Rank Dependent Expected Utility argues that they should not be observed.' In other words, no one theory explains everything.

6.6 Conclusions

The experimental work described in this chapter has come a long way: starting with rather *ad hoc* hypothetical choices involving rather arbitrary amounts of money, the experimental designs have evolved over the years: first, introducing relevant incentive mechanisms and then modifying and improving them; second, systematically exploring the whole range of parameter values; and third, carefully constructing tests which enable particular theories to be singled out from competing theories. At the same time, the theorists have responded by constructing new theories which take account of, and respond to, earlier experimental results.

It would be nice to say that a consensus is emerging. Perhaps one is, but not the kind of consensus that one would like: both the last two papers discussed in the preceding section have concluded that no one theory explains everything. That may be an improvement on the position of the 1950s when everyone believed that SEUT was infallible, but I suspect that it cannot be a final conclusion.

My recommendations for the way ahead are as follows. First, I would like to see experiments, along the lines of Camerer and Battalio et al., conducted with much larger sums of money – I suggest adding at least one zero to the amounts involved in the gambles which are played out. There is obviously a trade-off problem here: between the amounts of money involved in the gambles and the number of subjects used in the experiment. My own preference would be to cut down the number of subjects by a factor of 10 and increase the payments by the same factor. At the same time, I would introduce large real losses. I suspect that the strategy employed by most experimenters, of giving the subjects who are to play out gambles involving losses a sum of money at the start of the experiment at least as large as the magnitude of the largest possible loss, does not work: subjects do not treat the losses as real losses. I realize that I argued above that having real losses may cause difficulties, but I think these difficulties can be overcome, particularly with the kind of experiment considered in this chapter: subjects can be given the various questions in advance and have plenty of time to study them; the gambles can be chosen so that the expected values are positive, and indeed sufficiently so that only the most risk averse are discouraged from taking part; and the moral hazard problem can be overcome by employing a sufficiently transparent random device to determine the outcome.

Second, I would like to see experiments repeated, with several days and possibly some kind of group discussion intervening. A number of recent experiments carried out at EXEC, the Centre for Experimental Economics at the University of York, suggest that subjects make fewer mistakes on the second repetition and that their behaviour becomes more consistent with SEUT.

Third, I would like economists to think more carefully about the whole issue of randomness. There are two types: randomness across subjects and randomness for particular subjects. It is all too clear from recent evidence that subjects do make mistakes, but this is often conveniently ignored by experimenters. Instead, it is usually assumed that any randomness is across subjects: so, for example, some subjects obey SEUT, some obey regret theory, others obey Machina's generalized expected utility and so on. Indeed, some tests carried out on experimental data can be rationalized only on this basis.

If this is what is being assumed, then the next obvious step is to find out what proportion of the population obey SEUT, what proportion obey regret theory and so on. This calls for representative experiments.

If, however, it is assumed that individual subjects make mistakes, and that it is this which gives rise to randomness, then economists need to give much more thought to the process which generates the errors. While it is simple and convenient to assume, as I have done, that errors of valuation are white noise, it seems more sensible to argue that subjects are more likely to make errors of valuation with some problems than with other problems: a certainty, for example, is easy to assess, whereas a two-stage gamble with several possible outcomes is more difficult. We might expect a higher incidence and variance of errors with the latter valuation than the former. This, I feel, is the way ahead.

Notes

1 It is not clear that these terms are formally distinct. Nevertheless, the intuitive distinction described below is of use for expositional purposes.
2 Note that the word 'action' rather than 'choice' is deliberately used. This is to emphasize that if G_1 is chosen then G_2 is rejected, and vice versa.
3 Gambles involving losses create problems for experimenters. For various reasons, experimenters do not like to send subjects away from an experiment having made a loss. This is partly for goodwill; partly because such an experiment may attract only risk-lovers; and partly because the experimenters may be subject to a moral hazard problem – the temptation (particularly in University Britain of the late 1980s) to run a large experiment with large losses for the subjects – and then to retire early – could be overwhelming!

Part III

Experiments on Individual Economic Behaviour under Risk

7

An Example of a Simple Set of Search Experiments

7.1 Introduction

My very first experiments were on search. The motivation for them came from some rather enjoyable theory that I had been doing on optimal search with learning: I had written down the mathematics of a model with Bayesian learning about the parameters of the distribution over which the searcher was searching, and I was intrigued to discover the implications in terms of the actual numbers involved in a particular example. It was then that I discovered that, although I could write down the mathematics of the problem, the numerical difficulties involved with translating this into actual numbers defeated even the University of York computer. This got me wondering: if the computer finds it impossible, what hope for the man on the Clapham omnibus? What hope, indeed, for *homo economicus*?

So I set up my first experiment, based on the extreme position that subjects had no information whatsoever about the distribution over which they were searching. In other words, they were learning from an initial position of complete ignorance about the distribution. As it happened, all the distributions in my experiments were normal distributions; if the subjects had known this (or had assumed it) it would have simplified their decision problem somewhat, but it would still have been extremely complicated computationally. As I could not do the computation myself, even with the aid of the University mainframe, I had no optimal strategy with which to compare the strategies of the subjects.

However, if one was prepared to assume that the subjects were acting 'as if' they knew the distribution and were trying to optimize accordingly, then one could derive an 'optimal strategy' with which to compare the behaviour of the subjects. I will discuss how this is done later in the chapter. But first, I discuss the details of these early experiments.

7.2   The First Search Experiments

My first set of search experiments, reported in Hey (1982), appear in retrospect very primitive: they were not financially motivated; subjects were processed one by one; the software was rather user unfriendly; it ran on the University mainframe. Nevertheless, the experiments were instructive. I used 31 subjects, mainly economists. Because no actual money was involved, the subjects might have been motivated by considerations other than maximizing their expected winnings. Partly to counteract any such tendency, but also as a way of getting information about the subjects' thought processes, I asked the subjects to 'think aloud' as they did the experiment and I tape-recorded their responses. Subjects were alone in a room housing a computer terminal and a tape-recorder whilst doing the experiment. These tape-recorded protocols provided useful additional information.

Each subject was asked to envisage a situation in which he or she had decided to buy some item (a consumer durable, for example), and had decided on a specific make and model. Moreover, the subject had also made up his or her mind as to the maximum amount that they were willing to spend on this item. This maximum amount, $£x$, is a familiar concept in demand theory, particularly for indivisible goods: it is the limit price.

Subjects were then told to imagine that a very large (formally an infinite number) of shops sold this item, but at possibly differing prices. Initially, the searcher was given no idea of what prices were available but could get any number of price quotes (from different shops) by paying a cost of $£c$ per quote. Full recall was available (that is, the searcher could return to any shop at any stage and buy the item at the price quoted). Moreover, subjects were told that there was nothing special about the order in which quotes were obtained.

To enable the subjects to familiarize themselves with the search problem, they were allowed as many 'trial runs' as they required; it was emphasized that these trial runs were simply to demonstrate the mechanics of the experiment and were otherwise uninformative. After these trial runs, the subjects moved on to the 'real thing'; this consisted of four separate search problems. The subjects were told that $£x$, the maximum amount that they were willing to spend on the item, was to cover both purchase and search. In view of this, we necessarily had to give them the option of giving up searching without buying; in fact, just twice out of 124 repetitions did subjects exercise this option.

The software was designed so that each search problem (whether in the 'trial runs' or the 'real thing') began with the subjects being told x and c, and being given an initial price quote. After each quote, they were asked whether they wished to buy (at the lowest price so far encountered), to continue searching or to give up without buying. After each new quote was generated, the software reminded the subjects of x and c, the price quotes so far obtained (in chronological order) and the amount they would spend in total (purchase plus search) if purchase took place at the lowest price so far obtained. The program kept a record of all the subjects' responses.

In these experiments, the subjects were given no information about the distribution over which they were searching. If, in contrast, they had been given complete information, or if one was prepared to assume that they behaved 'as if' they had been given complete information, then one could derive the appropriate optimal strategy. On the assumption that the subjects were risk neutral in the relevant range, and hence that they were trying to maximize the expected net savings (relative to x), the optimal strategy is simply to keep on searching until a price quote is obtained which is less than the optimal reservation price $R*$ given by

$$\int_{-\infty}^{R*} F(x)\,\mathrm{d}x = c \tag{7.1}$$

where $F(.)$ is the distribution function (cumulative probability function) of the price distribution. (I shall prove a closely related result in section 7.3.) Given c and a specific distribution, it is a straightforward matter to compute $R*$ and hence to check whether a particular subject's behaviour is consistent with this (full information) optimal strategy: it is consistent if the subject stops searching after receiving the first price quote less than or equal to $R*$. In this first set of experiments, behaviour was consistent with this optimal rule 25 per cent of the time.

An alternative hypothesis is that subjects use a reservation strategy with a fixed, but non-optimal, reservation value. In such cases, the final price quote obtained by a subject in any search problem would be the lowest of all the price quotes obtained in that problem. In this first set of experiments, behaviour was consistent with such a rule 41.1 per cent of the time. Clearly, therefore, the use of a reservation strategy, and *a fortiori* the optimal reservation strategy, accounts at most for less than half the observed behaviour. Some subjects must be using some other strategies on some occasions.

This is where our tape-recorded protocols proved useful. From the remarks made by the subjects whilst doing the experiment, one can try to infer the types of alternative rules that the subjects might be using. These can then be compared with actual behaviour. Six rules, including the two reservation rules discussed above, were identified.

Rule A   ('reservation' rule): Stop searching if a price quote is received that is 'sufficiently' low.

Rule A*   ('optimal reservation' rule): Stop searching if a price quote is received less than the optimal (with respect to the true distribution) reservation value.

Rule B   ('one bounce' rule): Have at least two searches; stop if a price quote is received larger than the previous quote.

Rule C   ('two bounce' rule): Have at least three searches; stop if both the last quote and the next to the last are larger than the second to the last.

Rule D   ('modified one bounce' rule): Have at least two searches; stop if a price quote is received larger than the previous quote less the search cost.

Rule E   ('modified two bounce' rule): Have at least three searches; stop if both the last quote exceeds the second to last less twice the search cost and the next to last exceeds the second to last less the search cost.

Rules A and A* have already been discussed. Rules B to E are all rather bizarre in that they appear to imbue the order in which the quotes are obtained with some significance. This is particularly odd since subjects were specifically told that there was no significance in the order. Rules B and C are also rather odd in that they ignore the cost of obtaining the quotes; in contrast, rules D and E take these costs into account: if you like, rule D is rule B 'corrected for' the cost, and rule E is rule C 'corrected for' the cost.

Whilst rules B to E may appear rather odd, they do appear to be consistent with behaviour in quite a large number of cases: to be specific, rule B is consistent with behaviour in 24 per cent of cases, rule C in 18 per cent of cases, rule D in 29 per cent of cases and rule E in 19 per cent of cases.[1] There are, in addition, some cases which are not explicable by any of these rules; usually these are cases where it appears that the subject went on buying quotes for too long – a phenomenon which is only apparent too late of course!

More importantly, even though rules B to E appear rather odd, their implications are very interesting. A simulation study reveals that the use of such rules leads to quite good performances in terms of the realized value of the objective function (expected purchase price less search cost). Obviously the optimal strategy does best in terms of this objective, but rules B to E are not far behind (for details see Hey, 1982). Additionally, they appear quite robust. Finally, the implications of rules B to E for market behaviour almost exactly agree with the implications of the optimal strategy, rule A*.

7.3   The Pilot of a Second Search Experiment

At about the same time as I was carrying out this first set of experiments other economists, most notably Schotter and Braunstein (1981), were investigating search problems in which searchers were given much more information about the distributions from which they were searching. The typical discovery of such experiments was behaviour considerably closer to the optimal than that which I had observed. This lent provisional support to the intuitively appealing hypothesis that behaviour approaches the optimal as the information available to the searcher increases. Conversely, behaviour becomes increasingly subject to apparently arbitrary 'rules of thumb' as information decreases.

An alternative interpretation of my 'rules of thumb' findings revolves around the incentives present in my first set of search experiments. Recall that subjects were not paid in this first set. So in my second set I wanted to incorporate an appropriate financial incentive. This necessitated a slight change in the experimental design; as will be seen, this change was also a simplification and improvement.

In addition, I was intrigued to discover the effects on behaviour of a change in the 'rules of the game' which should (for a risk-neutral searcher with complete information) have no effect on behaviour. To be specific, I was intrigued to discover the effect of removing the recall option. Removing this option means that, when the searcher stops searching, he or she can accept only the last observation. Under risk neutrality and complete information, this should have no effect, since the optimal reservation value remains constant through time.

I therefore carried out four different sub-experiments a, b, c and d: a and c allowed recall, b and d did not; in a and b the searcher was provided with complete information about the distributions, whilst in c and d the searcher was provided with no information. As with the earlier experiments the subjects were given written instructions 24 hours in advance of the experiment, which they performed at a VDU terminal alone in a room with a tape recorder. As before, subjects could have as many trial runs as they wanted, to familiarize themselves with the mechanics of the experiment, before moving on to the 'real thing'. In this second set, this consisted of five search problems. In each problem, subjects were sequentially presented with random offers from an underlying distribution which was normal with mean μ and variance σ^2. The distributions were truncated below at £0 (to protect the subjects) and above at £30 (to protect me). The parameters μ and σ in each of the five problems, and the corresponding offer cost c, are given in table 7.1. In each problem, subjects were told the offer cost and were then given a random offer. They were then invited to obtain as many offers as they wished (at a cost c per offer). The outcome on any one round was the highest or last offer (as appropriate) less the offer cost times the number of offers. After each problem, the computer told them the outcome, and then moved on to the next problem. At the end of the five problems, the computer randomly selected one of the five outcomes. This, plus an appropriate bonus designed to make each of the four sub-experiments equally attractive

Table 7.1   The parameters of the second search experiment

Problem number	Offer cost c (£)	Mean offer μ (£)	Standard deviation σ (£)	Optimal reservation value R^* (£)
1	1.00	6.00	2.50	6
2	0.50	4.75	2.50	6
3	0.10	5.10	2.00	6
4	0.20	4.20	2.00	6
5	1.00	3.50	5.00	6

financially (£1 for a, £2 for b and c and £3 for d), was the subjects' payment. It was paid to them in cash.

So this second set differed from the first in at least three crucial respects: (a) it was financially motivated; (b) it was more straightforward – the objective was to maximize the last or highest offer less the search costs; (c) it incorporated two two-way splits – with and without information, and with and without recall.

I should perhaps spend a little time discussing the question of how the information concerning the price distribution was conveyed, as this is a question that crops up in other contexts. The information that we wanted to convey was the information that the offer distribution 'was normal with mean μ and standard deviation σ, truncated below at 0 and above at 30'. To statistically literate subjects we could simply say this. But we wanted the experiment to be accessible to all sorts of subjects, not just the statistically literate, indeed probably preferably not the statistically literate. So we needed to convey the above statement in a more accessible form. One obvious contender is a pictorial probability distribution – after all, a bell-shaped distribution is familiar to all, is it not? But here we anticipated the problem of what we would say to a subject who asked us what the two axes on the graph portrayed: the horizontal axis presents no problem – it portrays the offers themselves; but it is the vertical axis that causes the difficulty. Imagine trying to explain to a mathematically illiterate subject what probability density means! (It is bad enough trying to explain it to university students.) So we abandoned that idea.

What we finally used, though we appreciate that it is not perfect, is the following: for those subjects in sub-experiments a and b, that is, those with full information, they could, at any stage in the proceedings, ask the computer to tell them what proportion of future offer values would lie between any two values specified by them. They could costlessly repeat this interrogation as often as they liked, and by so doing could build up a picture of the probability distribution. They were told that this remained constant for the duration of a particular problem.

For a risk-neutral individual performing experiments a and b (those with full information), the optimal strategy is simply to keep on searching until an offer greater than the optimal reservation value R^* is obtained. In this second set of experiments, R^* is given by (cf. (7.1))

$$\int_{R^*}^{\infty} [1 - F(x)]\,\mathrm{d}x = c \tag{7.2}$$

where c is the offer cost and $F(.)$ is the distribution function of the offer distribution. Although equation (7.2) may appear unfamiliar, it is the usual type of optimality condition in economics: the right-hand side is the (marginal) cost of buying one more offer; the left-hand side is the (marginal) expected gain from buying one more offer when the best offer to date is R^*. The equation simply states that when the marginal cost is equal to the marginal benefit then the searcher should be indifferent between stopping and buying one more offer. Note that

$$\int_{R*}^{\infty} [1 - F(x)]\,dx = \int_{R*}^{\infty} (x - R*) f(x)\,dx$$

One interesting feature of the optimal strategy described above is the fact that the expected net payment (the expected outcome to use my terminology above) following the optimal strategy is $R*$. On reflection, this is obvious: at an offer of $R*$ one is indifferent between continuing and stopping. In my second set of experiments I deliberately chose the parameters μ, σ and c so that the optimal reservation value $R*$ in each search problem was £6 (see table 7.1). So subjects doing sub-experiment a, for example, could expect to earn £7 (£6 plus the bonus of £1) from the experiment if they behaved optimally; if they behaved suboptimally, the expected payment would be less.

In total 32 subjects performed the experiments, eight for each of the four sub-experiments. Table 7.2 gives some summary statistics. It can be seen that on sub-experiment c (that without information but with recall) 40 per cent had behaviour consistent with rule A and 32.5 per cent had behaviour consistent with rule A*; these results are remarkably close to the correspond-ing 41.1 per cent and 25 per cent observed in my first set of experiments, which were of the same basic type as sub-experiment c. The closeness may have something to tell us about the influence of financial incentives.

If we denote by p_e (p_e^*) the proportion of the subjects doing sub-experiment e whose behaviour was consistent with using rule A (A*), that is, the (optimal) reservation rule, then table 7.2 reveals that overall

$$p_b^* > p_a^* > p_d^* > p_c^*$$

and

$$p_b > p_a = p_d > p_c$$

Table 7.2   Analysis of rules A* and A

Sub-experiment	Percentage of A*[a]	Percentage of A[b]
a	57.5	80.0
b	65.0	95.0
c	32.5	40.0
d	52.5	80.0
All	51.875	73.75

[a] The percentage of those whose behaviour was consistent with using the optimal reservation rule.
[b] The percentage of those whose behaviour was consistent with using some reservation rule.

These results suggest that (a) having information (about the distribution) makes it more likely that the subject will follow a reservation rule and more likely that the subject will follow an optimal reservation rule, and (b) having the facility of recall makes it less likely that the subject will follow a reservation rule and less likely that the subject will follow an optimal reservation rule. Of these, (a) is not surprising, but (b) is: it seems that the extra freedom allowed by the recall facility was 'abused' by the subjects. Or perhaps that having recall makes the subjects more careless?

7.4   A Large-scale Implementation of the Second Experiment

The experiment described in section 7.3 – with just 32 subjects – was very much a pilot study. Having ascertained that the basic design and software did what I wanted it to do, I then proceeded to a full-scale study involving 200 subjects, 50 on each of the four sub-experiments. In this large-scale study, I dropped the tape-recorded protocols and used a simple questionnaire instead. The questionnaire was completed by the subjects themselves after they had finished the experiment. In addition to questions asking for factual information (age, sex and income), there were questions asking the subjects how they tackled the search problem in general and how they took into account certain aspects of the problem (the offer cost and the uncertainty in particular). I regard the information gleaned from such questionnaires as interesting and indicative, but potentially of rather dubious reliability; after all, there is no incentive for the subjects to treat the questionnaire seriously. A similar problem exists with the tape-recorded protocols, which we dropped for a variety of reasons. First, for purely practical reasons: when processing 200 subjects it is much easier to do them in batches of eight rather than individually, and this leads to practical difficulties in making tape-recordings. Second, for secretarial reasons: it is almost a guaranteed way of losing the goodwill of secretaries to ask them to transcribe tape-recordings, because the quality is usually extremely bad and it requires great skill and much patience to transcribe them accurately. Third, for analytical reasons: even when transcribed, tape-recorded protocols are difficult to process and require careful handling. Psychologists have considerable experience of doing this – and there are software packages available to assist in protocol analysis – but we simply felt overwhelmed by the magnitude of the problem. In addition, we were rather sceptical as to what might emerge at the end of the day; this brings me back to my point about incentives.

I had two main objectives in this large-scale study: first, to see whether the tentative results suggested by the pilot study ((a) and (b) at the end of section 7.3) would be confirmed by a larger number of subjects; second, to move on from tests of the absolute correctness or otherwise of the optimality theory to tests of the relative or comparative correctness. Perhaps I should explain. So far, the tests have looked to see whether subjects behave as the theory says they should behave. This is what I mean by an absolute test. But this is not the usual type of test carried out by economists when testing economic theories. On the contrary, standard econometric tests are almost always tests of the comparative statics predictions of the theory. In other words, standard tests are not tests of whether the theory is absolutely correct, but rather tests of whether economic agents respond to changes in the parameters of the decision problem in the manner indicated by the theory. So they are comparative tests. Quite clearly it is possible for a subject to fail an absolute test but pass a comparative one, though not, of course, vice versa.

In our simple search experiment, the optimal strategy for a risk-neutral subject with complete information is a reservation strategy with reservation value R^* given by equation (7.2). A test of whether a subject's behaviour is consistent with the use of such a strategy is an absolute test of that theory. In contrast, a comparative test is a test of the comparative statics predictions of the theory. In the case of our simple search experiment, the comparative statics implications are immediate: from equation (7.2) it can be seen that R^* increases with (a) a fall in the offer cost c, (b) a rightward shift in the offer distribution $F(.)$ and (c) a Rothschild–Stiglitz increase in the riskiness of the offer distribution $F(.)$. Since in our experiments all the distributions were normal with mean μ and variance σ^2, it follows that the last two of these comparative statics propositions can be restated as follows: R^* increases with (b) an increase in μ and (c) an increase in σ. So the optimally behaving searcher is more choosy (has a higher R^*) when c falls or when μ or σ rises. These are the comparative predictions tested in this large-scale study.

Each of the 200 subjects performed five 'real' search problems, as in the pilot. Half were given parameter set 1, and half parameter set 2. These are specified in table 7.3, along with the implied optimal reservation values. It should be noted that the truncation does not affect the value of R^* since the truncated density was all located at the truncation point (see equation (7.2)).

Table 7.3   Parameters in the large-scale experiment

Problem	c	μ	σ	R^*
Parameter set 1				
1	0.1	3.72	4.0	10.0
2	0.2	3.96	4.0	9.0
3	0.4	4.40	4.0	8.0
4	0.2	6.51	1.0	7.0
5	0.1	6.00	0.25	6.0
Parameter set 2				
1	0.1	− 0.28	4.0	6.0
2	0.2	1.96	4.0	7.0
3	0.4	4.40	4.0	8.0
4	0.2	8.51	1.0	9.0
5	0.1	10.00	0.25	10.0

c, μ, σ and R^* are all denominated in pounds.

Table 7.4   Percentage of cases in the larger-scale experiment with behaviour consistent with the use of the optimal (some) reservation rule

	With recall (%)	Without recall (%)	Total (%)
With information	15 (70)	2í (86)	18 (78)
Without information	13 (50)	17 (77)	15 (64)
Total	14 (60)	19 (82)	$16\frac{1}{2}$ (71)

It will be noted from table 7.3 that, in parameter set 1, R^* falls as one goes from problem to problem; in parameter set 2 the opposite happens. This was so designed to test for any trend effects; none were apparent.

Table 7.4 presents a simple test of the absolute predictions of the optimality theory. Overall, it shows that in just $16\frac{1}{2}$ per cent of all cases (1000 search problems in total, that is, 200 subjects with five search problems each) was behaviour consistent with the use of the optimal strategy. However, in 71 per cent of all cases behaviour was consistent with the use of some reservation rule – so although one should conclude that subjects' behaviour departed from that prescribed by the optimality theory, it appears that subjects were *trying* to do the right thing. It should also be noted that these results appear to confirm the tentative findings of the pilot study, that the facility of recall makes the subjects less likely to use the optimal (any) reservation rule, while the availability of information makes the subjects more likely to use the optimal (any) reservation rule. Once again, it appears to be the case that having the facility of recall makes the subjects less careful.

Let me now move on to the comparative tests. There is a slight difficulty here as it is not obvious what is the appropriate test. One possibility is simply to see whether the number of offers purchased was a decreasing function of c and an increasing function of μ and σ, but this would effectively ignore the particular offers received; it would therefore be inefficient (even if unbiased). An alternative is to try and estimate the search/stopping rule 'actually' used and see whether this is sensitive to the three parameters in the correct way. This is the strategy used here.

The information recorded by the experiment is whether the subject stopped or continued buying offers at each stage. One can therefore interpret the 'dependent variable' that the theory is trying to explain as the 0/1 variable indicating whether the searcher stopped or continued at that stage. Probit (or logit) analysis would therefore appear appropriate: one could think of the stopping rule as being stochastic in general (though deterministic in particular cases), with an implied probability of continuing p being some appropriate function of relevant variables; one could then interpret the 0/1 values observed as being the realizations of this stochastic stopping rule. If the searcher is following the optimal rule described above, then the stopping rule is given by

$$p_i = 1 \quad \text{if} \quad \max(x_1, x_2, \ldots, x_i) < R*$$
$$p_i = 0 \quad \text{if} \quad \max(x_1, x_2, \ldots, x_i) \geq R* \tag{7.3}$$

where x_j is the jth offer purchased by the searcher and p_i is the probability that the individual will continue searching (buy another offer) after having bought offers $1, 2, \ldots, i$. Further, given the fact that the reservation value $R*$ is independent of i, then this optimal rule can be written in the simpler format

$$p_i = 1 \quad \text{if} \quad x_i < R*$$
$$p_i = 0 \quad \text{if} \quad x_i \geq R* \tag{7.4}$$

This is clearly a special case of a more general formulation which can be written as

$$p_i = p(x_i; c, \mu, \sigma)$$

where $p(.)$ denotes a probability function (taking values between 0 and 1). This equation was estimated (for all the sub-experiments jointly and for each of the four sub-experiments separately) using probit methodology and the LIMDEP mainframe package. Adopting a linear function form within the probit model, the estimation results for all the subjects and all the variants combined were[2]

$$p_i = \phi \, (1.908 - 0.2626x_i - 0.7533c + 0.1250\mu - 0.0950\sigma) \qquad \chi^2 = 775$$
$$\quad\;\; (14.7) \quad (23.2) \qquad (2.5) \qquad (6.4) \qquad (3.1) \tag{7.5}$$

Here $\phi(.)$ denotes the normal distribution function, and the figures in parentheses are t-ratios which should be interpreted in the usual fashion. They show that all four variables and the intercept have coefficients which are significantly different from zero. The signs of the coefficients confirm the theory with one exception, that being the negative sign on σ, which suggests that search decreases as the spread of the distribution increases – an opposite conclusion to that of the theory. Otherwise, the coefficients have the right sign: search decreases with the magnitude of the last offer and with the offer cost, and it increases with the mean of the distribution.[3]

One possible explanation for the incorrect sign on the σ variable is that equation (7.5) lumps together the data for all four sub-experiments. One could legitimately argue that one should treat the four cases as being quite different, in particular distinguishing the information cases from the no-information cases. Accordingly, the equation was re-estimated for each of the four variants separately; the results are given in table 7.5. It should be noted that, although the coefficient on σ remains negative for all four variants individually, it is significantly negative only in the 'no-recall no-information' variant. This suggests that the overall significantly negative effect is being driven by the latter case. Note further that in each of the no-information cases the magnitude of the coefficient on σ is greater than in the corresponding information cases (0.0902 compared with 0.0519 in the recall cases, and 0.2227 compared with 0.0005 in the no-recall cases). In these no-information cases (unless one adopts the extreme 'as if' assumption discussed above) it

Table 7.5   Estimates of stopping equation

Group	Constant	x_i	c	μ	σ	χ^2	n
All	1.9076*	− 0.2626*	− 0.7533*	0.1250*	− 0.0959*	775	3582
a	1.4660*	− 0.2494*	− 0.7215	0.1489*	− 0.0519	165	793
b	1.9852*	− 0.4586*	− 1.2875	0.2975*	− 0.0005	323	807
c	1.6833*	− 0.1485*	− 0.1485*	− 0.9366	− 0.0902	90	1090
d	2.7770*	− 0.3389*	0.1927	0.0633	− 0.2227*	305	892

*Significant at the 5 per cent level.
a, recall, information; b, no recall, information; c, recall, no information; d, no recall, no information.

is not so obvious that the theoretical prediction (that search increases with the dispersion of the distribution) should hold. Instead, one could argue that there is an opposing effect, which more than offsets the hypothesized effect, which occurs in the no-information cases because offers have a twin role: the direct effect as an offer *per se* and an indirect effect giving information about the distribution. Since the subjects in the no-information cases were told nothing about the distribution, one could quite plausibly argue that a sequence of offers coming from a distribution with a high standard deviation could be interpreted as a good sequence of offers in the sense that the subject should stop buying offers having received the sequence. To put this point more concretely, consider the two sequences:

Sequence 1: £5, £6 and £7
Sequence 2: £1, £4 and £7

Given the small number of observations, it is not clear to someone who knows nothing about the distribution whether sequence 2 is a relatively good sequence from a distribution with the same mean and variance as the distribution generating the first sequence, or whether it is an equally good sequence from a distribution with the same mean but a larger variance than the first sequence. Given the small number of observations, it is unlikely that any sophisticated statistical analysis would help in this instance. So one could understand subjects who were more likely to stop after sequence 2 than after sequence 1 even though sequence 2 may in fact have come from a distribution with a higher variance than the distribution from which sequence 1 came. This kind of argument 'rationalizes' the negative coefficient on the standard deviation terms in the above probits, at least as far as the no-information cases are concerned.

There remain the negative coefficients on the standard deviation in the information cases. One clue as to how this might come about, and indeed additionally as to why the other two comparative statics predictions of the optimality theory are confirmed, comes from the subjects' responses to the questionnaires filled in at the completion of the experiment. One of the questions specifically asked the subjects to describe how they tackled the problem. Many of the subjects in the information cases specifically responded that they stopped when the chance of getting a better offer was appropriately small. The concept of a 'better offer' varied somewhat from subject to subject, though the majority agreed that this should be regarded as net of the offer cost expended to get that offer. The magnitude implied by 'appropriately small' also varied from subject to subject; indeed, this could often be interpreted in stochastic terms, so that the 'stopping rule' implicitly used was of the form discussed above. An algebraic approximation to the verbal descriptions made by many of the subjects would be as follows:

$$p_i = g[1 - F(x_i + c)]$$

where $g(.)$ is a monotonically increasing function on $[0, 1]$ with $g(0) = 0$ and $g(1) = 1$. Note that the subjects in the information cases were told the function $F(.)$.

If the function $g(.)$ in this equation is the identity $g(x) \equiv x$ for all x then the equation reduces to the stochastic stopping rule

$$p_i = \phi[(\mu - x_i - c)/\sigma]$$

where $\phi(.)$, as before, is the unit normal distribution function. This rule has remarkable similarities to the optimal and estimated rules; in particular, the comparative statics implications of changes in μ and c are precisely the same as for the optimal rule and identical with those found empirically. Further, the effect of changes in σ are ambiguous: for $\mu - x_i - c$ positive an increase in σ leads to a decrease in p, whereas for $\mu - x_i - c$ negative the opposite is true. If significant numbers of subjects were following this type of rule, then it would help to explain the unexpected sign on σ in our empirical analyses.

So the conclusion is as follows. It is quite clear that the behaviour of the subjects in these search experiments departed significantly from that predicted by the optimality theory (based on SEUT). Nevertheless, the comparative statics implications of their behaviour agreed with those of the optimality theory, at least in so far as the predictions concerning a change in the offer cost and a rightward shift in the offer distribution are concerned. However, the comparative statics effect of a change in the dispersion of the offer distribution was not in accordance with the theory. Alternative explanations were proffered for both the information and no-information cases. It is difficult to appraise the explanation for the latter case as the role of optimality is not clear, but at least the results here provide a description of behaviour. As far as the explanation for the information cases is concerned, the alternative presented here has certain aspects in common with the optimal case, yet is quite clearly a simpler rule for subjects to operate. Although the comparative statics implications depart from those of the optimality theory in one key respect (the dispersion effect is conditional rather than unconditionally positive), the implications for market stability are not dissimilar.

It should, of course, be noted that the finding that the comparative statics predictions of optimality theory (with the one exception) are confirmed is not a particularly strong finding. Other theories arrive at the same predictions. But the finding helps to calm the fears of those who worry about the accumulating experimental evidence against SEUT, while at the same time confirming the conventional econometric tests of search (and other) theories – which are, after all, tests of the comparative correctness of the theory, not the absolute correctness.

7.5   Conclusions

Sufficient evidence has now been accumulated by ourselves and others to indicate that the SEUT-based model of optimal search is not a particularly good description of absolute behaviour, and that behaviour worsens when information lessens and when the facility of recall is introduced. Nevertheless, the SEUT-based theory provides some reasonably accurate comparative statics predictions.

I have concentrated here on work carried out by myself. Other work includes that of Schotter and Braunstein (1981), Cox and Oaxaca (1986), Wilde (1986), Kogut (1988) and Harrison and Morgan (1990). In addition, there is a sizeable volume of literature in the psychology journals on experimental work on search carried out by psychologists in the 1970s; references to this can be found in Hey (1982). Taken together, this literature provides an impressive body of evidence indicating the strengths and weaknesses of the economic theory of search as a description of actual behaviour. It shows clearly the power of experimental methods.

Notes

1 Note that, in some instances, behaviour may be consistent with more than one of these rules.
2 There were 200 subjects altogether, each doing five rounds; the average number of offers purchased was 3.582 per searcher-round, giving us a grand total of 3582 observations on the equation above.
3 It may be useful to give some insight into the economic meaning of equation (7.5). To this end, substitute into it some specific parameter values and explore the consequences. For an initial example, take the parameters of the fifth round of the first data set: these were $c = 0.1$, $\mu = 6$ and $\sigma = 0.25$. Inserting these into (7.5) gives

$$p_i = \phi(2.5582 - 0.2627 x_i)$$

from which it follows that $p = 0.05$, 0.25, 0.50, 0.75 and 0.95 according as x is 16.00, 12.31, 9.74, 7.17 and 3.48. Recalling that the optimal reservation rule with these parameters was 6.00, it is clear that there was a general tendency for too much search to be conducted. Moreover, while the above equation could be termed a stochastic stopping rule, it is clear that the reservation value is not at all precisely defined; rather, it could be thought of as a stochastic variable with mean 9.74 and standard deviation 3.81. In contrast, if the optimal strategy was being followed, then equation (7.5) would have read

$$p_i = \phi(6a - ax_i)$$

where a was an appropriately large number (in theory infinity, but anything above about 1.645 would appear reasonable – leading to values of p of 0.95, 0.5 and 0.05 corresponding to x values of 5, 6 and 7).

8

A Consumption Experiment

8.1   Introduction

There must be many economists like myself who have been excited by the simplicity and elegance of the famous Hall (1978) solution to the dynamic consumption problem under income uncertainty. This seminal paper has inspired much further theoretical and empirical work, including the experimental work to be discussed in this chapter.

Hall (1978) examines the case of an individual, living for a random length of time in a discrete period world and facing uncertainty about future incomes, trying to decide on the optimal allocation of income between consumption and saving in order to maximize some lifetime objective function. On the face of it, this is an extremely complex problem; Hall, aided and abetted by dynamic programming techniques, solves it in a simple, neat and appealing manner. The implications for the optimizing consumption stream are initially rather surprising; on reflection they are eminently sensible. Moreover, they seem to have some empirical validity.

This latter is all the more remarkable when it is recalled that the Hall solution implicitly builds upon the subjective expected utility theory (SEUT) foundation – a possibly rather weak foundation, if the stories emanating from part II of this book are to be believed. Of course, the empirical tests of the Hall model – until my experimental tests came along – were all econometric tests of the conventional form: based on aggregate or average data that were generated under conditions different from those of the theory. No direct test of the Hall model had hitherto been carried out.

The purpose, therefore, of the experiments reported in this chapter was to carry out a direct empirical test of the Hall model. I would, as far as possible, replicate the Hall model in the laboratory, and hence investigate it under the appropriate *ceteris paribus* conditions. This in itself would be a useful exercise (see my arguments in chapter 2). In addition, it would provide a test somewhere along the spectrum between the two extremes of tests of the basic SEUT axioms at the one end and conventional econometric tests at the other. As such, it might help to explain why tests of SEUT are not very flattering to SEUT whilst conventional econometric tests of theories of economic behaviour built on a SEUT foundation are often quite favourable to those theories. In a sense, we revisit some of the concerns of chapter 7.

I begin by describing the theory. I then discuss a pilot experiment which we ran with just 14 students. This led me to modify the design in certain respects before running a large-scale experiment with 128 subjects. The whole exercise was highly instructive.

8.2 The Economic Theory of Optimal Consumption under Income Risk

I follow Hall's (1978) basic formulation, though with some slight notational changes. Imagine an individual in a discrete random-horizon world facing income uncertainty. He or she must decide each period how to allocate his/her realized income between consumption and saving. To make the latter potentially attractive we specify a positive and known real rate of return on savings. We assume for the time being that the individual can both freely save and freely borrow at this known rate. We further assume that the individual obeys SEUT and that the utility function is defined over the consumption stream $C_1, C_2, \ldots, C_t, \ldots$ where C_t is the consumption in period t. Moreover, we assume that this utility function is additively separable in C_1, $C_2, \ldots, C_t, \ldots$ so that we can specify the objective of the individual, as viewed from the first period, as the maximization of the expectation of

$$U(C_1) + \rho_1 U(C_2) + \rho_1\rho_2 U(C_3) + \ldots + \rho_1\rho_2 \ldots \rho_{t-1} U(C_t) + \ldots$$

$$\equiv U(C_1) + \sum_{i=2}^{\infty} \left(\prod_{j=1}^{i-1} \rho_j \right) U(C_i)$$

where ρ_j is the discount factor that applies between periods j and $j+1$. In a random-horizon world, this ρ_j should be interpreted as the product of the true discount rate (conditional on being alive) of utility in $j+1$ as viewed from j multiplied by the probability of being alive in $j+1$, conditional on being alive in j. Often it is presumed, to simplify notation, that ρ_j is independent of j. This may be a reasonable presumption for the middle stages of an individual's life, but is a rather poor one for the early stages (when the probability of surviving to the next period rises with age) and for the later stages (when the probability of surviving to the next period falls with age). My treatment allows ρ_j to vary with j; however, I do assume that it is known.

Given the above specification of the objective function, it follows that the individual's objective as viewed from the start of some intermediate period t is the maximization of

$$E_t \left[U(C_t) + \sum_{i=t+1}^{\infty} \left(\prod_{j=t}^{i-1} \rho_j \right) U(C_i) \right]$$

$$(8.1)$$

where the expectation E_t is taken with respect to information available at the beginning of t.

Denote the income stream by $Y_1, Y_2, \ldots, Y_t, \ldots$ where Y_t is the income received in period t. We assume that Y_t is *ex ante* uncertain and that its realized value is revealed after the decision on C_{t-1} is made but before the decision on C_t is made. Moreover, Y_t is received at the beginning of period t and C_t is chosen and spent immediately afterwards. Denote wealth at the beginning of period t by W_t and let r_t denote the certain rate of return between t and $t+1$; r_t equals 1 plus the rate of interest between t and $t+1$. We have the accounting identity

$$W_{t+1} = r_t(W_t - C_t) + Y_{t+1} \qquad (8.2)$$

This completes the specification of the problem. We now move on to its solution which involves the sequential choice of $C_1, C_2, \ldots, C_t, \ldots$ to maximize the objective function: for the choice of C_t this is given by equation (8.1). I use familiar dynamic programming methods.

First, I need to introduce some notation to denote the maximized value of the objective function (8.1). I shall write it as $V_t(W_t)$ to recognize explicitly that its value depends upon the individual's wealth at the beginning of period t. It also depends upon $r_t, r_{t+1}, \ldots$, upon $\rho_t, \rho_{t+1}, \ldots$, upon the individual's utility function $U(.)$ and upon the joint distribution of $Y_{t+1}, Y_{t+2}, \ldots$; for notational clarity I shall not explicitly signal these dependences, but they should be borne in mind.

Thus, definitionally, we have

$$V_t(W_t) \equiv \max_{C_t, C_{t+1}, \ldots} \left\{ E_t \left[U(C_t) + \sum_{i=t+1}^{\infty} \left(\prod_{j=t}^{i-1} \rho_j \right) U(C_i) \right] \right\} \qquad (8.3)$$

That is, $V_t(W_t)$ is the maximized value of expected lifetime utility as viewed from the beginning of period t.

From this, since C_t is non-stochastic at time t (it is the decision variable) and using equation (8.3) with t replaced by $t+1$ throughout, it follows that we can write

$$V_t(W_t) = \max_{C_t} [U(C_t) + \rho_t E_t V_{t+1}(W_{t+1})] \qquad (8.4)$$

where W_{t+1} is given by equation (8.2).

Now the optimal choice of C_t, which I denote by C_t^*, is simply the value which maximizes the term in square brackets on the right-hand side of equation (8.4). The first-order condition, found by differentiating the expression in square brackets with respect to C_t and putting the resulting expression equal to zero, gives

$$U'(C_t^*) = \rho_t r_t E_t V'_{t+1}[r_t(W_t - C_t^*) + Y_{t+1}] . \qquad (8.5)$$

It can be shown that the second-order condition is satisfied if U is concave ($U'' < 0$), that is, if the individual is a risk-averter, and if V_{t+1} is concave

$(V''_{t+1} < 0)$, which it will be under our assumptions. The proof, which is tedious, is omitted.

We want to explore the implications of equation (8.5). To do this, we need to eliminate the term in V_{t+1}. This can be done as follows. First, use equation (8.4) to write

$$V_t(W_t) = U(C_t^*) + \rho_t E_t V_{t+1}[r_t(W_t - C_t^*) + Y_{t+1}] \tag{8.6}$$

Second, differentiate equation (8.6) with respect to W_t, taking into account the obvious fact that C_t^* is a function of W_t, and use the first-order condition (8.5) to simplify the resulting expression. This gives

$$V_t'(W_t) = \rho_t r_t E_t V_{t+1}'[r_t(W_t - C_t^*) + Y_{t+1}] = U'(C_t^*) \tag{8.7}$$

From this we get trivially that

$$V_{t+1}'(W_{t+1}) = U'(C_{t+1}^*)$$

which enables us to eliminate V_{t+1} from equation (8.3). So doing gives

$$U'(C_t^*) = \rho_t r_t E_t U'(C_{t+1}^*). \tag{8.8}$$

This is a familiar type of optimality condition: it states that the ratio of the expected marginal utility of period $(t+1)$'s consumption to the marginal utility of period t's consumption should equal the inverse of $\rho_t r_t$. This product is effectively the price of period $(t+1)$'s (utility of) consumption in terms of period t's (utility of) consumption: r_t indicates the rate at which money in t is converted into money in $t+1$ while ρ_t indicates the rate at which (utility of) consumption in $t+1$ is discounted to make it comparable with (the utility of) consumption in t. Note, as a special case, that when $\rho_t r_t = 1$, that is, when the individual discounts the future at the same rate as 'the market' does, then the optimality condition simply requires equality between the expected marginal utility of future consumption and the marginal utility of present consumption.

Now 'de-expectationalize' – to use a hideous Americanism – equation (8.8); that is, remove the expectations operator, though note that there is not a unique way of doing this. One way gives[1]

$$U'(C_{t+1}^*) = (\rho_t r_t)^{-1} U'(C_t^*) + u_{t+1} \tag{8.9}$$

where $E_t u_{t+1} = 0$, of course. Equation (8.9) states the rather remarkable result that the optimal consumption strategy implies that the marginal utility of consumption follows a random walk (with drift, given by the factor $(\rho_t r_t)^{-1}$). The random term captures the effect of the unexpected part of income – the 'surprise' component, as it has come to be called.

One approximation to equation (8.9) is of interest: suppose marginal utility is approximately linear, that is, suppose that the utility function is approximately quadratic. Suppose further that $\rho_t r_t$ is constant. Then an approximation to equation (8.9) is

$$C_{t+1}^* = \alpha + \beta C_t^* + v_{t+1} \tag{8.10}$$

where $E_t v_{t+1} = 0$. Hall (1978) estimated this equation using quarterly US data for the period 1948II to 1977I, with the following result:

$$C_{t+1} = -0.014 + 1.011 C_t + \hat{v}_{t+1} \qquad \begin{array}{l} R^2 = 0.999 \\ \text{DW} = 1.70 \\ n = 120 \end{array}$$
$$(337)$$

(where the t statistic is in parentheses and DW is the Durbin–Watson coefficient). Here C_t denotes actual consumption in period t. Similar results have been found for other countries and other times, though considerable controversy surrounds the question of whether other economic variables prove significant when introduced into the equation. According to the theory, they should not: all expectations are already incorporated into the C_t^* and therefore only the unexpected part of income enters into the equation – through the error term v_{t+1}. But note how strong the assumptions of the theory are: in addition to knowing r_t and p_t for all future periods, the individual knows the joint distribution of Y_t, Y_{t+1}, ... extending into the possibly infinite future. This is rational expectations in an extremely strong sense. Moreover, the individual can solve the optimal strategy as specified above. The purpose of my experiment was to investigate whether this was indeed the case.

8.3 A Pilot Experiment

Because of the complexity of the problem, my initial impulse was to try to make it as simple as possible. To this end, I decided to make the appropriate assumptions which would make the optimal strategy stationary, that is, time invariant. One obvious way of doing this is to make all the parameters and distributions constant. Thus if $r_t = r$ for all t, $p_t = p$ for all t and Y_1, Y_2, ..., Y_t, ... are independently and identically distributed then the optimal strategy is stationary.

A further simplification can be made if the utility function is taken to be constant absolute risk averse, that is, if

$$U(x) = -\exp(-Rx) \tag{8.11}$$

where R is the individual's index of absolute risk aversion. This implies that the optimal strategy is given by

$$C^*(W) = a + bW \tag{8.12}$$

where the parameters a and b are given by

$$b = (r-1)/r \tag{8.13}$$

and

$$pr\ E\{\exp[R(r-1)(a - Y/r)]\} = 1$$

For a proof see Hey (1980).

A point of clarification may be necessary at this stage concerning the distinction between the optimal strategy itself (which, under the simplifying assumptions above, is given by equation (8.12)) and the implications of the optimal strategy (which is given by equation (8.9) or (8.10)). Note that the latter does not provide the individual with instructions on how to choose the optimal value of consumption, whereas the former does. The latter simply expresses the form of the relationships between successive values of consumption if the individual follows the optimal strategy. Note particularly that the optimal choice of consumption is not random (as equation (8.9) suggests); rather, it is a deterministic function of wealth (as given by equation (8.12)).

One final simplification was adopted for the pilot study: all the distributions were normal[2] with mean μ and variance σ^2. In this case, the parameter a is given by

$$a = \frac{\mu}{r} - \frac{R(r-1)\sigma^2}{2r^2} - \frac{\log(\rho r)}{R(r-1)} \tag{8.14}$$

The purpose of the pilot was to test this special case (equations (8.12), (8.13) and (8.14)) in the laboratory. However, it is immediately clear that the consumption story as told above cannot be replicated easily in the laboratory – we cannot keep subjects in the laboratory for the whole of their natural lives! So we need to construct an experiment that has precisely the same structure (i.e. the same objective function and the same constraints) as the consumption story, though with different details. This we did as follows.

First, we cast the subjects in a discrete world with a random horizon. To make it stationary, we invoke a constant stopping probability $1 - p$; so at the end of each period there is a probability p that the experiment will continue into the next period. The use of the notation p is deliberate. Second, we give the subjects a random income each period. The distribution of income in each period is normal with mean μ and variance σ^2 and is independent of income in all other periods. This income is denominated in tokens, not money. Tokens can be accumulated or decumulated and a rate of return r is imposed on any token balance carried over from period to period. Third, tokens can be converted into money through a concave conversion scale pictured in graphical form: if C tokens are converted they become $U(C)$ in money. Again, the notation $U(.)$ is deliberate. Fourth, the subject's payment for taking part in the experiment is the amount of money converted from tokens in the final period of the experiment. Thus, any tokens converted in earlier periods and any tokens left unconverted in the final period are lost.

Finally, suppose the subject is risk neutral. Then the subject is interested in devising a conversion strategy that will maximize his or her expected payment from the experiment. Let C_t denote the amount of tokens converted to money in period t. If period t is the final period then the individual would get paid $U(C_t)$. As the probability of period t being the final period (as viewed from the beginning of the experiment) is $p^{t-1}(1 - p)$ it follows that the expected payment as viewed from the beginning of the experiment is the expectation of

$$(1-p)U(C_1) + p(1-p)U(C_2) + p^2(1-p)U(C_3) + \ldots + p^{t-1}(1-p)U(C_t) + \ldots$$

$$= (1-p)[U(C_1) + pU(C_2) + p^2U(C_3) + \ldots + p^{t-1}U(C_t) + \ldots]$$

By a similar argument it follows that the subject's objective as viewed from the start of some intermediate period t is the maximization of

$$E_t(1-p)[U(C_t) + pU(C_{t+1}) + p^2U(C_{t+2}) + \ldots]$$

Except for the innocuous factor $1-p$, this is precisely the same as equation (8.1) with $p_j \equiv p$ for all j. It therefore follows that the optimal solution to the subject's problem in my experiment is that specified above: the experiment is entirely congruent to the consumption problem.

In the pilot experiment, we used just one set of parameters: the rate of return on savings r was 1.12; the continuing probability p was 0.9 (this implied a stopping probability of 1 in 10); the mean token income μ was 10; the standard deviation σ of token income was 4; and the 'utility function'/ conversion scale was

$$U(x) = 30[1 - \exp(-0.022314x)]$$

Thus the 'index R of absolute risk aversion' was 0.022314.

Substituting these parameter values in equations (8.12), (8.13) and (8.14) gives us the optimal conversion strategy

$$C^* = 5.936 + 0.107W \tag{8.15}$$

where W is token wealth. The hypothesis under test in this pilot study was that subjects' converted tokens into money according to equation (8.15).

The pilot study consisted of just 14 subjects. All were economists, either staff or postgraduate students. They performed the experiment using a VDU connected to the University mainframe. They were given the written instructions in advance and had the opportunity to discuss any ambiguities or confusions before they were left on their own to carry out the experiment. In addition, as with the pilot search experiments, they were asked to think aloud and to record their thoughts on a tape-recorder. As before, the idea of this was to obtain some supplementary information on how they tackled the problem. In the large-scale study (see section 8.4) we dropped the tape-recordings in favour of written questionnaires, for much the same reasons as before.

The details of the pilot experiment are reported elsewhere (Hey, 1987); let me confine myself to the broad messages that emerged, and the main changes in the experimental design that resulted from it. First, it was abundantly clear that the behaviour of the subjects departed significantly from the optimal strategy specified in equation (8.15): when, for each subject, a linear regression of the actual conversion against wealth was performed, the intercept was significantly different from 5.936 and the slope was significantly different from 0.107. However, rather interestingly, when a simulation study was carried out on the implications of the actual relationships (between C and W) for the expected payment, it was found that most did not do much worse than the optimal strategy. Clearly, the optimal strategy was better, but not significantly better.

Second, the tape-recordings revealed some rather unexpected strategies: some subjects converted one-tenth of their wealth at any time; others converted the mean (token) income plus or minus some small amount dependent on current wealth. The tape-recordings also revealed some strange misunderstandings of basic probability laws, particularly relating to the stopping probability. At the beginning of the experiment many subjects argued – quite correctly, with the stopping probability equal to 0.1 – that the expected duration of the experiment was 10 periods and that it would most probably last between 5 and 15 periods. Unfortunately, many did not also realize that these calculations remained relevant however many periods they had already survived. So some became very confused when 15 periods had passed with the experiment still ongoing. Others became very agitated when the experiment stopped after just one period!

There are a number of problems here: first, there is the question of correctly conveying to the subjects the nature of the stopping mechanism and its implications; second, there is the practical experimental question of whether one is prepared to cope with the implications of a genuinely random stopping mechanism – namely, that some subjects will survive just one period while some others will last a very large number of periods. The former creates disutility for the experimenter; the latter creates disutility for the subject. One way out of this second difficulty is the deliberate 'fixing' by the experimenter of the random device: that is, tell the subjects one thing about how the experiment ends but actually do something different. This can usually be done with computerized experiments, but I am very loath to do it. I feel that it is crucially important that economics experiments actually do what they say they do and that the subjects believe this. I would not like to see experiments in economics degenerate to the state witnessed in some areas of experimental psychology where it is common knowledge that the experimenters say one thing and do another. This would be very harmful to experimental economics. We did not 'fix' the stopping mechanism in this experiment; but this meant that some subjects lasted just one period while others went on for rather a long time (over 40 periods).

As far as the correct perception by the subjects of the stopping mechanism was concerned, we tried to improve things between the pilot and the large-scale study. To be specific, we altered the way that the 'ending of the experiment' was displayed on the computer screen: at the end of each period, 10 random digits were (slowly) printed out on the screen, with the experiment stopping if the *last* of these was a zero. (One could hear the cries of excitement!) However, as we shall see, this did not cure the problem. It is not clear what would, which is a pity as a constant-stopping-probability random-horizon model is a very attractive framework for many dynamic experiments. I will return briefly to this issue in the next chapter when a finite-horizon model is discussed.

The pilot experiment also highlighted a problem with the theory, relating to the borrowing option. Although not explicitly raised, it was implicit throughout the theoretical section (8.2) that borrowing was freely allowable, at the rate of return r_t. In Hall's original model, the horizon was finite and there was an additional implicit constraint imposed, to the effect that the individual could not die in debt. Things are not quite so easy in a random-horizon world since, if the individual ever borrows, there is no guarantee that he will not die in debt. I must admit that I had not thought this through fully when we carried out the pilot experiment, though I did have some unease at the back of my mind. My intuition told me that if I put no constraint on the magnitude of borrowing, then the optimal thing to do in a random-horizon world must surely be to borrow an infinite amount and hence die infinitely in debt. The mathematics of the solution above rule out such a strategy as it is confined to interior solutions. So I vaguely realized that some constraint on borrowing was necessary, even though I had not fully worked out quite what the constraint was. Rather arbitrarily, therefore, I imposed a maximum overdraft limit of 40 tokens; if any subject exceeded this, he or she would be immediately ejected from the experiment with zero payment. A couple of subjects fell foul of this rule; in particular, one 'went for broke', borrowing and converting a lot in the hope that the experiment would end before he hit the borrowing constraint. This reflects badly on my risk-neutrality assumption (see below) and on the borrowing constraint.

Between the pilot and the large-scale experiment, I had time to think more carefully about the borrowing constraint. If we were to impose the implicit Hall constraint, that the individual could never die in debt, it effectively meant that borrowing at any stage could never exceed the minimum income in the following period. If, as was indeed the case, this minimum was zero, then the condition implied that no individual could ever borrow. We therefore imposed this as a condition in the large-scale study. Obviously this has implications for the form of the optimal strategy: with a no-borrowing restriction equation (8.12) is no longer the optimal strategy.

In addition, we realized from the pilot study that our assumption of risk neutrality of the subjects was an unsafe assumption: the subject who was 'going for broke' was clearly displaying risk-loving behaviour and others were quite clearly risk averse. This created a problem. The identification of an individual's utility function is a tiring and time-consuming business: it requires the individual, in general, to answer a moderately large number of questions. In the context of our experiment this was in addition to the 'playing of the game' itself. We decided, rightly or wrongly, that we should try and minimize the number of questions, and do this after the playing of the game proper. Moreover, we decided we needed to ask the question(s) in such a way that the subjects had an incentive to answer honestly. This created a further layer of complexity.

To simplify things we decided on a drastically simplifying assumption (though less drastic than simply assuming that subjects were risk neutral): we assumed that all subjects had utility functions that displayed constant absolute risk aversion. Utility functions therefore had just one parameter. At a minimum, one question would be sufficient to estimate this one parameter. Accordingly, we appended one question to the end of the experiment; I shall give details in the next section.

An alternative procedure which I plan to use in future experiments is to get subjects to do two experiments: the consumption experiment and a utility-function-calibration experiment (like that in chapter 5). On the assumption that the utility function remains constant and that wealth has not changed significantly between the two experiments, one could use the results of the second experiment to help analyse the results of the first.

8.4 A Large-scale Experiment

I have discussed at some length the various messages that emerged from the pilot study and the consequent changes in the experimental design that were implemented before the large-scale experiment was conducted. Let me now turn to the details of the latter.

There were two main aims of the large-scale study: to see whether actual behaviour agreed with the optimal behaviour, and to see whether the comparative statics implications of actual behaviour coincided with the comparative statics implications of the optimal strategy. For the latter, repetitions with different parameter sets were required. This could be done in two ways: give the same subject different parameter sets, or give different subjects different parameter sets. Because we did not want to confuse learning effects with comparative statics effects, and because we were using subjects who were visitors to the University of York, we decided to use the second method. This, in part, determined the number of subjects we needed.

In the special case of the consumption problem discussed above, there are four key environmental parameters (in addition to the risk-aversion parameter of the subjects): p, the continuing probability; r, the rate of return; μ, the mean of the token income distribution; and σ, the standard deviation of the token income distribution. For each of these parameters we selected two values: for p, 0.8 and 0.9; for r, 1.1 and 1.2; for μ, 11 and 7; and for σ, 1 and 5. These gave us considerable variability. They also gave us a combination of $2 \times 2 \times 2 \times 2 = 16$ parameter sets if each is permed with all the others. For each of these sets we had eight subjects, giving us a total of 128 subjects altogether. Payment averaged just under £8 per subject, giving a total expenditure of approximately £1000. Finance was very kindly provided by the Leverhulme Trust to whom I am most grateful.

This large-scale study, which was carried out jointly by myself and Valentino Dardanoni (and published in Hey and Dardanoni, 1988a), was carried out in a terminal classroom of the University of York. Subjects were mainly visitors to the University, and they were processed on a continuous basis. As with some other of my experiments, the subjects were asked to complete a short questionnaire (at the end of the experiment, but before being paid). This asked them to state (a) their age, (b) their sex, (c) their income, (d) the maximum they would be prepared to pay there and then for the chance of winning £10 on the toss of a fair coin, (e) their strategy, (f) how they took the stopping probability into account, (g) how they took the rate of return into account and (h) how they took the distribution of token income into account. As elsewhere, subjects were invited (costlessly) to interrogate the computer about this distribution. (It is surprising that very few subjects took much advantage of this feature: most subjects were content with finding the median and range; very few tried to discover anything more.)

A sample of the data generated by the experiment is pictured in figure 8.1. This portrays the behaviour of four subjects all performing the experiment with parameter set b ($p = 0.8$, $r = 1.1$, $\mu = 7$, $\sigma = 5$). The amount converted/

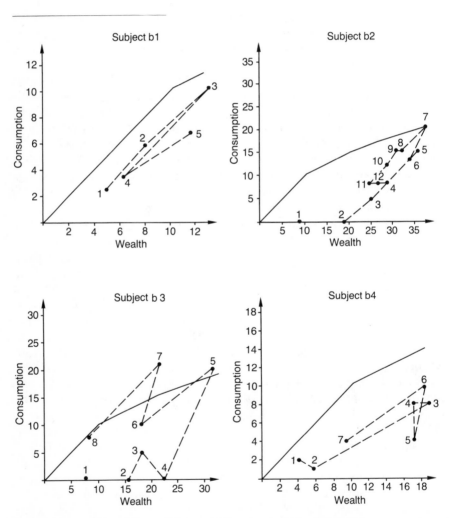

Figure 8.1   Behaviour of four subjects on the consumption experiment: − − − − − , actual; ———— , 'optimal'.

consumed (I shall use the terms interchangeably) each period is shown on the vertical axis and this is plotted against wealth (the token stock) at the beginning of the corresponding period on the horizontal axis. Each cross represents one period, and the crosses are numbered and joined together in chronological order. The unbroken line in each graph indicates the optimal strategy for a risk-neutral subject.

At the end of the experiment, we generated a data matrix containing 1291 rows, formed as follows: the rows consisted of all the time periods for all the subjects stacked up on top of each other. Thus, if n_i denotes the number of periods for which the experiment lasted for subject i, then the first n_1 rows to the data matrix consist of the n_1 periods for subject 1, the next n_2 rows the observations for the n_2 periods of subject 2 and so on. The columns were variables: actual consumption/conversion; wealth; time period; continuing probability; rate of return; mean (of token distribution); and standard deviation (of token distribution). We then appended extra columns giving the optimal conversion/consumption, and the various characteristics of the subjects obtained from the questionnaire (age, sex and income).

The optimal strategy for any subject was calculated numerically, since with the imposition of a no-borrowing constraint it is not possible to obtain an explicit solution (even under the assumption of risk neutrality). The numerical algorithm computed the optimal solution iteratively, starting from a fixed horizon and working back (using backward induction and assuming interior solutions throughout) until convergence was obtained. To do this, we needed an estimate of each individual's utility function; this we took (as already noted) to be constant absolute risk averse with parameter S, namely

$$V(x) = -\exp(-Sx) \qquad (8.16)$$

To obtain an estimate of S – one we could reasonably trust – we added a 'sting in the tail' to the experiment: at the end of the experiment (and without advance warning) the computer offered the subject the chance to increase their earnings from whatever they were, say £x, to £$(2x-2)$. What they were asked to do was to specify a number between 0 and 1. They would then go to the experimenter and spin a pointer on a circular disk with circumference continuously calibrated from 0 to 1. If the pointer stopped at a number q less than p, then the subject would get paid £x; otherwise the subject would spin the pointer again. If, on this second spin, it stopped before q, the subject would get paid £$(2x-2)$; otherwise (that is, if it stopped between q and 1 on the second spin) they would get paid £2. (We decided that £2 was the minimum we could reasonably pay anyone for half-an-hour of their time.)

If the subject obeyed SEUT, then the answer p would be the value that maximized

$$V(x)F(p) + \int_{q=p}^{1} \{V(2)[1-F(q)] + V(2x-2)F(q)\}\, dF(q) \qquad (8.17)$$

where $F(.)$ denotes the distribution function of the spinner. The first-order condition for the maximization of equation (8.17) yields, if $F(q) = q$ (that is, if the spinner is uniform),

$$V(x) = pV(2x - 2) + (1 - p)V(2)$$

Using equation (8.16) this gives

$$-\exp(-Sx) = -p\exp[-2S(x - 1)] - (1 - p)\exp(-2S)$$

which is satisfied by a unique value of S for given x and p.

We also have an estimate of S obtained from question (d) on the questionnaire, though we feel much less confident about the accuracy of this estimate. We thus have two point estimates of S and a numerical algorithm to calculate the optimal strategy for a constantly risk-averse subject for any value of S and for any set of parameters. This enables us to calculate two new columns of data, which we denote by C_1^* and C_2^*, which give the optimal consumption level for each individual and each time period given the values of the relevant variables: W, p, r, μ and σ. C_1^* was calculated using the answers to the 'sting in the tail' question, and C_2^* using the answers to the question on the questionnaire.

Before proceeding to the empirical results, I should note two things. First, if the individual is not risk neutral but has utility function (8.16) then all the theory of section 8.2 needs to be modified so that $U(.)$ is replaced by $V[U(.)]$ everywhere. Second, the numerical algorithm that we used to compute C_1^* and C_2^* is 'driven' by the relevant first-order conditions, and hence implicitly assumes that (apart from corner solutions imposed by the no-borrowing constraint) the optimal solution is an interior one. If this assumption is not correct, the algorithm does not converge to a meaningful solution. In such cases, the optimal strategy is of a reservation form: 'consume all or nothing depending on whether wealth is above or below a given reservation value'. We decided to exclude such cases from the analysis that follows – mainly on the grounds that in the real world we do not observe them, but also partly on the grounds that the nature of the appropriate comparison of actual with optimal differs from that in the 'conventional' case. Using this criterion, we excluded 30 subjects in the C_1^* case (of whom nine were risk-lovers and 21 were faced with $pr > 1$ and were insufficiently risk averse), and we excluded 18 subjects in the C_2^* case (of whom three were risk-lovers and 13 were faced with $pr > 1$ and were insufficiently risk averse). After these exclusions we were left with a data matrix containing 956 rows with a valid C_1^* and 1096 rows with a valid C_2^*. The behaviour of the excluded subjects still remains to be analysed.

The main empirical results are summarized in table 8.1. First examine the columns headed $C - C_1^*$ and $C - C_2^*$. These columns show the results of regressing these two variables in the data matrix against various other variables. Under the null hypothesis that actual behaviour departs from optimal behaviour only by a random (white noise) term we would expect that $C - C_1^*$ and $C - C_2^*$ would not depend on any other variables in the data matrix. The null hypothesis is decisively rejected. Most crucially, the time

Table 8.1 Regression results from the larger-scale consumption experiment

Independent variables	Dependent variables					
	C	C^*	$(C-C^*)_1$	C	C^*_2	$(C-C^*)_2$
Constant	-27.3 (2.0)	-8.5 (1.6)	-17.8 (1.1)	-0.7 (0.1)	69.0 (4.5)	-67.8 (2.4)
t	0.14(10.8)		0.14(10.7)	0.14(10.9)		0.13 (7.4)
W	1.9 (2.3)	1.1 (4.0)	0.65(0.7)	0.6 (0.6)	4.7 (5.2)	5.12 (3.1)
ρ	4.3 (0.5)	4.5 (1.6)	-2.24(0.3)	-9.3 (0.9)	-40.1 (4.9)	32.76 (2.1)
r	20.4 (2.5)	0.8 (0.3)	19.1 (2.1)	7.6 (0.8)	-30.5 (4.4)	36.5 (2.8)
μ	0.7 (3.9)	1.3 (13.3)	-0.6 (3.3)	0.5 (2.6)	0.7 (5.6)	-0.17 (0.7)
σ	-0.6 (3.5)	-0.8 (16.2)	0.33(1.9)	-0.5 (2.8)	-0.5 (4.0)	-0.04 (0.2)
$W\rho$	-0.5 (1.0)	-0.6 (4.0)	0.21(0.4)	-0.1 (0.2)	2.3 (4.6)	-2.2 (2.4)
Wr	-1.1 (2.2)		-1.0 (1.8)	-0.4 (0.8)	2.6 (6.3)	-2.9 (3.8)
$W\mu$	-0.01(1.6)	-0.02(0.1)	0.02(1.8)	-0.01(1.0)	-0.01(0.2)	-0.001(0.6)
$W\sigma$	0.04(4.2)	-0.03(7.8)	0.03(2.8)	0.03(3.1)	0.7 (0.9)	0.03 (1.0)
a	0.03(1.2)	0.01(3.3)	0.04(1.3)	0.03(1.4)		-0.06 (1.8)
s	-0.9 (2.7)		-1.15(3.1)	-0.9 (3.0)		-1.3 (3.8)
i	-0.1 (4.7)		-0.04(1.4)	-0.1 (2.8)		0.02 (0.5)
R^2	0.38	0.81	0.22	0.38	0.71	0.22
n		956			1096	

t statistics in parentheses.

t, time period; W, wealth; ρ, continuing probability; r, rate of return; μ, mean of token distribution; σ, std. of token distribution; a, age of subject (years); s, sex (0 male, 1 female); i, income (in thousands); n, sample size.

period is significant, which indicates (since the optimal strategy is not time dependent) that actual behaviour is. This was an obvious feature of our subjects' behaviour. (Note that the above test of the null hypothesis may not have been sufficient: if none of the t statistics had been significant, then we could not have concluded that $C - C_1^*$ and $C - C_2^*$ were white noise. However, the fact that some t statistics *are* significant is sufficient to reject the white noise hypothesis. Note also that all the regressions reported in table 8.1 were estimated using the White correction for heteroscedasticity; heteroscedasticity, not surprisingly, was always present.)

The second hypothesis under test was the correspondence between the comparative statics of actual behaviour and the comparative statics of optimal behaviour. To test this hypothesis, we proceeded as is normal in economics: we first used the data on actual behaviour to estimate the effect of changes in the various potentially explanatory variables on actual behaviour. Then we estimated the same relationship using the optimal behaviour. The results are given in the four remaining columns of table 8.1.

Let me begin by comparing the first two columns, where the data come from the restricted sample of 956 observations. If we look at the signs of the coefficients in the two equations we see that in all cases the signs are the same. In other words, the comparative statics implications of actual behaviour agree in qualitative terms precisely with those of the optimal behaviour. Thus, if we had used optimality theory to predict how changes in some parameter affected actual consumption, we would have predicted perfectly the direction of the actual consumption changes, even though in absolute terms the two consumption strategies are quite different. Note that the same proposition is not quite true when we use C_2^* instead of C_1^*, but this is hardly surprising in view of the rather less reliable nature of the estimate of the index of absolute risk aversion S underlying C_2^*. In this respect, it might be of interest to note that the correlation between the two point estimates of the index of risk aversion was just 0.1777!

The main conclusions from this large-scale study are twofold: first, that actual behaviour differs significantly from optimal behaviour; second, that nevertheless the comparative statics implications of actual behaviour appear to agree with those of optimality theory. The first of these is not surprising given the complexity of the decision problem. Whether the second is surprising is a matter for some debate. As one of the referees on Hey and Dardanoni (1988a) remarked:

> To have a view, I ought to know, not only the comparative statics for the optimal consumption trajectory, but also the comparative statics for a wide variety of other (non-optimal) consumption trajectories. If nearly all trajectories yield more or less the same comparative statics as the optimal case ... then I ought not to be surprised at all.

This statement has important implications for the way theorizing in economics ought to proceed; but whether the profession will take any note is another matter.

8.5 Conclusions

Much was learnt from these experiments, though there remain some unsatisfactory features. The first and most obvious is the use of the random-horizon
constant-stopping-probability framework. This was deliberately used so that
the implied optimal strategy was time invariant (stationary). If, instead, we
had used a finite deterministic horizon framework, then the optimal strategy
would have been time dependent. Subjects would have needed to calculate a
different consumption function ($C^* = C_t(W_t)$) for each period of the experiment, instead of just one consumption function ($C^* = C(W_t)$) which would
have been applicable for all periods. This seemed to us to make the problem
more complex. However, the subjects in these experiments were quite clearly
using a time-dependent strategy, as the regressions in table 8.1 bear witness.
Subjects clearly did not perceive the stationary nature of the problem. We are
now sceptical as to whether the design can be changed to make them perceive
it correctly; until it can we fear we must abandon random-horizon experiments. In the context of our consumption experiments, however, this could
have the offsetting advantage of allowing us to relax our very strict borrowing
constraint.

The position concerning the utility function of the subjects also remains
unsatisfactory. We feel unhappy about using just one question to determine
a subject's attitude to risk, and yet we are equally unhappy about assuming
that all subjects are risk neutral. Moreover, the 'sting in the tail' question,
although incentive compatible, created difficulties for the subjects – many
reported that they simply did not understand it. This is ironic since it is a
much simpler decision problem than the consumption/savings problem
which they had just completed! Perhaps they were just tired. Perhaps we
made the mistake of pointing out to them that if they put p equal to 1 they
could guarantee a payment of x. This, of course, was true, but a subject who
genuinely preferred p equal to 1 rather than some number less than 1 was
revealing himself or herself to be infinitely risk averse ($S = \infty$) which would
appear to contradict the fact that the individual turned up to do the
experiment in the first place!

What I now think is a better procedure is to carry out two experiments with
the same subjects: the basic consumption experiment, and a utility-function-
revealing experiment of the type discussed in chapter 5. In other words, one
first identifies the utility function of the individual; then one carries out the
experiment of interest. The question remains as to whether one should do the
two experiments one after another or to let some time elapse between them.
The former may be rather tiring for the poor subjects, while the latter may
be affected by changing wealth levels between the two experiments. Assuming
constant absolute risk aversion is one theoretically consistent way around the
latter problem.

Finally, I should return to the interesting finding of the pilot study: that
actual behaviour departed quite significantly from optimal and yet the
expected payments from following the actual strategies did not appear to be
very much lower than the expected payment from the optimal strategy. This

may have resulted from a rather flat-topped objective function, and may be a characteristic of this particular decision problem. It leaves open the possibility that actual behaviour departed significantly from the optimal precisely because it did not make much difference whether it did or not. To test this proposition, we need to explore behaviour in decision problems with sharper-peaked objective functions. This is one of the concerns of the next chapter.

Notes

1 An alternative gives $U'(C_{t+1}^*) = (\rho_t r_t)^{-1} U'(C_t^*) v_{t+1}$ where $E_t v_{t+1} = 1$; there are clearly other ways still.
2 Truncated below at zero to protect the subjects and above to protect the experimenter.

9

A Broad Survey of Other Experimental Studies

9.1 Introduction

This part of the book is concerned with experimental investigations into individual economic decision-making. For reasons connected partly with the economics profession's view of the quality of its theorizing in this area and partly with experimentalists' preoccupations elsewhere, this has generally been a rather neglected area, especially as far as experiments with human subjects have been concerned. There has been a sizeable volume of experimental work with animals, to which I shall briefly refer in section 9.3, but work with humans has been conspicuous by its relative absence. This chapter reviews, rather selectively, what little there is. I start in section 9.2 with my own work on expectations, uncertainty variables and the dynamic competitive firm, before turning to the work of other experimentalists in section 9.3. Of prime interest there is the work of David Ansic, from EXEC, investigating a number of demand for money theories. Also in section 9.3 are references to a number of other studies and to animal studies. Conclusions, as well as a useful warning from Harrison (1988) about the construction of economics experiments, are contained in section 9.4.

9.2 Expectations, Uncertainty Variables and the Dynamic Competitive Firm

Expectations

The section title refers to three distinct sets of experiments. I shall discuss them in turn, beginning with one which appears most ideally suited for experimental investigation but which has been subject to remarkably little such investigation (for references to other work, see Bolle (1988), Dwyer et al. (1989) and Bergman (1988)) – namely expectations formation. This is particularly pertinent at the present time, with the rational expectations paradigm pre-eminent in the world of economic theory, especially since the profession seems to have lost sight of the fact that the paradigm's insight is into what might occur if economic agents' expectations are rational in the strict sense of the theory, rather than what will occur. Clearly if expectations are not rational in this sense, then some other outcome will probably occur. Surely, therefore, it behoves us to try to discover how expectations are formed?

This was the motivation behind a set of very simple expectations experiments which I have just completed (Hey, 1990b). The experiment was computerized and had a straightforward design: subjects were asked to make predictions (in sequence) of a time series; they were given information about past values. The payment they received was linked to the accuracy of their predictions in such a way that if they were risk neutral their optimal prediction was their expectation. Thus the experiment enables us directly to observe people's expectations, and hence to test hypotheses about how these expectations are formed. Let me be more precise: the payment for each prediction was given by

$$\text{payment} = a - b(Y - X)^2 \qquad (9.1)$$

where Y denotes their prediction and X is the actual value of the time series. It should be clear from equation (9.1) that the value of Y which maximizes the expected payment received by the subject is given by

$$Y = EX \qquad (9.2)$$

where the expectation is taken with respect to their current information set. The subjects were first told the values of $X_1, \ldots, X_{50}$; then for $i = 51, \ldots, 70$ they were asked to predict X_i; after each prediction they were told the outcome. Thus they made a total of 20 predictions in sequence.

This was repeated three times, the first series being a practice series and the second and third being 'real series' for which they were paid. If the subjects' predictions were unbiased with respective standard deviations σ_2 and σ_3 (for series 2 and 3 respectively) then their expected earnings from taking part in the experiment would be $a - b\sigma_2^2$ for series 2 and $a - b\sigma_3^2$ for series 3. I chose a, b and the σ_i so that the total expected earnings for a subject under these assumptions would be £10. The maximum possible payment (if all predictions were perfect) was £20. This would appear to be an appropriate incentive – our subjects were undergraduate students at the University of York.

Since the experiment was computerized, it enabled us to display information in attractive and flexible ways and to keep it constantly up to date. In particular, it allowed us to give subjects the facility of observing the past observations on X in a variety of different formats depending upon their predilections. Four basic formats were offered:[1] a table of k past values in chronological order; a table of k past values in reverse chronological order; a scatter time series graph of k past values; and a time series graph of the past k values. The subject could choose the value of k. Such displays could be made at any time and as frequently as desired – no charge was made. Some subjects preferred the tabular displays; some the graphical; most a combination of the two.

To make the experiment as fair as possible to the rational expectations hypothesis, I made it as simple as possible, and deliberately chose the simplest possible forms for the actual time series, namely first-order autoregressive processes. If a particular expectational hypothesis does not perform well under these simple conditions, it is unlikely that it will fare better under more complicated scenarios. So each of the three series was a first-order autoregressive process but with different parameters. To add a twist to the story, we put a structural break in the middle of the predictive part of the third series; unfortunately, very few of the subjects seemed to notice it! However, they did appear to notice certain key differences between series 2 and series 3.

A total of 48 subjects (mainly on EXEC's register) performed the experiment. A little under £400 in total was paid out, with a mean payment of £8.13 and a standard deviation of £1.61. The maximum payment was £13.73 and the minimum £4.99. All subjects were given precisely the same sequences (they were all given the same random number seed), and so direct comparisons between subjects could be made. The data generated by the experiment were 20 predictions for each of the two 'real series' for each of 48 subjects (a total of 1920 observations) and information on the subjects' reviewing of past observations, as well as the responses to a brief questionnaire completed by subjects at the end of the experiment.

The analysis of the results was interesting, and led us into considerations that had not occurred to us at the outset. Essentially, we wanted to test whether the rational expectations hypothesis, or the adaptive expectations hypothesis or some other expectations hypothesis fitted the data best; at the outset we had no clear idea as to what this third hypothesis might be, and so in a strict statistical sense we could not use the data both to generate some new hypothesis and to test it: that would be 'double-counting' the data. Nevertheless, we were forced to introduce *some* third alternative – not 'too' data determined – as it soon became clear that neither of the first two hypotheses were particularly good at explaining the data. A further difficulty was that none of the three hypotheses was nested inside either of the others, so that non-nested statistical tests were required. As is well known, such tests can lead to ambiguous conclusions.

A final difficulty was the specification of the rational expectations hypothesis itself. There is no difficulty with the adaptive expectations hypothesis, which can safely be written as

$$Y_t = \lambda X_{t-1} + (1 - \lambda)Y_{t-1} + \text{white noise error} \tag{9.3}$$

but the rational expectations hypothesis appears to have at least two interpretations. One such interpretation is that

$$Y_t = X_t + \text{white noise error} \tag{9.4}$$

In other words, expectations are correct on average.[2] A second interpretation of the rational expectations hypothesis is that people make predictions (form expectations) as if they knew the true model. So if the true process was $X_t = \alpha + \beta X_{t-1} + \text{white noise error}$, then rational expectations would be specified as

$$Y_t = \alpha + \beta X_{t-1} + \text{white noise error} \qquad (9.5)$$

Superficially, it would appear that equations (9.4) and (9.5) (combined with the true data-generating process) are the same, and hence that their implications for the statistical testing of the various competing hypotheses are the same. But that is not the case; unfortunately, I cannot go into detail here. Suffice it to say that rational expectations does rather better under equation (9.5) than under equation (9.4), but that it generally performs much worse than the other two hypotheses. It is difficult, on the basis of the data we have, to distinguish between these other two hypotheses. The message is that we did not ask for enough predictions. Nevertheless, the basic design worked well. In particular, it showed that subjects were trying to act rationally, and did indeed perceive broad differences between series 2 and series 3, but that they were not being precisely rational in either of the strict senses discussed above.

Uncertainty Variables

A rationality of a rather different type was the objective of an early experiment motivated by the many stimulating works of George Shackle. This related to the choice of an appropriate uncertainty variable, to use Shackle's own terminology, for use in economic models of decision-making under risk and uncertainty. The conventional wisdom in economics, as embodied in subjective expected utility theory (SEUT), states that the 'rational' decision-maker (that is, one who obeys the axioms of SEUT) will always attach subjective probabilities to the various risky or uncertain states of the world, and will use these subjective probabilities when deciding between various actions; in SEUT there is no distinction between risk and uncertainty. Not so, says Professor Shackle, who introduced two additional uncertainty variables to the economics profession: possibility and potential surprise. His arguments are intuitively attractive and intellectually appealing. The purpose of my experiments was to investigate the practical appeal of these two uncertainty variables, and to compare them with probability and the minimum selling price of a lottery ticket as competing uncertainty variables.[3]

The experiment, details of which can be found in Hey (1985a), was computerized and involved three separate uncertain situations: (a) the weather on the York University campus the following day; (b) the subject's employment status in June of the year following graduation; and (c) the Prime Minister of the United Kingdom in June 1989 (some five years after the experiment). In each uncertain situation there were several possible outcomes (specified by me in the first two situations and by the subjects in the third). In each uncertain situation, subjects were asked to attach a number from 0 to 9 to each outcome representing his or her view of (a) the possibility, (b) the potential surprise and (c) the probability of that outcome. In addition they were asked to specify the minimum amount for which they would sell a lottery ticket (which would yield £10 if the outcome were to occur and £0 otherwise). So, on the possibility scale, 0 indicated completely impossible, 4 or 5 moderately possible and 9 perfectly possible; on the potential surprise scale, 0 indicated complete absence of surprise, 4 or 5 moderate surprise and 9 total amazement; on the probability scale, 0 indicated completely improbable, 4 or 5 moderately probable and 9 certain. Subjects were specifically asked to do the various scalings independently of each other as we did not want to suggest the need for any kind of consistency check.

I had difficulty in devising an incentive-compatible payment mechanism for his experiment. In fact I cheated – in the written instructions to the subjects I rather vaguely asserted: 'Your payment will depend upon your answers to the questions, so it is in your interest to be as careful as possible in your answers. All will be revealed after the experiment.' I had to be vague because the only sensible way to link payment to answers was through their answers to the minimum selling price question in the first uncertain situation: I chose one of the possibilities at random, chose 'lottery' or 'minimum selling price' at random, observed the actual weather at noon the next day, and paid them accordingly. However, if the subjects had actually known this, then they might have restricted their careful responses. I can see no way round this problem with this particular experiment.

The experiment, unfortunately for Professor Shackle, revealed rather little support for his position. Indeed, all four uncertainty variables moved closely together. This could have been a consequence of the nature of the experiment; in particular, it could have resulted from the rather vague remarks about the payment system – subjects could have misinterpreted it to mean that they had to supply answers which were in some sense internally consistent. This would have led to an increased correlation between the various variables. We did, in fact, give subjects the option of not giving a value for any one of the uncertainty variables in any of the uncertain situations, but none of the subjects chose to exercise this option. Again, they might have misinterpreted the remarks about the payment system. On reflection, it might have been better to give a simple flat-rate payment and get different subjects to give responses for different uncertainty variables. This would be a possibility for some future experiment.

The Dynamic Competitive Firm

My experiments on the dynamic competitive firm (Hey, 1990a, c) take me back to the concerns of chapter 8: how do people take dynamic decisions under risk? Do they behave in accordance with the (SEUT-based) theory? The experiments on consumption under income risk reported in chapter 8 were instructive, but they kept encountering two major criticisms: first, the subjects had little incentive to perform well since the objective function appeared to be fairly flat-topped; second, the subjects had no opportunity to learn and to perform well since they were 'thrown in at the deep end' and performed the experiment just once. Surely, it was repeatedly asserted, if subjects were to do the experiment a second time, then they would perform much better, and approach the optimum.

   The main aim of these experiments on the dynamic competitive firm was to answer these two objections. The switch from the individual to the firm was, in a sense, coincidental, though it did help cure the first problem, but it introduced a new type of criticism: 'OK, I may buy your story that individuals do not behave optimally, but I cannot see the relevance for a firm – a firm will always be able to solve the optimal strategy, employing an operations research specialist if necessary'. Taken seriously, this is an objection to the use of naive subjects; would the use of firms' managers as subjects disarm this criticism I wonder?

   In these firm experiments (carried out with 96 subjects after two pilot studies involving 24 and 16 subjects) the main innovation was that each subject did the experiment twice (with a different parameter set and seed) with several days intervening. Sixty-four of the 96 subjects performed the experiment in eight groups of eight; these subjects also took part in a group discussion between the first and second repetition. As is now usual with my experiments, all subjects completed a brief questionnaire after each repetition. They were paid (for both repetitions) after the second repetition; in addition, group leaders were paid a small organizational bonus.

   The basic story was as follows. Subjects were asked, in each of eight periods, to take the output and sales decisions of a price-taking firm operating under output price uncertainty. Stocks could be held to help offset some of the uncertainty, although there was a constant unit cost to such stock holding. For each repetition the subject was paid in cash the total profits made by their firm over the eight periods; so if the subjects were risk neutral their objective would be to design and implement an output and sales strategy that would maximize their expected total profit. It can be shown (see Hey, 1985b) that this is as follows.

Optimal output strategy

Produce in period t output X_t^* given by

$$C'(X_t^*) = P_t^* + \int_{P_t^*}^{\infty} [1 - F(p)]\,\mathrm{d}p \qquad (9.6)$$

where $C(.)$ is the firm's cost function, and P_t^* is a reservation value defined recursively by

$$P_{t-1}^* = P_t^* + \int_{P_t^*}^{\infty} [1 - F(p)]\,\mathrm{d}p - k, \qquad (9.7)$$

where $F(.)$ is the distribution function of the (independently and identically distributed) output price and $k\ (>0)$ is the per unit storage cost. On the assumption that $F(0) \geq 0$ it is clear that the recursion is started by $P_T^* = 0$ where T is the final period.

Optimal sales strategy

Sell in period t the amount S_t^* given by

$$S_t^* = \begin{cases} 0 & \text{if } P_t \leq P_t^* \\ X_t + I_t & \text{if } P_t > P_t^* \end{cases} \tag{9.8}$$

where I_t is the level of the firm's pre-production stocks at the beginning of period t and the reservation price P_t^* is as defined in equation (9.7). It is assumed that the firm must decide on output in t before the price in t is known, but decides its sales in t after the price in t is revealed.

The intuition behind this optimal strategy is appealing. It is optimal to sell all or nothing – all when the current price is higher than the price that one can expect to get on future sales, nothing otherwise. It is optimal to produce at the point where marginal cost equals the expected price on sales. Note that the (conditional) expected price on sales exceeds the (unconditional) mean price because sales are made only when the price is sufficiently high. Inspection of the optimality conditions reveals that the reservation price P_t^* falls as the horizon T approaches, reaching zero in the final period. Likewise, the optimal output level falls as the horizon approaches, reaching the level at which marginal cost equals the (unconditional) mean price in the final period. These properties are a consequence of the finite-horizon nature of the problem; if, in contrast, it had been a random-horizon model (with constant stopping probability) then both the output level and the reservation price would remain constant through time. This illustrates neatly the difference between finite-horizon and random-horizon models. As I have remarked earlier, I would prefer to use the latter because of the much simpler nature of the optimal strategy, but the experimental difficulties involved with random-horizon models encountered in chapter 8 led me to use a finite-horizon framework for these firm experiments. Nevertheless, there is one interesting spin-off which can be exploited to good effect: this relates to the difference between the optimal strategy defined above and what one might term a myopic strategy. The latter might be defined as one that ignores the dynamic aspect of the problem, instead treating it as a sequence of one-period problems. This would lead to a constant output strategy (at the level at which marginal cost equals the mean price) and a sales strategy which would involve selling all the production regardless of the price. So there are two aspects that enable us to distinguish the fully optimal dynamic strategy from this inferior myopic strategy: (a) the use of a reservation sales strategy; (b) the use of a declining output strategy and (associatedly) the use of a declining reservation price on the reservation sales strategy. Our results suggest that most subjects were fairly good at identifying (a) but rather poor at identifying (b), particularly on the first attempt.

As with the consumption experiments, I was interested in testing the comparative statics propositions of the theory, particularly those relating to the dynamic aspects of the model. These consisted of changes in the storage cost k and (since all the distributions in my experiment were truncated normals) in the standard deviation σ of the distribution. As should be readily apparent, an increase in σ or a decrease in k leads to an increase in the optimal output and an increase in the optimal reservation price in all periods except the last. These experiments were designed *inter alia* to test these theoretical predictions.

In the large-scale study, four different values for σ (5.0, 4.5, 4.0 and 3.5) and four different values of k (0.1, 0.2, 0.4 and 0.8) were used although not all $16(= 4 \times 4)$ pairwise combinations were employed. In fact, a subset of eight of these 16 pairs was used; these were chosen in such a way that all subjects got similar possibilities for making a reasonable amount of money. Recall that all subjects performed the experiment twice; we gave each subject a different parameter pair on the second repetition from that on the first; we chose the pairings so that there was symmetry, and so that subjects who had a 'bad' parameter pair on their first attempt got a 'good' pair on their second attempt, and vice versa. Details are given in table 9.1. The 'expected profits' figures in the table are those computed using the optimal strategy and the myopic strategy as specified above. Note the very large difference between them, indicating a relatively sharp-peaked objective function. Note also that these are average profits; the actual profits on any particular price sequence will naturally be different – indeed on any particular price sequence one may be able to do better using the myopic strategy, or even some other strategy, than the optimal strategy. So, in order to be fair to the subjects we chose random number seeds that would produce good profits for someone following the optimal strategy. Moreover, in order to maintain the sharp-peakedness of the objective function, we deliberately chose seeds which maintained the sharp differential (usually of the order of a threefold difference) between the profits behaving optimally and the profits behaving myopically. The subjects, presumably, were unaware that the seeds were deliberately selected to yield 'representative' price sequences; if they had been aware, then their behaviour might have been affected.

As already noted, 64 of the subjects performed the experiment in eight groups of eight: so there were eight who had parameter pair 2 on their first repetition and parameter pair 13 on their second; eight who had parameter pair 3 on their first repetition and parameter pair 11 on their second; and so on. The remaining 32 subjects performed the experiment in eight groups of

Table 9.1   Parameter sets in dynamic competitive firm experiment

Parameter pair	σ	k	Expected profit (£) Optimal	Myopic	Parameter pair on second repetition
2	5.0	0.2	17.27	5.00	13
3	5.0	0.4	15.89	5.00	11
4	5.0	0.8	13.69	5.00	5
5	4.5	0.1	16.30	5.00	4
6	4.5	0.2	15.57	5.00	9
9	4.0	0.1	14.66	5.00	6
11	4.0	0.4	12.80	5.00	3
13	3.5	0.1	13.08	5.00	2

four but did not have an intervening group discussion. We term the first 64 as the group subjects and the last 32 as the individual subjects, though it should be emphasized that all 96 subjects actually performed each repetition on an individual basis; the only group activity was the intervening group discussion.

Each of the 96 subjects did the experiment twice, giving a total of 192 repetitions of the experiment. A total of £1322 was paid out to the subjects: £481 on the first repetitions (an average of £4.89 for each group subject and an average of £5.25 for each individual subject) and £841 on the second repetitions (an average of £8.98 for each group subject and an average of £8.34 for each individual subject). So the payment increased on average by 75 per cent between the first and second repetitions, while the group payments rose from 93 per cent to 108 per cent (of an individual payment) – clear evidence of a learning effect and slight evidence of a group effect. Further analysis suggests that the group effect is insignificant although the learning effect is significant. The reason for the latter is quite clear: on the first repetition very few subjects managed to get even output myopically correct, though quite a few were adopting a reservation sales strategy; on the second repetition many were getting output at more reasonable levels, many more were adopting a reservation sales strategy and a few were even using a declining output and reservation price strategy.

Let us now turn to some more formal analysis. The main hypotheses under test are the absolute correctness of the optimality theory specified above and its comparative correctness. The former can be dismissed quite easily,[4] though it is apparent that behaviour is closer to the optimal on the second repetition than on the first. In Hey (1990c) I give some summary measures to indicate the extent of the discrepancies.

The comparative statics tests are of more interest. Let us start with the output variable. As all subjects had the same cost function and the same mean for the price distribution, the comparative statics propositions tested concern σ and k: an increase in σ or a decrease in k lead to an increase in X_t^* for all $t \neq T$. In addition, we know that X_t^* falls as t approaches T (the horizon). To test these we proceed by constructing a large data matrix in much the same fashion as in the consumption experiment of chapter 8. First, for each subject on each repetition, we start with a data matrix of seven columns and eight rows: g, a dummy taking the value 0 or 1 depending upon whether the subject did the experiment in a group or individually; a, a dummy indicating the attempt/repetition number (1 or 2); t, the time period; X_t, the output chosen by that subject on that repetition and in that time period; p_t, the proportion of post-production stock sold by that subject on that repetition and in that time period; σ, the relevant standard deviation of the price distribution for that subject on that repetition; and k, the relevant storage cost for that subject on that attempt. Then all such data matrices for all subjects on both repetitions are stacked on top of one another to form a grand matrix of seven columns and 1536 rows (8 rows for each subject on each attempt × 2 attempts × (64 group subjects + 32 individual subjects)). We then try and explain the X (and later p) column(s) of this matrix.

One point emerges immediately – that the two repetitions should be treated separately since behaviour is quite different in them. It is also tempting to treat the group subjects and the individual subjects separately, but no significant differences were found. Accordingly, group and individual subjects are lumped together in the analyses that follow. One final preliminary remark concerns the question of outliers: a glance at the data on output reveals a smallish number of such outliers. These relate to subjects whose output decisions were 'in the wrong ball park': whereas the optimal and myopic output values lie in the range 250–500, there were five X observations in the data matrix of 10,000 (all on the first repetitions), two of 2000, two of 1500 and 19 of 1000. One is tempted to regard the five values of 10,000 as outliers and the rest as not, though clearly this is a fairly arbitrary decision. Thus in the analysis below all rows with X-observations equal to 10,000 are excluded.[5]

Let us begin with the obvious (linearized) test of the comparative statics predictions stated above. Standard regression in LIMDEP gives the following.

First repetitions (five outliers excluded)
$$X_t = -126.7 - 0.5123t + 87.25\sigma - 194.1k \qquad R^2 = 0.43$$
$$(1.8) \quad (0.2) \qquad (5.2) \qquad (5.0) \qquad\qquad n = 763$$

Second repetitions (no observations excluded)
$$X_t = 690.3 - 6.948t - 101.0\sigma + 198.5k \qquad R^2 = 0.119$$
$$(14.7) \quad (3.2) \quad (9.1) \qquad (7.6) \qquad\qquad n = 768$$

(t ratios in parentheses).

These results are intriguing. On the first repetitions, the t term is not significantly negative (as it should have been if the subjects had been exploiting the opportunities presented by the dynamic aspects of the problem) whereas the σ term is significantly positive (as it should be) and the k term is significantly negative (as it should be). On the second repetitions things are different, however: the t term is now correctly significantly negative, but the σ and k terms, though both significant, have the wrong signs. So behaviour 'improves' in some respects between the first and second repetitions but 'worsens' in others.

Testing the comparative statics propositions of the optimal sales strategy is not so straightforward since this strategy is characterized by a reservation rule but the reservation price used (if indeed one is used) is not observable. One way round this problem is to estimate a probit model on the subset of the data consistent with the use of a reservation rule. In other words, rows with p_t not equal to 0 and 1 are excluded from the analysis. Rows where $t = T (= 8)$ are also excluded, for obvious reasons. Probit analysis using LIMDEP then reveals the following.

First repetitions (243 non-zero p values and $96t = 8$ values excluded)
$$z_t = -6.567 - 0.0078t + 0.0783\sigma + 0.2017k + 0.3638P_t \qquad \chi^2(4) = 260$$
$$(5.9) \quad (0.2) \qquad (0.4) \qquad (0.4) \qquad (11.4) \qquad\qquad n = 429$$

Second repetitions (96 non-zero p values and $96t = 8$ values excluded)

$$z_t = -10.59 + 0.0944t + 0.5508\sigma - 1.447k + 0.4378P_t \qquad \chi^2(4) = 425$$
$$\quad\;\; (10.3)\;\;(2.4)\qquad(3.3)\qquad\;(3.4)\qquad(13.8)\qquad\quad n = 576$$

(t ratios in parentheses). Note that the model implies $p_t = 1$ if $z_t > 0$ and $p_t = 0$ if $z_t \leq 0$.

The first repetitions are poor: the signs on k and P_t are correct, but only the latter is significantly different from zero. Nor are the coefficients on t and σ significant – which is just as well as the signs are wrong. Things are in some respects better with the second repetitions: all coefficients are significant; the signs on t and P_t are correct, but those on σ and k are the opposite of what they should be. This mirrors our findings on the output equations.

So some interesting results emerge. As already noted, it is clear that behaviour improves with repetition – some subjects have clearly understood the nature of the problem. But what is particularly intriguing are the wrong comparative statics signs on σ and k: while the σ effect and the k effect go in opposite directions, as predicted by the theory, they unfortunately both go in the wrong direction. A similar result concerning σ will be recalled from the experiments reported in chapter 7. Perhaps the same explanation applies?

9.3   Money, Search Again and Animals

Money

In this section I report rather briefly on a number of other experiments carried out by other experimentalists using both human and animal subjects. I begin with some very interesting experiments, by David Ansic of EXEC, into the demand for money. Following Keynes, Ansic considers three separate basic motives for holding money (transactions, speculative and precautionary) and has designed three separate experiments, one on each of these three motives. Two of the experiments have now been run; the third is about to be run. In a broad sense, they are of the same basic genre as the other experiments discussed in this chapter, though their execution has some particularly nice features.

Ansic's first experiment, what he terms the bond experiment, is an investigation into the speculative demand for money. It is built around the following simple story. Subjects are told that they are in a 20-period decision problem and are given an initial stock of 1000. There are two assets: money and a bond which has a fixed dividend but a variable price. Subjects can move freely and costlessly between money and bonds each period, at the price prevailing in that period. The price is a random variable, identically and independently distributed each period. Ansic portrays the distribution as in figure 9.1.

Once the subject seeds the 'wheel' the arrow pointer rolls round the numbers in the frame, quickly at first, and then slowly glides to a halt at one of the possible bond prices. The frame is certainly very impressive and subjects seem happy with it. It is perhaps ironic, therefore, that Ansic 'fixes'

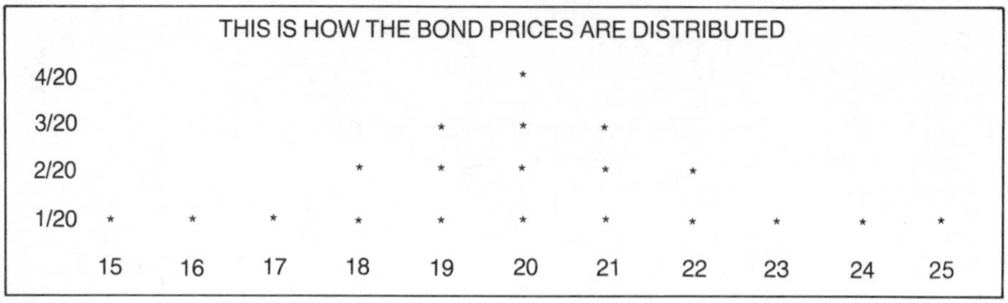

THIS IS HOW THE BOND PRICES ARE DISTRIBUTED										
4/20						*				
3/20					*	*	*			
2/20				*	*	*	*	*		
1/20	*	*	*	*	*	*	*	*	*	*
	15	16	17	18	19	20	21	22	23	24	25

Figure 9.1   Screen for price distribution.

his software to give each subject one of two possible predetermined price sequences! The advantage, of course, is that one can study the behaviour of several subjects under precisely the same conditions. There are potential disadvantages though: if subjects get to know that all subjects get the same sequence then collusion becomes profitable. Alternatively, if subjects become aware that the price sequence is 'fixed' in some fashion, then they might wonder whether it is fixed conditional on their own earlier responses. This could change behaviour.[6]

Ansic exploits the possibilities offered by PC software most effectively: writing in TURBO PASCAL his programs consist of a set of screens which the subject moves between by his or her responses. Help screens and 'what if?' screens can easily be built into this type of program. In Ansic's second experiment, which he terms the Miller–Orr experiment, he exploits the software possibilities to even greater effectiveness. This experiment is an investigation into the transactions demand for money; it involves the subject managing the financial affairs of an absent individual who is subject to a random cash inflow/outflow. Cash outflows must be met but any spare cash can be put into the bank where it earns interest. The economic problem results from the fact that taking money out of or putting money into the bank incurs a transactions cost.

The subject is paid interest earned less transactions costs incurred. The whole experiment is run in continuous time and revolves around the screens pictured in figure 9.3. The rather nice feature of this experiment is the middle screen: once initiated, parts of this screen begin to move. The time bar shrinks slowly and continuously, the cash bar fluctuates continuously up and down as cash inflows and outflows occur and the bank balance bar increases slowly as interest is accumulated. This process continues until either the subject presses a key to initiate a trip to the bank or the cash balance hits zero (when the subject is forced to go to the bank to make a withdrawal).

The optimal strategy for a risk-neutral subject in this experiment is easily stated. It is characterized by an upper bound on the cash balance h^* and an optimum target level z^*; if the cash balance hits the upper bound h^*, then the subject should deposit the amount $h^* - z^*$ in the bank; if the cash balance hits

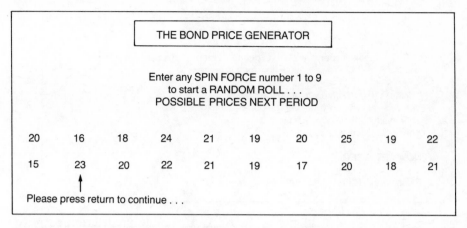

Figure 9.2   Screen for random generator.

zero, the subject should withdraw the amount z^* from the bank. The target z^* is given by

$$z^* = (3bv/4i)^{1/3} \tag{9.9}$$

where b is the transactions cost per transfer, i is the interest rate charged per day and v is the variance of the distribution of daily changes in the cash balance. Ansic adopted an experimental design with two values for each of these three parameters (but using just six of the $2^3 = 8$ possible combinations). This enabled him to test not only the absolute correctness of the theory but also the comparative statics implications. Details of the results can be found in Ansic (1990), and details of his bond experiment are given in Ansic and Loomes (1990).

Search Again

The search experiments reported in chapter 7 are just the tip of an iceberg. Psychologists were doing search experiments in the late 1960s and early 1970s with economists moving into the area in the early 1980s. Even in the late 1980s and early 1990s experiments on search were still being carried out, though naturally the focus of interest had shifted somewhat. I mention here two rather interesting examples of such recent research. The first is a paper by Harrison and Morgan (1990) which considers a search situation which is somewhat different from that of chapter 7, the difference being that the cost of obtaining an offer is not simply a linear function of the number of offers obtained at the one time. Under such circumstances, it is not necessarily the case that the sequential strategy employed in chapter 7 is the best; it might be better to employ a strategy which is a combination of that sequential strategy and a fixed sample size strategy. In other words, a sample of n_1 offers is taken in the first instance; if none of them is acceptable then a sample of n_2 offers is taken; and so on. (Of course, n_1, n_2, ..., are chosen optimally.)

PRESS A KEY AT ANY TIME TO START OR GO TO THE BANK

THE TIME	YOUR CASH	BANK BALANCE
end –	0 –	0 –
100 –	10 –	50 –
200 –	20 –	100 –
300 –	30 –	150 –
400 –	40 –	200 –
500 –	50 –	250 –
600 –	60 –	300 –
700 –	70 –	350 –
800 –	80 –	400 –
900 –	90 –	450 –
strt –	100 –	500 –

SPRING

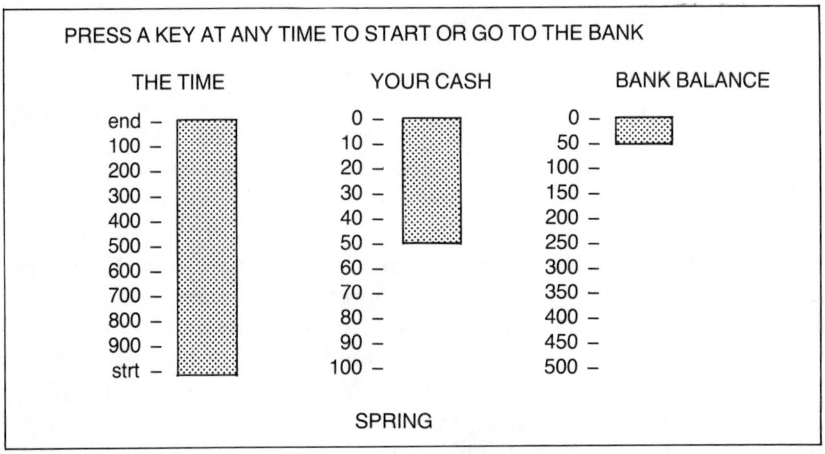

ACCOUNT STATEMENT

Your current bank balance is	55.10
The interest you have accumulated so far is	3.20
Your current cash on hand is	21.00
The charges you have paid so far are	1.00
Your net earnings for the season so far is	2.20

HOW MUCH DO YOU WANT TO DEPOSIT (WITHDRAW)?

Please press RETURN to continue . . .

Figure 9.3 Screens from the Ansic Miller–Orr experiment.

Such a strategy is termed a variable sample size (VSS) strategy. Harrison and Morgan's experiments were designed, *inter alia*, to see whether subjects were able to employ a VSS strategy when it was indeed optimal to do so. Their paper contains a wealth of detail. In addition, it contains some rather interesting material relevant to my quest for a 'theory of errors', although the issue is tackled in a somewhat different manner. Harrison and Morgan begin with the question: 'What is the perceptive threshold of experimental subjects? If it is deemed to be a penny (per observable action) then any observed decisions that result in the loss of less than a penny to the subject are not *perceptually* significant deviations from theory using this proposed metric.' This is a rather neat way of looking at the issue: it enables errors to be assessed in relation to this perception threshold. So, for example, it enabled the authors to conclude one section of their results with the statement: 'a perceptive threshold (per sampling decision) of over 18 cents per decision would be required before one could say that our subjects behaved consistently with the theoretical predictions in this case'. The implications should be followed through.

Search experiments have also been conducted by Moon and his collaborators: Moon and Martin (1989) and Moon and Keasey (1989). The first of these follows up my earlier experiments while the second takes us into relatively uncharted waters with the first serious attempt at an ill-defined experiment in this area. Subjects were formed into seven teams of three, 'each team representing an identical, but competing high-quality garden gnome manufacturer'. Each team was asked to formulate a tender for a block order of gnomes for delivery within three months. The problem, deliberately, was left ill-defined, or unstructured, with certain key elements left unspecified. Although not entirely successful, this experiment does point the way forward in this important new research direction.

Animals

The question of the appropriate choice of subjects for use in experiments is one that is frequently encountered. When giving seminars on my dynamic competitive firm experiments, for example, I am often asked whether it is meaningful to draw inferences from the behaviour of relatively young inexperienced subjects: would not real managers be better subjects? In the converse direction, I am often reluctant to use economics students as subjects since they might act as economists in the experiment rather than as 'human beings'.[7] Nevertheless, many experiments are run with student subjects, some with school subjects, simply because students are relatively cheap: their marginal wage rate, and hence the level of payments one needs to make, is relatively low. Most experimentalists would argue that results generated from such subjects do indeed generalize to other contexts.

Similar arguments can be made for the use of animals as subjects in experiments. Powerful evidence of the insights obtained by so doing can be found in the numerous studies carried out by John Kagel and his associates (including Battalio, Dwyer and Green). Useful references are contained in

Green and Kagel (1987) and Kagel (1987). The latter provides a helpful introduction and overview. In addition to arguments for the use of animal subjects, Kagel provides three illuminating examples of recent experimental work with animals. The first of these relates to the welfare trap hypothesis concerning dynamic responses to guaranteed-income programmes. By using pigeons who had to peck a response key in order to get additional food (over and above some 'unearned consumption' level), and by varying the number of pecks required to obtain an amount of food, the experimentalists could study the effect of the wage rate (the number of pecks per unit of food) and the level of unearned consumption on labour supply (i.e. the number of pecks per unit of time). They found a clear tendency (as predicted by the welfare trap hypothesis) for the labour supply to fall when unearned consumption rose.

Kagel's second example relates to the 'cycle of poverty hypothesis' of temporal choice behaviour. This effectively states that individuals on low incomes discount the future more heavily than those on high incomes. To investigate this hypothesis, Kagel and his associates used a design involving rats subjected to a decision involving a choice between a small amount of food with very little delay and a larger amount of food with a somewhat longer delay. To operationalize the difference between high-income and low-income conditions, they effectively starved the low-income group of rats so that their average body weight was just 244 grams compared with 542 grams for the high-income group. Rather surprisingly, the initial results of the experiment suggest that the converse of the hypothesis is true: the low-income rats opted for the long-delay option with greater frequency. The research continues.

Kagel's third example brings us back to the concerns of part II of this book; it concerns Allais-type violations of the independence axioms. Again rats were used, but now the two-option decision problem was between two risky prospects. Table 9.2 gives details of the three choice problems. This was operationalized by presenting the rat with two levers to press: in choice

Table 9.2   Kagel's test of the independence axiom

Choice problem	Option 1		Option 2	
1	A: 8 pellets, $p = 1.0$		B:	$\begin{cases} 13 \text{ pellets}, p = \frac{3}{4} \\ 1 \text{ pellet}, p = \frac{1}{4} \end{cases}$
2	C:	$\begin{cases} 8 \text{ pellets}, p = \frac{1}{2} \\ 1 \text{ pellet}, p = \frac{1}{2} \end{cases}$	D:	$\begin{cases} 13 \text{ pellets}, p = \frac{3}{8} \\ 1 \text{ pellet}, p = \frac{5}{8} \end{cases}$
3	E:	$\begin{cases} 8 \text{ pellets}, p = \frac{1}{3} \\ 1 \text{ pellet}, p = \frac{2}{3} \end{cases}$	F:	$\begin{cases} 13 \text{ pellets}, p = \frac{1}{4} \\ 1 \text{ pellet}, p = \frac{3}{4} \end{cases}$

problem 1, for example, pressing lever A gave eight pellets of food with certainty, whereas pressing level B gave 13 pellets three-quarters of the time and one pellet one-quarter of the time. The rats were 'taught' this information during a pre-experiment period in which just one or other of the two levers was operational. No food was available between experimental sessions. SEUT theory predicts that A is preferred to B if and only if C is preferred to D if and only if E is preferred to F. Kagel et al. interpret this as implying that A, C and E should be chosen equally often in repeated trials. They find that this is not the case. Here, the behaviour of rats mirrors that of humans.

9.4 Conclusions

In this chapter we have discussed a *mélange* of experiments with a mixture of conclusions. In many cases, where both the absolute correctness of a theory and its comparative statics predictions were under test, it appeared that the former was rejected by the experimental evidence while the latter was not. In a sense, this second finding is not too surprising, as the predictions of the theory are often rather weak and could have arisen from a number of competing theories.

It is the rejection of the absolute correctness that gives grounds for further thought. I have already discussed the difficulty of testing the absolute correctness and, associatedly, of constructing a 'theory of errors'. The remarks of Harrison discussed in section 9.3 should be noted in this respect. He amplifies these remarks in an insightful paper (Harrison, 1988) which should be read by all experimental economists. His basic point is that 'many experiments suffer from design features that make any inferences from them problematic'. The key deficiency relates to the precept of dominance which requires that the experimental 'rewards have motivational relevance'. This takes us back to the flatness of the objective function. As I have already noted, if the objective function is 'too flat' in the neighbourhood of the optimal point, then one should not be too surprised if subjects stray rather a long way from optimal behaviour.

Harrison gives four illuminating examples. One relates to the Becker–Degroot–Marschak (BDM) elicitation procedure for a certainty equivalent of some risky prospect; this I discussed in chapter 6. Recall that the procedure works by asking the subject to state a minimum selling price for the prospect and then randomly choosing a buying price for the prospect. If the buying price exceeds the stated selling price, the subject receives the former; if not, the prospect is played out. As I have already demonstrated, an individual who obeys SEUT will announce his certainty equivalent as his minimum selling price. This defines the optimal response. But the objective function is very flat-topped: as Harrison shows in a simple numerical example, the loss to the individual in income is just 1, 2, 3, 4 or 5 cents if the individual over-reports his minimum selling price by 45, 64, 78, 90 or 100 cents. In other words, large differences in the individual's decision have relatively minor effects on the individual's payoff.

Other examples (concerning the measurement of risk attitudes, the consistency of choice, preference reversals and the inducement of risk attitudes) are presented by Harrison. In each case, instances of experiments are discussed wherein large differences in subjects' responses could be induced with remarkably little impact on the subjects themselves. In other words, the experiments provided very little incentive for accurate reporting. It seems mandatory that all planned experiments be subject to a similar analysis before their implementation. Otherwise, as Harrison remarks, any inferences drawn from their execution might be problematic.

Notes

1 In future experiments, additional formats might be offered, such as regression or time series analyses, but we were wary of offering things that might alter behaviour. Ideally, one would have a computer program which was so sophisticated that it would react passively but would provide whatever was requested.

2 Some economists would write equation (9.4) as $X_t = Y_t +$ white noise error, and would correctly argue that the statistical difference is crucial. I have trouble with this reverse formulation, however, since I programmed the experiment myself and *know* that the actual values of the time series were not determined by the subjects' predictions!

3 Under SEUT the last two move together.

4 Formally this requires some notion of statistical significance, which in turn requires a 'theory of errors', but as with the material in chapter 5 the theory does not provide one. If you were a hard-liner you could simply argue that the theory as specified in the text is a deterministic one, and that, since no subject's behaviour exactly agrees with it, it is therefore rejected. A softer approach would allow some error, but how that should be specified is not clear. On this see later.

5 One might also be tempted to regard very low values of X (near or at zero) as outliers, but here one is on much less sure ground. Fortunately, excluding them seemed to make very little difference to the general shape of the results reported, and so no downward exclusions were made.

6 One way of getting round this problem is to give them at the start of the experiment a sealed envelope containing a listing of their price sequence, which they can open at the end to check that it truly was independent of their responses. The problem with this, of course, is that subjects may then begin to wonder whether the sequence was truly random. (And what particular sequence actually is?)

7 Actually, it appears to be the case that this concern is misplaced: many economists, particularly academic economists, perform rather badly in experiments! Nevertheless, one is reminded of the public goods experiments of Marwell and Ames which appeared to indicate that economists tended to free-ride significantly more than non-economists.

Experiments on Interactive Economic Behaviour

10

The Economic Theories of Games and Bargaining

10.1   Introduction

The four chapters of part IV of this book are in two pairs, the first pair (this chapter and the next) being devoted to games and bargaining, and the second pair (chapters 12 and 13) to auctions and markets. In each pair, the first of the pair is devoted to the relevant economic theories, the second to a survey of the corresponding experimental material. As will become apparent, the role for experimental work in the two pairs is quite different because of the nature of the theory in the two areas. In games and bargaining theory, economics effectively says that it does not know which outcomes will occur, because there are so many theoretical possibilities. In markets, in contradistinction, there is plenty of theory to say that particular outcomes are equilibrium outcomes (in the sense that, if market participants experienced that outcome, they would all be content with it), and indeed some theory to say that in particular circumstances there will be a unique equilibrium outcome, but there is virtually no theory to say whether a particular outcome will be attained. So, in games and bargaining, the role for experimental economics is to try and discover which of many potential equilibria will actually be attained, whereas, in markets, the role for experimental economics is to try and discover whether a particular (usually unique) outcome will actually be attained.

In this chapter, I consider the economic theories of games and bargaining and their application in two important areas of economics: industrial organization theory (as currently practised) and public goods theory. The distinction between games and bargaining problems is often blurred in the literature, and any attempt to distinguish the two is somewhat artificial. Here, I shall use the term 'games' to refer to non-co-operative strategic contests between two or more individuals or groups. In contrast, 'bargains' usually involve a period of pre-decision discussion which may result in some explicit or implicit agreement or collusion. In some bargaining situations, such pre-decision agreements might be formalized in some kind of contract between the two players. Of course, how this is done is itself a matter for negotiation: one might think in terms of a 'supergame' which incorporated all the pre-play negotiation, although in principle this process of extending the game backwards could go on indefinitely. I shall avoid such complications in what follows.

I begin simply, in section 10.2, by considering simple static (one-shot) games, building upon the now-hoary example of the Prisoner's Dilemma. This leads, as is well known, to an economic solution which offends intuition. Things do not get much better in section 10.3 where these one-shot games are repeated, unless they are repeated infinitely often or randomly often. Intuition remains offended. Nevertheless, we move on into sections 10.4 and 10.5, where applications of this theory to two key areas of economics are considered. Finally, a brief look at bargaining theory is found in section 10.6. Section 10.7 concludes the chapter.

10.2   Static (One-shot) Games

The essence of the type of decision problem that I want to consider in this section is captured in the very simple two-person non-zero-sum game pictured in figure 10.1. This is a generalized example of the famous Prisoner's Dilemma. Note that $a > b > c > d$. This means that if player 2 chooses action 1, then player 1 would get more (c instead of d) by choosing action 1 than action 2; likewise, if player 2 chooses action 2, then player 1 again would get more (a instead of b) by choosing action 1 than action 2. Thus, as far as player 1 is concerned, action 1 dominates action 2 because it leads to a better outcome for player 1 whatever action player 2 chooses. Similarly, as far as player 2 is concerned, his action 1 dominates his action 2 because it leads to a better outcome for player 2 whatever action player 1 chooses. This, according to game theory, is sufficient to ensure that both players choose their action 1, and hence that they each experience outcome c.

So far so good. The essence of the problem is simply that this outcome is Pareto dominated by outcome b, b which is achievable by both players choosing their action 2. But, if one player knows that his opponent is to choose action 2, then he has a natural incentive to choose his action 1 (and thus get a instead of b whilst suffering his opponent to experience d instead of b). In other words, the outcome b, b (achievable by both choosing action 2) is likely to be an unstable outcome: both players have an incentive to change to action 1; yet if they both do so they will both be worse off than if they had stuck with action 2.

```
                              Player 2
                           1          2
                        ┌─────────┬─────────┐
                      1 │  c, c   │  a, d   │
          Player 1      │         │         │
                      2 │  d, a   │  b, b   │
                        └─────────┴─────────┘
```

Figure 10.1   A generalized Prisoner's Dilemma. Note that $a > b > c > d$ and payoff x, y means that player 1 gets x and player 2 gets y.

Let me restate the argument using the concept of a Nash equilibrium of a game. This simply a situation where every player is happy with his or her decision given the decisions of the other player(s) in the game. So, in the context of our simple game, both players choosing action 1 is a Nash equilibrium because, given that player 2 chooses action 1 then action 1 is the best response for player 1, and similarly given that player 1 chooses action 1 then action 1 is the best response for player 2. So if both players choose action 1 then both will be happy with their choice given the choice of their rival – neither would want to change their decision.

Neither would want to change their decision – yet both would prefer to end up in the situation where both players choose action 2, for by so doing both would end up with a better outcome than if both chose action 1 (*b* instead of *c*). This is the essence of the problem: game theory points to an equilibrium which is Pareto dominated by another outcome. (Of course, this is not necessarily the case: not all Nash equilibria of games are so dominated, but this is the essence of the Prisoner's Dilemma.) Why this is a problem for economics will be seen later, in sections 10.4 and 10.5: society may end up in a situation which is Pareto dominated by another outcome which is not a Nash equilibrium and which therefore could not be considered as a possible contender for the set of possible equilibria.

But are Nash equilibria the only possible contenders for this set? Consider again our simple game of figure 10.1 and ask whether action 1 is really the only rational response of either player to any decision of the rival. Suppose a super-sophisticated economic agent noted that *b, b* dominated *c, c* and therefore chose action 2, arguing that the other player would think likewise; and suppose the other player did indeed think likewise. They would then end up at the Pareto-dominating outcome. Could one seriously argue that this was irrational, particularly compared with a pair of less sophisticated players who argued *à la* Nash and hence ended up at the Pareto-dominated outcome? I am not sure that one can; nor that rationality must be confined to a player's response to his rival's decisions rather than applied to the game as a whole. This, perhaps, is what the experimental evidence suggests, as we shall see in the next chapter.

10.3   Repeated Games

Things are perhaps different when some pre-decision discussion and commitment are possible or when a game is repeated; for if a game is to be played just once and the players are not allowed to converse, there is little left to consider. I will discuss pre-decision discussion (bargaining) in section 10.6; here I consider the question of repeated games. In particular, I ask whether the concept of Nash equilibrium leads to more acceptable conclusions.

I begin with finitely repeated games, but stay with the decision problem of figure 10.1. Suppose now that our two players are to play the game a total of T times, with their total outcomes being the cumulation of the individual outcomes on the T repetitions. Even if we continue to exclude the possibility of explicit discussion and agreement, our intuition suggests a role for implicit collusion: if both players learn to trust each other, then the repeated outcome b, b may occur. But let me first see what formal analysis tells us. Let us work with the Nash equilibrium concept and use backward induction.

Consider first the final repetition, the Tth repetition. At this point, all the previous $T - 1$ games have been played, and there is just the one game remaining. The Nash equilibrium is that already discussed: namely, for both players to choose action 1. So far so good. Now consider the $(T - 1)$th repetition. Both players know that, after playing this $(T - 1)$th game, they will both choose action 1 in the final game. Thus what they do in this $(T - 1)$th game has no influence on the final game, and so they can consider it in isolation. Familiar arguments show that the Nash equilibrium in this $(T - 1)$th repetition is when both players choose action 1.

The argument is repeated, showing that the Nash equilibrium in all repetitions is for both players to choose action 1. Once again, they end up at the Pareto-dominated outcome; the repetitions do not appear to help. This is even more counter-intuitive than the result for the one-period case.

Consider now an infinitely repeated game. In order to have a finite objective function with which to work, I need to introduce a discount factor; let me denote this by p. So a stream of payments x_t ($t = 1, 2, \ldots$) has a present discounted value of

$$\sum_{t=1}^{\infty} p^{t-1} x_t$$

As before, if both players choose action 1 in every repetition this is a Nash equilibrium. But there may now be other Nash equilibria. Consider, for example, the following symmetric strategies: at any repetition (date) t, a player chooses action 2 if the rival has always chosen action 2 from repetition 1 through repetition $t - 1$; otherwise he or she chooses action 1. This may be a Nash equilibrium strategy, for if player 2 is playing this strategy then player 1 gets

$$b(1 + p + p^2 + \ldots) = b/(1 - p) \text{ over the infinite future}$$

if he or she plays the strategy. If, however, he or she does not, then the payoff over the infinite future is

$$a + c(p + p^2 + \ldots) = a + pc/(1 - p)$$

The former exceeds the latter if $b/(1 - p) > a + pc/(1 - p)$, that is, if $p > (a - b)/(a - c)$. So for sufficiently high discount factors the strategy of mutually choosing action 2 is a Nash equilibrium. The essence of this example is that 'anti-social' behaviour can be 'punished' by the rival if the future is not discounted too heavily.

We thus get a discontinuity: mutually choosing action 2 is not a Nash equilibrium strategy in *any* finitely repeated game, however large T is, but it may be a Nash equilibrium in an infinitely repeated game.

Moreover, the same analysis shows that there may be several Nash equilibria in randomly repeated games. The same algebra applies if we now interpret p as denoting the product of a true discount factor and the probability of continuing to another repetition of the game.[1] For example, suppose the true discount factor is 1 and the probability of continuing to another repetition is p. Suppose further that $a = 15$, $b = 10$, $c = 5$ and $d = 0$. Then the above analysis demonstrates that mutually choosing action 2 is a Nash equilibrium strategy if

$$p > 0.5$$

that is, if the stopping probability is less than one-half. Once again, 'anti-social' behaviour is punishable when the probability of the game continuing is sufficiently high.

So, in infinitely repeated games and randomly repeated games, both mutually choosing action 1 and mutually choosing action 2 may be Nash equilibria. Unfortunately, the list does not stop there: indeed there are many other Nash equilibria – possibly infinitely many – in such cases. (Tirole, 1988, p. 432, gives some useful discussion and references.) So we have a rather unsatisfactory conclusion: in the finitely repeated game there may be a unique Nash equilibrium, but it is an intuitively unacceptable one; in the infinitely repeated and randomly repeated games there are infinitely many Nash equilibria, some intuitively appealing, others less so, but theory sheds very little light on which are the 'better' equilibria. This is where experimental methods can shed some light.

There is one final point that I should make before concluding this section. This relates to the backward induction argument used above. Consider figure 10.2, which is taken from Binmore (1987) and which consequently is frequently referred to as Binmore's centipede (though he refers to it as Rosenthal's centipede). This illustrates a game played by two players who take decisions sequentially. The decision nodes in figure 10.2 are labelled with the number of the player to take a decision at that node. The numbers are the payoffs (think of them as pounds or dollars), the top number being the payoff to player 1 and the bottom the payoff to player 2.

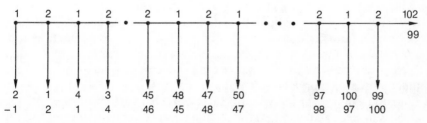

Figure 10.2   Binmore's centipede (•, decision nodes).

The 'solution' to this centipede game as suggested by Nash equilibrium backward induction is found as usual. Consider the final decision node and ask what player 2 would choose to do if he or she found himself or herself at that node: choosing to play 'across' would give a payoff of 99; choosing to play 'down' would give a payoff of 100; accordingly, player 2 should rationally choose to play 'down'. Now consider the penultimate decision node: here player 1 must choose 'across' or 'down' knowing that, if 'across' is chosen, player 2 will play down at the next node. The possible payoffs to 1 are thus 99 ('across') and 100 ('down'); accordingly, he should rationally choose to play 'down'. The logic continues backwards, with the conclusion being that, at any node, the player should play 'down'. In particular, player 1 should play 'down' at the very first node.

This analysis is disturbing: it suggests that supposedly rational players would end up with payoffs of 2 and -1, rather than the 102 and 99 they could have got if they had persevered to the end. This is counter-intuitive, and seems to offend against what one might consider as rational. However, there is a logical difficulty, which Binmore (1987) spells out with some care. The above logic requires the players to base their decisions on what they would do if they reached a particular node in the game and if their opponent was rational; yet both players know that they would never reach any node down the centipede if their opponent was rational: the game would end after just one move from one or other player. We have a logical contradiction.

10.4   Applications to Industrial Organization Theory

Notwithstanding the above, it is clear that game theory in recent years has radically transformed industrial organization theory. Many applications of simple games have found their way into the literature. A useful introduction can be found in Tirole (1988) which illustrates perfectly the way that games have permeated into economic theory. Of particular importance and interest are (of course) oligopoly models of various kinds with especial reference to entry and exit, competition and collusion, and invention and innovation. The last category has particular interest for experimental economists.

Consider two simple examples, the first being a model of a 'memoryless' patent race. Such races, despite their rather unreal nature, enjoy a rather vogue status amongst economists: typically they involve two or more firms competing to be the winner in a race to the discovery of some patentable idea. The first firm that makes the discovery earns some rent from the patent; the rest earn some consolation prize (which may be valueless). Although models vary in terms of their assumptions, the basic story is straightforward: the probability of a particular firm being the winner is some function of their R&D expenditure (this could be current or cumulative). Consider the continuous-time memoryless model discussed by Tirole (1988, pp. 394–6); this is a good example of its type. In this model there are two firms, one the monopolist in some industry and the other a potential entrant. The patent for which the two firms are competing is a cost-reducing innovation. It is assumed that the research technology is characterized by a relationship between a firm's probability of making the discovery (and obtaining the patent) at some point in time and that firm's current R&D expenditure. By making the probability independent of a firm's past R&D expenditure it follows that the solution is time independent; as Tirole remarks 'this assumption has the merit of simplifying the analysis by abstracting from the investment aspects of R&D expenditures'. Indeed, it reduces each firm's decision problem to the choice of an expenditure level for R&D which remains fixed until one or other firm makes the discovery. Let me denote the R&D expenditure levels by x_1 and x_2 for firm 1 (the monopolist) and firm 2 (the potential entrant) respectively. Then the problem reduces to the optimal choice of x_1 by firm 1 and x_2 by firm 2. Obviously, the problem is a strategic one, but Tirole solves it using the Nash equilibrium method: (x_1^*, x_2^*) is a Nash equilibrium if x_1^* is optimal for firm 1 given that firm 2 chooses x_2^* and if x_2^* is optimal for firm 2 given that firm 1 chooses x_1^*. Tirole then studies the properties of (x_1^*, x_2^*) and the implication for the market structure consequent on the innovation.

This type of patent race model is now very prevalent in modern industrial organization theory, and there has been a lot of recent literature extending the basic model: for example, by allowing the probability of discovery to depend not only on current R&D expenditures but also on past expenditures; by operating in a discrete-time world where simultaneous discovery becomes a possibility; by allowing the 'discovery distribution' to vary in terms of its riskiness; and so on. But the basic solution methodology, based on game theoretic solutions constructed on the foundation of Nash equilibrium, has remained largely unchanged. In this context, my remarks in sections 10.2 and 10.3 become relevant: is the Nash equilibrium concept the (only) appropriate solution concept? The problem of Pareto-dominated Nash equilibria is obviously relevant in this context: it is clearly wasteful for both firms to be chasing after the same patent when expenditures do not reinforce each other. This is particularly true in the real world: ask any pharmaceutical company! It is also of particular importance if any policy prescriptions handed out by economists originate from Nash-equilibrium-based models. So one crucially wants to know whether actual outcomes of these types of game are indeed the Nash equilibrium outcomes. This is where experimental methods come into their own; and note how suited the simple patent race model discussed above is for experimentation.

Let me give one further example, which is, in fact, a model which I shall shortly be testing experimentally with Riccardo Martina. This is a particularly nice model as the actual structure of the model is entirely deterministic – any randomness is introduced by the players themselves. Again it is a 'patent race' model between two firms/players, but here the difference is that the winning post is a finite discrete number of steps away from the starting line. The race takes place in discrete time, and in each period the two firms simultaneously announce their decisions concerning the number of steps that they will be taking that period. To keep life simple, assume that they can choose to go zero, one or two steps in each period: choosing no steps costs nothing (but does not get you very far!), choosing one step costs c_1 and choosing two steps costs c_2. The essence of the problem is that c_2 is more than twice c_1, so it is inefficient to go two steps at a time. If there was just one 'competitor' it would be optimal to proceed to the winning post one step at a time. With two competitors, however, combined with the fact that the prize, if shared equally, is not sufficient to offset the cost of getting to the winning post two steps at a time, there is a strategic problem. This is analysed in depth by Fudenberg et al. (1983), who solve it using backward induction and Nash equilibrium. Once again, my earlier comments apply, both as to the relevance of these solution concepts and as to the appropriateness of experimental investigation. I shall make some brief comments about the experimental implementation of this simple deterministic patent race in chapter 11.

10.5   Applications to Public Goods Theory

Public goods theory is a second area in which game theoretic solutions have been prescribed for economic problems, and in which much good experimental work has been done. I shall describe the latter in chapter 11; here I consider some of the basic theory.

Consider the simplest public goods problem: a society consists of I members; individual i has income z_i ($i = 1, \ldots, I$); there are two goods, a private good and a public good; the price of the former is 1 and that of the latter is p, which is greater than 1. Each individual must decide how much of his or her income z_i to devote to consumption of the private good and how much to devote to the public good. Denote the respective amount x_i and y_i. Note that these must satisfy

$$x_i + y_i = z_i \qquad (i = 1, \ldots, I) \tag{10.1}$$

The essence of a public good is that all can consume it; thus the total supply of the public good available for consumption by each member of society is

$$\sum_{i=1}^{I} \frac{y_i}{p}$$

Now suppose for simplicity that the utility function of the ith individual in society is

$$U_i \equiv U_i(a,b) = a + b \tag{10.2}$$

where a and b are the consumptions of the private good and the public good respectively. I choose this form to demonstrate the public goods problem in its starkest form.

Consider the problem faced by individual j. If she is to choose her values of x_j and y_j so as to maximize her utility given the decisions of the others in society, then she faces the following decision problem:
choose x_j, y_j to maximize

$$U_j(x_j, y_j) \equiv x_j + \sum_{i=1}^{I} \frac{y_i}{p}$$

subject to

$$x_j + y_j = z_j$$

and subject to given y_i ($i = 1, \ldots, I; i \neq j$).

This can alternatively be written
choose y_j to maximize

$$U_j(x_j, y_j) = (z_j - y_j) + \sum_{i=1}^{I} \frac{y_i}{p} \qquad (10.3)$$

subject to given y_i ($i = 1, \ldots, I; i \neq j$).

Inspection of problem (10.3) shows that the objective function is linear in the decision variable y_j with coefficient $-1 + 1/p = (1 - p)/p$. Since p is assumed to be larger than 1, it follows that the optimal choice of y_j is that which makes y_j as small as possible, namely zero. In other words, for any given public good contributions of the other members of society, it is optimal for individual j to contribute nothing to the public good. We thus get the result that the Nash equilibrium in this public goods game is for no-one to contribute anything to the public good. Public good provision will therefore, according to this theory, be zero: everyone will try to free-ride; as a consequence the public good will not be provided.

The reason, of course, in this stark setting is clear: to an individual who values the private and public goods equally (see the utility function given by equation (10.2)) it is relatively more expensive to derive utility from the public good than the private good since the price of the former is greater than the price of the latter. However, the Nash equilibrium, to which the members of society seem inexorably driven by their selfish optimizing, is once again Pareto dominated by other outcomes. Consider the social optimum.[2] From equation (10.2) it is clear that this is determined by the maximization, with respect to x_i and y_i (for all i), subject to $x_i + y_i = z_i$ (for all i), of

$$\sum_{i=1}^{I} x_i + \frac{I}{p} \sum_{i=1}^{I} y_i$$

Substituting in the I constraints, we get that the social optimum is determined by the maximization, with respect to y_i (for all i), of

$$\sum_{i=1}^{I} (z_i - y_i) + \frac{I}{p} \sum_{i=1}^{I} y_i$$

This objective function is linear in each y_i ($i = 1, \ldots, I$) each with coefficient $-1 + I/p$. If we assume[3] that society is sufficiently large for I/p to exceed 1, then it follows that the optimal choice of y_i (for each i) is that which makes y_i as large as possible, namely z_i. In other words, it is optimal for society for each member of society to contribute the whole of his or her income to the public good.

That this outcome may Pareto dominate the Nash equilibrium outcome can easily be seen by calculating the utility of individual j under the two outcomes. These are respectively

$$\left(\sum_{i=1}^{I} z_i\right)\Big/ p \qquad \text{and} \qquad z_j$$

If all incomes are equal (and given the presumption that I/p exceeds 1) it is clear that the first of these is larger than the second. If incomes are unequal, then the poorer still do better under the social optimum although some of the rich may do worse. In the latter case, it is not necessarily true that the social optimum Pareto dominates the Nash equilibrium.

Public goods theory, based on Nash equilibrium, thus predicts that free-riding will occur, possibly to the mutual detriment of all members of society. In the simple case discussed here, we get the extreme result that all members of society will totally free-ride and no public good will be provided; less extreme models give less extreme results, but the basic free-riding story remains. Nor is it solved by finitely repeating the public goods decision, as my discussion in section 10.3 demonstrates. Free-riding may be reduced, or even eliminated, in infinitely repeated or randomly repeated decision problems, but not even this is guaranteed by the theory.

10.6   Bargaining

As with games, the word 'bargaining' is intimately associated with the name of Nash, who in the 1950s published a solution to the bargaining problem. This is an axiomatic derivation leading to 'the Nash bargaining solution'; as such it should properly be considered as a normative rather than a positive solution. Nevertheless, some economists tend to think of it as a descriptive solution; this motivates some of the experimental material discussed in chapter 11.

An excellent account of Nash bargaining theory is given by Binmore and Dasgupta (1987); the basic story can be found in chapters 1 and 2. Consider two individuals bargaining over some decision. The outcome of any decision will be a utility pair: x_1 for individual 1 and x_2 for individual 2. There are constraints on the bargaining process, and so any outcome must be a member of some convex set of (x_1, x_2) values. If agreement is not reached, then the outcome is some status quo outcome in which individual 1 gets utility ξ_1 and individual 2 gets utility ξ_2. Let the set of (x_1, x_2) values which satisfy the constraints and are such that $x_1 \geq \xi_1$ and $x_2 \geq \xi_2$ be denoted by χ. Nash starts by assuming that any bargaining problem has a solution (which may, of course, be the status quo outcome). He then imposes certain axioms on the solution. The key axioms are feasibility, invariance and independence of irrelevant alternatives. Feasibility appears harmless: it simply requires that the solution lies in χ. Invariance is somewhat less innocuous, but still appealing: it requires that the solution is independent of the calibrations of the utility functions of the two bargainers. Independence of irrelevant alternatives also seems normatively appealing (but remember a similar-sounding axiom of SEUT also appeared normatively appealing): it simply requires that if a solution to a particular problem is contained within a more constrained problem then that solution is also the solution to the more constrained problem. As Binmore remarks (Binmore and Dasgupta, 1987, p. 37) this axiom 'is a consistency condition – i.e. it is a condition which assets that the "same" convention is to be used in solving two games'.

These three axioms are sufficient to imply that the solution to the bargaining problem is the pair (x_1, x_2) which maximizes the product

$$(x_1 - \xi_1)^\tau (x_2 - \xi_2)^{1-\tau}$$

subject to (x_1, x_2) contained in χ, for some τ $(0 < \tau < 1)$. If one further imposes the axiom of symmetry (that the two players should be treated symmetrically) then it follows that $\tau = 0.5$ and the solution to the bargaining problem is the pair (x_1, x_2) which maximizes the product

$$(x_1 - \xi_1)(x_2 - \xi_2) \tag{10.4}$$

subject to (x_1, x_2) contained in χ. This is called the Nash bargaining solution to the game.

Let me emphasize that this is an axiomatic-based solution. One should perhaps envisage two bargainers who meet and agree on the axiom set and then ask for some arbitrator to suggest a decision consistent with the axioms. The arbitrator would then choose the Nash bargaining solution. However, it is questionable whether one can extend this solution to other situations; indeed, it is not clear how one can envisage it operating in other circumstances. It is not really relevant to simultaneous announcements of decisions by the two bargainers, nor indeed to some kind of sequential process (although some theorists envisage the Nash bargaining solution as the outcome of some dynamic sequential bargaining process). If one wants to consider a process, one needs to describe carefully the 'rules of the game' for the outcome can be very sensitive to them.

Consider now an example of what some theorists call one-period ('ultimatum') bargaining games. There are two players. Player 1 starts by proposing the division of some fixed sum of money between the two players; player 2 then accepts or rejects that division. If the former, the division is as player 1 suggests; if the latter, neither player gets anything. The backward induction solution to this bargaining game is that player 1 demands (and gets) all except ε of the fixed sum of money (where ε is a very small positive amount of money). Clearly there is a strong first-mover advantage, if this backward induction solution is to be believed. The Nash solution could be imposed, but this quite clearly changes the rules of the game; nor is it apparent that the players would agree to its imposition. In a sense, we are back to games, not bargaining. All the material of the earlier parts of this chapter remain relevant.

10.7 Conclusions

This has been a rather frustrating chapter, particularly compared with earlier chapters. The key difference is that this chapter has been concerned with strategic interaction between two or more economic agents; in contrast, earlier chapters have been concerned with 'games' between an individual and nature. Crucially, these have been non-strategic games: nature does not respond strategically to the decisions of the individual; hence the individual does not need to worry about any response from nature when taking his or her decisions. In such contexts, the concept of rationality seems rather more straightforward than when dealing with strategic games. As I have already emphasized, while it may seem rational (for the economic theorist) to restrict attention to states in which each individual is optimizing given the decisions of the other individuals, it does leave open the possibility that actual human beings may be even more sensible and realize that by so doing they might all end up at Pareto-dominated positions. It seems to me that theory alone cannot resolve the difficulty (though I still believe that there is a Nobel Prize in Economics awaiting the first economist who proves an impossibility theorem about mutual rationality in strategic games); we need some experimental evidence to shed some light on what real people actually do. This is the concern of the next, more satisfying, chapter.

Notes

1 Recall a similar discussion in chapter 8.
2 This I define here as the allocation which maximizes $\Sigma_{i=1}^{I} U_i$.
3 If this assumption was not true it would simply mean that for society as a whole the public good was too expensive relative to society's evaluation of it.

11

Experiments on Games and Bargaining

11.1 Introduction

This is an area into which I am only just beginning to venture myself, and so most of the material in this chapter consists of surveys and reports of experimental investigations by others. Good surveys can be found in several works by Roth, particularly Roth (1987, 1988), while Plott (1982, 1989) will be found especially useful for those interested in applications to industrial organization theory. Much of the material in the Plott papers also overlaps with the concerns of Chapters 12 and 13 of this book.

The organization of the material in this chapter follows that of the preceding chapter to a large extent, though I combine the two sections on games since many of the early experiments investigating, for example, the one-period Prisoner's Dilemma actually involved several repetitions of the Prisoner's Dilemma problem and hence were effectively repeated Prisoner's Dilemmas. I also incorporate into section 11.2 some material that other economists sometimes consider as relevant to bargaining; as I noted earlier, the division between games and bargaining is somewhat blurred. The distinction I use here is primarily based on whether the players/bargainers are able to communicate explicitly with each other before coming to their decisions. If they are, then I consider that to be a bargaining problem and put it in section 11.5; if not, I call it a game problem and put it in section 11.2. Accordingly, several items which Roth, for example, calls a bargaining situation are considered in my section on games. In essence, his distinction is between 'experimental tests of axiomatic models' and 'experimental tests of strategic models'. I consider the former under bargaining and the latter under games. I should note, though, that Roth's usage is followed by others: Binmore et al. (1985), for example, refer to a sequential two-period game between two players (which I shall discuss in section 11.2) as a bargaining problem – though they do qualify it with the adjective 'noncooperative'; perhaps that is what turns it back into a game!

11.2 Games

I start with 'games proper', both one-period and repeated, before moving on to bargaining (sequential) games. As is not surprising, the earliest experiments on games, conducted both by psychologists and economists, were concerned with Prisoner's Dilemmas in various forms. Early examples include Lave (1962, 1965) and Rapoport and Chammah (1965).

In principle, it is a straightforward matter to set up an experimental investigation of the one-period Prisoner's Dilemma. Such an investigation could be computerized or non-computerized, though the former is much easier to administer and control. Moreover, since in a one-shot game there is no future, there is no real need for human subjects actually to play against each other; they can play against the computer. Of course, it could be argued, if the actual payoff resulting from the choices of the subject and his or her opponent is to be given to the subject, that a subject may choose differently if he or she knows that the rival is a machine rather than another human being. But there is nothing in the theory that says that this should be so, so one could argue that there is nothing that the subject could complain about should his or her rival be the machine rather than another human being. Nevertheless, the possibility that computerization might change behaviour should be borne in mind.

In carrying out a test of the game-theoretic conclusion concerning the one-period Prisoner's Dilemma (that both players choose option 1, in the example of section 10.2), there is no need to worry about the subjects' attitudes to risk. Clearly one wants to confirm that the four potential payoffs a, b, c and d are ranked in that order by the subjects themselves, but by using monetary payoffs which are sufficiently different from each other one can usually guarantee this.[1] But risk aversion should not matter since the behaviour predicted by the theory for both players consists of a pure strategy (rather than a mixed strategy), in which case there is, of course, no risk to either player. Option 1 dominates all other strategies, in the Nash sense.

Roth (1988) reports that 'the Prisoner's Dilemma has motivated literally hundreds of experiments', and accordingly does not attempt to review them individually. I shall follow his lead and simply note his conclusion, to the effect that 'typical experiments concerning the one-period game reported a level of cooperation which responded readily to various kinds of experimental manipulation but which was bounded well away from either zero or one hundred percent'. However, I also note a disquiet with these experiments that Roth shares. This concerns the actual experimental implementation of the tests of the one-period Prisoner's Dilemma.

In practice, in most of these experiments, subjects did not come to the laboratory, take one decision with respect to one Prisoner's Dilemma problem, and leave. Such a procedure would have been considered inefficient: while you have the subjects there you might as well get them to take a number of decisions, and hence to participate in a number of Prisoner's Dilemmas.[2] Whether this makes the problem a repeated Prisoner's Dilemma depends on the experimental procedure; here one needs to be very careful.

Some cases are very clear: if subjects make decisions in several Prisoner's Dilemma problems against the same opponent then both are in a repeated-game situation. Further, if they both know how many problems they are to play, then they are in a finite-horizon situation and the theory pertinent to that becomes relevant. Alternatively, if subjects know that they are to play a given number of problems, each against a different opponent, then they are in a sequence of (independent) one-period Prisoner's Dilemma problems. However, if subjects are in some doubt as to the number of decision problems they are to face, and as to the constancy or otherwise of their opponents, then it is no longer clear what the 'rules of the game' are, nor what the predictions of the theory are. Many experimental studies have suffered from such ambiguities (see Roth and Murnighan (1978) for a good discussion on the design of Prisoner's Dilemma experiments).

If the experimental rules are not clear about the number of games that the subjects are to play, then the subjects will be forced to attach their own subjective probabilities to the hypothesis that any particular play will be the final one. This is unsatisfactory, since the experimenter cannot control nor observe these subjective probabilities. A better procedure is to impose an objective, known continuing probability. Then the theory of section 10.3 can be used to make predictions: recall that, in the context of the simple Prisoner's Dilemma of chapter 10, the Nash equilibrium if this continuing probability was 'too low' was mutual choice of option 1; however, if the continuing probability became 'sufficiently high', the mutual choice of option 2 became another Nash equilibrium.

This prediction has been tested in a number of studies. Roth and Murnighan (1978) report on a pilot study they carried out with a payoff matrix which implied the possibility of the second Nash equilibrium if and only if the continuing probability was greater than $1/3$. The subjects in this pilot study played three different random-horizon games (against different opponents in the three games) with continuing probabilities of 0.1, 0.5 and 0.9. (Half the players played in that order, half the players in the opposite order.) Note what the theory predicts. In the 0.1 case, the only Nash equilibrium is mutual choice 1, so all players should always choose option 1. In the 0.5 and 0.9 cases, both mutually choosing option 1 and mutually choosing option 2 are Nash equilibria, so we might expect (over a large number of subjects) that roughly half the time option 1 is chosen and half the time option 2 is chosen. In fact, option 2 was chosen significantly more often in the 0.5 and 0.9 cases than in the 0.1 case, but even in the 0.9 case the percentage of subjects choosing option 2 was only 36 per cent. So the theory is supported, even though not completely.

There are two possible difficulties with this experiment. First, subjects may not understand or believe in the stopping/continuing mechanism: even though they are told that, at the end of every decision problem, there is a probability p of continuing to another problem, and that p is constant, they may intuitively feel that p changes with time. This, it will be recalled, was a problem with my random-horizon consumption experiments. Second, once randomness is introduced, we should take into account the attitude to risk of the subjects; the theory of section 10.3, on which the above predictions were based, assumed risk neutrality. So the experimental anomalies may simply be the result of risk aversion. A rather clever way round this problem – though in another context – is described in section 11.5.

Possibly the granddaddy of all Prisoner's Dilemmas experiments is that carried out relatively recently by Selten (himself the granddaddy of games, both theoretical and experimental) and Stoecker (1986). In the experiment reported in this paper, subjects played 25 'supergames' each of which was a ten-period repeated Prisoner's Dilemma. So this was a repeated repeated game, and subjects could gain plenty of experience of playing the ten-period game. The payoffs in the matrix, all in German marks, were 1.45, 0.6, 0.5 and 0.1, so mutual co-operation (choice of option 2) would give each player 0.6 marks (in any period of any 10-period game of any of the 25 supergames) while mutual non-co-operation (choice of option 1) would give each player 0.1 marks. The penalty for co-operating when the rival defected was 0.1 marks while the gain from defecting when the rival co-operated was 0.85 marks.

The most common pattern of behaviour observed in these experiments was some initial co-operation (for at least four periods), followed by defection by one or other of the players, followed thereafter by mutual non-co-operation. By around supergame 16, this form of behaviour was typical in most plays. So players learn to co-operate, but then they learn to defect. Interestingly, the defection point sets in earlier and earlier in later supergames; as Roth remarks (1988, p. 999) 'the cooperation starts to unravel from the end'. Selten and Stoecker (1986, p. 54) note, however: 'even if it is very clear from the data that there is a tendency of the end-effect to shift to earlier periods, it is not clear whether in a much longer sequence of supergames this trend would continue until finally cooperation is completely eliminated'. Nevertheless, the picture is clarified by Selten and Stoecker's experiments: at the beginning players do learn to co-operate and hence display increased co-operation during the early stages, but as experience accumulates, players get more and more aware of the dangers of not defecting first and, as a consequence, co-operation begins to unravel. In a sense, this appears to be empirical confirmation of a rather unstable effect: perhaps the theory is telling us something of the truth ... but not the whole truth?

Selten and Stoecker's experiments extended the one-period Prisoner's Dilemma to a doubly repeated setting. In contrast, a recent paper by Cooper et al. (1990) extended the analysis to what is now termed a co-ordination game. A co-ordination game is one which exhibits multiple Nash equilibria which are Pareto rankable. An example is given in figure 11.1; in this the first entries in the payoff matrix are the payoffs to player 1, and the second entries are the payoffs to player 2. Note that the payoff matrices of the two players are the transpose of each other. Note also[3] that both (1, 1) and (2, 2) are Nash equilibrium strategies (if player 1 (2) plays 1 (2) then player 2 (1) should play 1 (2)) and that (2, 2) Pareto dominates (1, 1). Note finally that (3, 3) Pareto dominates both (2, 2) and (1, 1) but is

Player 2

		1	2	3
	1	350, 350	350, 250	700, 0
Player 1	2	250, 350	550, 550	1000, 0
	3	0, 700	0, 1000	600, 600

Figure 11.1   An example of a co-ordination game. Matrix entries are payoffs to players 1 and 2 respectively.

not itself a Nash equilibrium (if player 1 (2) plays 3 then the optimizing response by player 2 (1) is to play 2).

   Cooper et al. (1990) were interested in testing three hypotheses with respect to such games: first, that the outcome will be a Nash equilibrium; second, that the Pareto-dominating Nash equilibrium will be selected; third, that dominated strategies are irrelevant to equilibrium selection. Their experiment was computerized and involved seven cohorts of players, each cohort consisting of 11 different players. Each player played a sequence of one-shot games against different anonymous opponents within his or her cohort. The incentive mechanism used was that introduced by Roth and Malouf (1979) and deserves some discussion, though it is not altogether clear that such a mechanism is necessary for this particular experiment. The idea is to control for attitude to risk: if the payoffs in figure 11.1 were denominated in money, and if either player perceived that the other player might be playing a mixed strategy, then calculations of expected utility would be needed to determine the optimal strategy if the player was not risk neutral. Generally, the experimenter does not know the subjects' utility functions although they could, in principle, be discovered. The alternative proposed by Roth and Malouf is the following: let the payoffs in figure 11.1 be denominated in points, and let the actual payoff to any player be determined as the outcome of a lottery (conducted after each play) which yields some given monetary amount x with probability q and some lesser monetary amount y ($y < x$) with probability $1 - q$. Then the expected utility of this lottery is

$$qU(x) + (1 - q)U(y) = q[U(x) - U(y)] + U(y)$$

which is maximized for any $U(x) > U(y)$ by the highest attainable value of q. Now let q equal the number of points earned by the player divided by 1000. This mechanism therefore induces the player to go for the strategy with the highest payoff in terms of the entries in figure 11.1.

   Cooper et al. conclude that their 'experimental evidence strongly supports the hypothesis that the outcome will be from the set of Nash equilibria. It does not support, however, any of the other proposed hypotheses regarding equilibrium selection.' Rather interestingly, they observed that the variations in a player's payoff from the rival's play of a co-operative dominated strategy influences the equilibrium selection. In other words, once again, the theory gets some bits right, but not all.

Let me now turn to sequential non-co-operative bargaining games, termed by Roth strategic models. Of particular interest here is a large number of experiments carried out on what is now termed the 'shrinking cake-eating problem'. Consider a simple model involving two bargainers who have to decide on the division of some amount of money. The rules of the game specify that the two players take it in turns to make demands (i.e. suggestions for dividing the money) which can either be accepted or rejected by the rival. If the demand is accepted all well and good; if the demand is rejected, the amount of money to be divided shrinks,[4] possibly to zero (in which case the game ends). If there is a finite horizon, that is, if the 'cake' shrinks to zero in a finite time (or after a finite number of demands), then backward induction can be applied in the usual fashion to find the optimal strategy for both players.

Consider first the simplest such game: a one-period one-demand model called the ultimatum game. This was subjected to experimental investigation by Guth et al. (1982). Players were divided into two groups of equal size, to be matched at random with players of the other group. One group consisted of the players 1, the other group players 2. In any game, the player 1 would make a suggestion for division of the fixed sum of k German marks by filling out a form saying 'I demand DM x'. Player 2 could either accept, in which case he got $k - x$ and player 1 got x, or reject, in which case neither player got anything. The backward induction solution is that player 1 demands, and gets, $k - \varepsilon$ while player 2 accepts ε; here ε is an arbitrarily small positive amount of money. The argument is simply that player 1 'knows' that player 2 will accept any demand that gives him/her (player 2) any amount of money which is strictly positive, and hence more than the zero he/she (player 2) would get by rejecting the demand.

Guth et al. observed very few instances of this 'optimal' solution: out of 21 games played by inexperienced subjects, just two offers were for k (one of which was rejected), while the modal offer was a 50–50 split (the mean offer was $0.65k$ for player 1 and $0.35k$ for player 2); out of 21 games played by experienced subjects (the same subjects one week later), there were three 50–50 proposals and one for $k - \varepsilon$, while the mean offer was $0.69k$ for player 1. The authors concluded that bargaining theory was not a very good predictor of observed behaviour, and the subjects appeared to be using other criteria, such as fairness.

This view was challenged by Binmore et al. (1985) who extended the game to a two-period game. The cake started at 100 pence, shrank to 25 pence after one offer and to zero pence after two offers. Following the same reasoning as that used above and working back, we can deduce the optimal strategy: at the second stage, player 2 should demand (and get) $25 - \varepsilon$; accordingly, at the first stage player 1 should demand (and get) between 75 and $75 + \varepsilon$. Binmore et al. used a computerized design with subjects linked anonymously by networked micros. Two games were played: game A, as described above; and game B, where the subject who was player 2 in game A became player 1. However, in game B just the opening demand was recorded.[5]

Binmore et al. observed a sharp change in behaviour between games A and B: whereas the modal demand in game A was for a 50–50 split (with a smaller mode at a 75–25 split), in game B the mode had shifted, in a very emphatic fashion, to a 75–25 split. They concluded that Guth et al.'s remarks about fairness were premature, and that the 'gamesmanship' solution would emerge after sufficient experience.

Not surprisingly, matters did not rest there. In quick succession there were responses by Guth and Tietz (1988), by Neelin et al. (1988) and by Ochs and Roth (1989). The first of these looked at two two-stage games of the type examined by Binmore et al. with shrinkage of 10 per cent and 90 per cent respectively. These are deliberately more extreme than the 75 per cent used by Binmore et al. Using the same argument as before, it can be seen that the 'optimal' predictions are for effectively a 10–90 split in the first game and a 90–10 split in the second. Guth and Tietz arranged their experiment in such a way that each subject played two games, each with a randomly chosen other subject; subjects who played the first game as player 1 played the second as player 2 and vice versa. Guth and Tietz found that, in the game with a shrinkage of 90 per cent, the average first demand was 76 per cent in the first game and 67 per cent in the second, and in the game with a shrinkage of 10 per cent, the average first demand was 70 per cent in the first game and 59 per cent in the second. These are hardly results that support the game theory's predictions.

Neelin et al. (1988) reported two experiments: in the first, 80 students played two-period, three-period and five-period games of the above type against different opponents; in the second, 30 students played three five-period games. They observed that behaviour was not everywhere consistent with the game-theoretic predictions nor with equal-split predictions.

The Ochs and Roth (1989) paper is probably the most systematic and comprehensive to date. It examined both two-period and three-period games with four different shrinkage scenarios. Ochs and Roth particularly wanted to explore the impact of different discount factors for the two bargainers. In my discussion above, I have treated a common discount rate and a (common) shrinkage of the cake as the same – as indeed they are – but if we want to use different discount rates for different players we need a different procedure. The one that Ochs and Roth adopted was the following. The cake to be divided was denominated in 'chips'. These chips were worth different amounts to the two players, and were worth different amounts in different periods: subjects were given a schedule showing how chips mapped (linearly) into money depending upon the period in which agreement was reached. This is quite ingenious, but I wonder how transparent it was to the subjects.

Ochs and Roth's experimental design also allowed them to follow a procedure similar to that used by me in my experiments reported in part III of this book: to test not only for the absolute correctness of the game-theoretic predictions, but also for the comparative statics correctness. Of particular concern in this latter respect was the comparative statics effect of changing discount factors. Roth (1988) in summarizing their results remarks: 'the perfect equilibrium predictions do poorly both as point predictions and in predicting qualitative differences between cells [comparative statics effects], such as mean first period offers'. He goes on to note that 'perhaps the most interesting ... concerns what happens when first period offers are rejected'. About 15 per cent of first offers met with rejection; oddly enough, well over half of these were followed by counter proposals in which player 2 asked for less than he had just been offered and rejected! This suggests that relative shares, as well as absolute shares, might be considered important by the players. If this is indeed the case, then the predictions discussed above, which are based on the assumption that utility is derived from absolute shares, are no longer relevant. This indicates a possible direction for future experimental and theoretical work.

11.3   Applications to Industrial Organization Theory

Many experimental investigations of topics which could be considered as part of industrial organization theory are described and discussed by Plott (1982, 1989). I report on them in chapter 13 as they come under the heading of auctions and markets according to the taxonomy that I have adopted for this book. In this section, I shall confine myself to those aspects of industrial organization theory that are specifically built on the foundation of modern game theory; the book by Tirole (1988) beautifully characterizes this branch of the literature. Of particular concern to me here is the modern theory of R&D, invention and innovation as found in chapter 10 of Tirole (1988). I should note, however, that much of part II, entitled 'Strategic interaction' and consisting of seven out of 11 chapters of the book, is built on game-theoretic foundations. It is therefore ripe for experimental investigation.

In section 10.4, the discussion concentrated on applications of modern game theory in the study of industrial organization with particular concentration on recent theories of R&D, invention and innovation. The discussion in this section will be similarly concentrated. I begin by examining the study of Isaac and Reynolds (1988), one of the few published experimental studies of R&D. As the authors remark, the use of experimental techniques enables empirical testing of theories in this area to come closer to the theoretical specification than is usually the case: often empirical work relies on the use of empirical proxies which are rather far removed from the theory itself. (The cynic might also remark that the Isaac and Reynolds study is of interest as it emphasizes the rather unrealistic nature of the theory in this area!)

Let me begin by discussing the theoretical structure investigated by Isaac and Reynolds. It is a model of R&D within the stochastic invention genre of models. It can be considered as a static one-shot model, even though it might be repeated over several periods (as indeed it is in the experimental implementation), since dynamic considerations do not enter into any of the solutions. The basic structure of the model envisages a set of N potential innovators (or firms), each of which simultaneously and privately chooses an R&D investment level without knowing the decisions made by the rivals. A random process then determines which, if any, is the successful innovator: more generally, the vector of the returns to the N firms is a well-specified stochastic function of the vector of R&D investments of the N firms. Clearly, the expected return to a particular firm is an increasing function of its investment expenditure and a decreasing function of the investment expenditures of its rivals. Within this general framework, there are various specifications that one can implement depending upon the focus of one's interests. Isaac and Reynolds choose an implementation that enables them to focus on two things of particular interest to them: N (the number of firms/subjects) and the 'appropriability' of the successful innovation. The latter depends on the gap between the rewards to the successful innovator and the rewards to the unsuccessful imitators; this, in turn, depends on spillover effects.

The Isaac and Reynolds implementation is particularly simple. Subjects are told how many subjects there are in their group. They are then told that in each period (of a ten-period experiment) they all start out as 'type B sellers'; this entitles them to a certain income V_l. However, they are given the opportunity each period to become a 'type A seller' which increases their income (to V_w) for that period. Note that all periods are independent: even if they become a type A seller in a particular period, they revert to being a type B seller at the beginning of the next period. The process by which they might become a type A seller in any period is a random one and is specified as follows: each subject can select how many draws to buy (at a given, pre-specified, positive cost) from a random device which has a probability of success (that is, of becoming a type A seller) of 1 in 10. Successive draws are independent. So, if a subject chooses to have x draws in any period, the chances of him or her becoming a type A seller in that period is simply $1 - (0.9)^x$. Clearly it is possible for any number of subjects, between 0 and N, to become type A sellers in any period, depending upon their choices of their x. The payoff V_w to type A sellers depends upon the number of type A sellers in that period.

In terms of the original R&D context, the two items of key concern to Isaac and Reynolds are the number of subjects N and the appropriability of the invention/success, which depends upon the value of V_l relative to V_w. Full appropriability is captured by putting V_l equal to zero, partial appropriability by putting V_l positive and non-appropriability by putting V_l and V_w equal. In the latter case, of course, firms have no incentive to invest money in R&D expenditure (i.e. in buying random draws).

Isaac and Reynolds adopted a 2×2 design; two values of N (four or nine) and two values of appropriability (full or partial). For each of these four cases, they calculated the optimal Nash equilibrium strategies, as specified in the optimal number of draws from the random device, and the socially optimal number of draws. These are specified in table 11.1.

Table 11.1 Solution implications for Isaac and Reynolds' experiment

Group size	Appropriability	Nash equilibrium		Social optimum	
		Draws for subject	Expected profit per subject ($)	Draws for subject	Expected profit per subject ($)
4	Full	9	0.542	4	0.802
4	Partial	5	0.796	4	0.802
9	Full	5	0.150	2	0.357
9	Partial	3	0.317	2	0.357

It should be noted that the solution has similar properties to that of the Prisoner's Dilemma: individual rewards are higher under the social optimum, but private incentives pull subjects away to the Nash equilibrium. Note that an increase in the group size decreases returns, and as a consequence lowers the optimal number of draws (both privately and socially), and that full appropriability (compared with partial) increases the (privately) optimal number of draws but lowers (as a consequence) expected private returns. Appropriability does not affect socially optimal behaviour.

The experiment showed that the Nash equilibrium comparative statics predictions concerning privately optimal behaviour were generally confirmed by the experimental evidence: as appropriability increased, so did actual draws; as group size increased, actual draws decreased. Moreover, subjects tended to over-invest (purchase too many draws) relative to the social optimum. There were some departures from the optimally specified levels of behaviour, but the changes were always in the correct direction. This echoes findings reported elsewhere in this book in other contexts. Isaac and Reynolds suggest that some of the discrepancies in levels can be attributed to risk aversion, though they do not provide a formal test of this proposition. (They show that Nash equilibrium strategies for particular constant-absolute-risk-averse utility functions fit the observed data quite closely, but make no claims that their subjects had these particular utility functions.) An alternative explanation could be built around strategic considerations and/or learning behaviour. First, note that the theory being tested each period is the Nash equilibrium theory which, definitionally, pre-supposes that each subject is happy with his or her decision given the decisions of the others. Given the nature of the experimental design (with one-shot announcements each period) there is no guarantee that this is in fact the case. One could try to guarantee that by implementing an iterative procedure each period, wherein subjects iteratively announce decisions but the decisions are binding only when all subjects agree to them. A hard-line theorist might argue that this would be unnecessary since the iteration goes on in the minds of the subjects, but it would nevertheless be interesting to explore. A second consideration concerns the ten-period repetition in the Isaac and Reynolds experiments: although there is no dynamic link between the various repetitions (which means that the finitely repeated Prisoner's Dilemma argument is applicable), subjects may introduce dynamic elements as part of their strategic responses. If they can get the other subjects to play the social optimum, so much the better. So we could get departures from the Nash equilibrium for such reasons. Clearly there are various lines of enquiry that emerge from this experiment.

Note that the experiment is very straightforward; the only tedious aspect of it is in the implementation of the random draws. For example, in the large-group full-appropriability case, each of the nine subjects would select five draws under the Nash equilibrium, requiring up to 45 draws from the random device. Isaac and Reynolds were aware that these needed to be carried out in an obviously transparent fashion; they chose to use a bingo cage with ten balls, numbered 1 to 10, with the number 10 ball counting as a success. Since the draws were with replacement, the bingo cage had to be reset after each draw; 45 such draws would thus take rather a long time! Such practical considerations need always to be borne in mind when designing an experiment.

In section 10.4 I discussed another R&D patent race model, that of Fudenberg et al. (1983). One advantage of this from an experimental point of view is that it involves no exogenous risk; all the risk or uncertainty is endogenous. This means that there is no need of any randomizing device (such as a bingo cage, die, pack of cards or roulette wheel) to implement the experiment. Indeed, the Fudenberg et al. (1983) model is extremely straightforward to reproduce in the laboratory; we at EXEC have software which enables up to 16 subjects to play a sequence of games against different opponents (including the computer, programmed to play the Nash equilibrium or some other strategy). We are about to pilot this. The only remaining worry concerns how far the theory departs from real-life R&D practices. But that is another story . . . !

11.4   Applications to Public Goods Theory

The experimental literature on the public goods problem, starting in a fairly serious fashion in the late 1970s and developing rapidly thereafter, provides an excellent example of how experimental design evolves over the years, focusing on contentious issues and learning from past mistakes. Over the past few years, experimental emphasis has increasingly been devoted to the investigation of the impact of repetition and learning on the extent of free-riding and to the examination of the desirability of certain 'mechanisms' which may help to get round the free-riding problem. Much of this recent work has used the 'stark setting' of section 10.5; earlier work, however, employed a somewhat less stark setting, which implied that some of the early conclusions were necessarily rather blurred.

Early work included a series of papers by two sociologists, Marwell and Ames (1979, 1980, 1981). Their modelling of the public good allocation mechanism differed from the stark setting of section 10.5 in that there was a non-linear (indeed S-shaped) relationship between the aggregate investment in the public good and the payoff to the public good. So the payoff as a function of the aggregate investment increased quite slowly until a certain point, where it accelerated sharply for a while before once again resuming a slow rate of increase. The point at which the payoff function accelerated sharply was termed the 'provision point' by Marwell and Ames; once aggregate contributions reached this point, collective net payoffs to further contributions were large and positive (at least for a while). As a result of this specification, the Nash equilibrium was not at zero public provision, nor was the social optimum at zero private provision, although the Nash equilibrium did imply substantial free-riding behaviour (as in our 'stark setting'). Marwell and Ames carried out a series of studies using this specification. They contacted subjects by telephone, and subjects phoned in their decisions. Marwell and Ames used a $2 \times 2 \times 2$ design with three independent variables: group size (large/small), the 'distribution of interest' (equal/unequal) specifying the differential payoff rates across the subjects, and the 'distribution of resources' (equal/unequal) specifying the differential allocations across the subjects. The striking feature of Marwell and Ames's findings was that free-riding existed, but not nearly to the extent predicted by the Nash equilibrium theory. Indeed, except in one study where economists were specifically selected as subjects (and in which public contributions were significantly lower), public contributions through Marwell and Ames's experiments were usually in the 40–60 per cent range. These findings are sharply at odds with public goods theory; possible explanations are discussed later.

Another early public goods experiment was a rather unusual one carried out by Schneider and Pommerehne (1981) at the University of Zurich. Although interesting in the sense that it was 'more real-life' than other experiments, its design inevitably suffers from a greater lack of experimental control than usual. The subjects in this experiment were a group of final-year economics students, who were approached by an experimenter posing as a publishing company representative. She explained that their professor was writing a book relevant to their course which would not be published until after the exam, but which might be made available in advance to the group of students. The students were invited to submit written bids for (individual) advance copies, with such copies going to the ten highest bidders. The students were then told that there was another way that they could get the book – by jointly raising a certain amount, they could each get a copy. Again written bids were solicited – now, of course, for the book as a public good. The key test, therefore, was whether the second bids were lower than the first bids; this is the prediction of public goods theory. Schneider and Pommerehne found they were, but not by much. So, as with Marwell and Ames, there was some free-riding, but not as much as predicted by the theory.

An experiment with a markedly different conclusion was one carried out by Kim and Walker (1984). This was one of the earliest experiments to consider the effect of repetitions on behaviour: they got their subjects to take one public good investment decision each day for 11 days. The idea behind this was to see whether repetition/learning drove the outcome to the Nash equilibrium. (Since Kim and Walker used the 'stark setting' of section 10.5, this Nash equilibrium consisted of zero public provision.) In fact, they found that convergence to this Nash equilibrium did occur, and did so remarkably quickly. Incidentally, and partly because of the rapid convergence, the experimenters changed the payment structure twice during the 11 days of the experiment; it should be noted that this changes the 'rules of the game' of the experiment, implying that it was not strictly a repeated version of the same public goods problem. Subjects may have become suspicious as a consequence of the changes in the payment structure; this may have affected their behaviour.

Subjects in Kim and Walker's experiment were told that there were 100 subjects participating in the experiment; in fact, there were only five. Elaborate precautions were taken to try to sustain the fiction, although, as far as the theory was concerned, it was unimportant. However, this practice does raise a wider issue, which I have discussed elsewhere, concerning the importance of the subjects' believing what the experimenters tell them. As I have remarked before, this seems to me to be of paramount importance: once subjects start to distrust the experimenter, then the tight control that is needed is lost. This makes me rather uneasy about the Kim and Walker 'deception' although I appreciate that other experimenters follow similar practices.[6] More generally, and particularly in the area of public goods experiments, one has to be careful that the subjects believe all the information they are given: for example, what would be the implication if subjects were not 100 per cent sure that the public good investment revealed to them was in fact the actual investment? And in how many public goods experiments could subjects check (afterwards if necessary) that this was actually the case?

Two papers from overlapping stables that take up some of the Marwell and Ames design features (but in the 'stark setting' of section 10.5) and concentrate also on the effect of repetition/learning on behaviour are Isaac et al. (1984, 1985). The 1984 paper is also of interest for being one of the first to describe the use of the computerized PLATO system for conducting the experiments; as the authors observe, this system 'allows for minimal experimenter–subject interaction during experimental sessions as well as insuring that all subjects see identical programmed instructions and examples .... The use of the computer system also facilitates the accounting process that occurs in each decision period and minimises subject's transactions costs in making decisions and recalling information ....' True, but there remains the problem discussed above of whether subjects believe what the computer is telling them about the decisions of the other subjects.

Isaac et al. (1984) used a $2 \times 2 \times 2$ design. The three treatment effects were group size (four and ten, and these were genuine values), per-capita return from the group investment (the counterpart of Marwell and Ames's 'distribution of interest') and degree of experience of the subjects (experienced/inexperienced). Each group was given ten repetitions of any given decision problem. As with Kim and Walker, these experiments revealed increased free-riding with repetition, though in this case the increase was not so sudden and dramatic. Indeed, significant continued public good provision was frequently observed, even in the tenth and final period of a given decision problem. More generally Isaac et al. conclude that 'free riding is neither absolutely all pervasive nor always non existent': their results showed considerable diversity.

In Isaac et al. (1985) (a non-computerized experiment with similar design features) rather more free-riding was observed and the rate at which free-riding increased with repetition was somewhat higher. Nevertheless, sporadic attempts by subjects to get others to increase their public good contributions (by increasing their own dramatically) were observed. Of course, without communication between the subjects it is difficult to see how this might rationally be achieved. Isaac et al. (1985) did explore, to a limited extent, the effect of communication on contributions; they concluded tentatively that communication does lead to an increase in contributions, albeit a small one.

A recent contribution by Andreoni (1988) looked in more detail at the effect of repetition on behaviour. His intention was to try to distinguish a strategic effect from a learning effect. These are clearly different: in a repeated game with given players, it may make strategic sense to make public good contributions in excess of the single-period Nash contribution; in contrast, subjects may simply learn through time that public good contributions are not worthwhile. To separate out these two effects, Andreoni adopted a rather clever design, with all subjects playing the game ten times but with subjects divided into two groups. One group, the Strangers, switched groups each repetition (so that they got a different set of players in each repetition), whereas the other group, the Partners, kept the same players in each repetition. The Partners group could be expected to play strategically; the Strangers group should not – any change in their behaviour could be attributed solely to learning. Andreoni found that Strangers free-rode more than Partners with the gap increasing with repetition. Nevertheless, once again, free-riding was neither all-pervasive nor non-existent.

A rather different line of attack was followed by Smith (1979, 1980) and Banks et al. (1988). These experimental designs were specifically policy oriented and were constructed to answer the question of what might be the appropriate decision mechanism for the provision of a public good when the voluntary contribution mechanism (studied in the experiments already discussed) seems to lead to substantial free-riding. Banks et al. had a specific policy problem in mind: the allocation of space on a space station to be put into orbit by NASA in the mid-1990s.

These studies therefore differed from those reported above in the nature of the decision mechanism to be operated by the subjects. One such mechanism is the 'Smith process with unanimity'; in this, subjects announce a personal public good contribution and a suggested quantity of the public good. If the sum of the bids exceeds the cost of the average suggested quantity, then the announcements are feasible. Under the 'unanimity' rule, however, all subjects must agree to any feasible outcome before it is implemented. A 'Smith process without unanimity' was also investigated. It had been expected that the enforcement of unanimity would lead to a significant increase in social efficiency (i.e. outcomes close to the social optimum) but this turned out not to be the case. It was also discovered, rather worryingly, that the performance of the Smith process 'decreases with repeated use rather than increases as one might have hoped'. Nevertheless, the Smith process did perform significantly better (in terms of social efficiency) than the voluntary mechanism. Banks et al. conclude that 'these experiments leave no doubt that the quality of public goods decisions can be substantially affected by the choice of mechanism'. This underlines the potential importance of experiments for economic policy analysis.

11.5 Bargaining

In chapter 10, I noted that the distinction between games and bargaining in the literature is sometimes rather blurred, and that I would rather arbitrarily use the term 'games' to refer to non-co-operative strategic contests between two or more individuals, and to confine 'bargains' primarily to situations where there was a period of pre-decision between the various individuals. For Roth's (1988) terminology, I refer to the material under his 'Experimental tests of strategic models' as games, and the material under his 'Experimental tests of axiomatic models' as bargaining problems. Accordingly, the experimental material under discussion in this section relates to the theoretical material of section 10.6, particularly Nash bargaining theory. A fuller discussion can be found in Roth (1987).

From section 10.6, it can be seen that the Nash solution to the Nash bargaining problem requires knowledge of the players' utility functions. Some of the early experimental work, however, tried to dodge this problem by making the simplifying assumption that the players were risk neutral. Unfortunately, the findings of these early experiments – that players were not following the Nash rules – were then uniformly discounted by theorists on the grounds that the utility functions were mis-specified. There are two ways round this problem: first, to discover, by some prior experiments, the utility functions of the players; second, to work with problems involving just two outcomes, so that the utility function is unimportant. The latter is much simpler, and was used in a path-breaking study by Roth and Malouf (1979).

Such games are termed binary lottery games. Consider, for example, a two-person game. Player 1 ends up with one of two monetary amounts, x_1 or x_2; player 2 ends up with one of two monetary amounts, y_1 or y_2; x_1 is smaller than x_2 and y_1 is smaller than y_2.[7] The actual outcomes are determined by a random device: player 1 gets x_1 with probability $1 - p$ and x_2 with probability p; player 2 gets y_1 with probability $1 - q$ and y_2 with probability q. The rules of the bargaining game specify that bargaining is conducted over the values of p and q subject to the constraint that

$$p + q = 1 \qquad\qquad (11.1)$$

so that there is a trade-off problem: the higher is the probability that player 1 gets his/her better outcome, the lower is the probability that player 2 gets his/her better outcome.

Let me be a little more formal. Since the players' utility functions are arbitrary up to a linear transformation, we can specify the two utility functions, $u(.)$ and $v(.)$ respectively, so that

$$u(x_1) = v(y_1) = 0 \qquad u(x_2) = v(y_2) = 1$$

That is, for each player the utility of his best outcome is 1 and the utility of his worst outcome is 0. Now the expected utility of the outcome of any bargain (p, q) is

for player 1: $(1 - p)u(x_1) + pu(x_2) = p$

for player 2: $(1 - q)v(y_1) + qv(y_2) = q$

So player 1 simply wants to maximize utility p and player 2 simply wants to maximize utility q, which equals $1 - p$ because of equation (11.1).

On the assumption that the players get their least preferred outcomes if agreement is not reached (so that the disagreement utilities are zero for both players), the Nash solution to this bargaining game is (see section 10.6, equation (10.4)) the value of p which maximizes

$$pq = p(1 - p)$$

The solution, clearly, is $p = q = 0.5$; that is, for the probability cake to be shared equally. Note that this is the case whatever the values of the prizes.

Roth and Malouf's (1979) experiment was designed to test these predictions: in particular it was designed to test whether changes in the values of the prizes, and whether the players knew one another's prizes, influenced the outcome of the bargaining process. The experiment was computerized, with players seated at separated terminals. They could send messages to each other via the computer, but they were not allowed to identify themselves nor send messages of a threatening or intimidating nature. (This is an issue to which some considerable attention has been paid, because of the rather muddy issues it raises. Clearly in a bargaining problem one wants the players to be able to bargain with each other in a reasonably realistic manner, yet at the same time one wants to exclude certain matters which one considers 'irrelevant'. In this category, of course, are threats of physical violence and other phenomena which would take the bargaining problem outside the implicit legal framework within which it is set. In addition, most economists, for better or worse, would want to exclude certain 'sociological' or 'psycho-logical' aspects of actual bargaining situations: for example, in face-to-face discussions, the physical sizes of the bargainers, the sexes of the two bargainers and so on; in telephonic discussions, the sound of the players' voices, the quality of the phone line and so on. For such reasons, many economic bargaining experiments have adopted the Roth and Malouf technique of computer-transmitted experimenter-censored text messages.

However, there have been a number of recent experiments involving face-to-face bargaining. This seems to make a significant difference.)

Roth and Malouf (1979) found that when the players' prizes were equal (that is, $x_1 = y_1$ and $x_2 = y_2$) and when they were unequal but the players were unaware that that was so (because they were not told the prizes of the rival), the Nash prediction that the probability cake would be split 50–50 was almost always confirmed. However, when the prizes were unequal, and the players knew what the rivals' prizes were, the 'agreements tended to cluster around two "focal points": the equal probability agreement, and the "equal expected value" agreement that gives each bargainer the same expected value' (Roth, 1988, p. 979). The observations clustered around this second focal point clearly violate the Nash predictions.

Further experiments carried out by Roth and various associates reinforced this simple message: the outcome of the bargaining process depends crucially on what each player knows about the prizes of the other player and, moreover, on what each player knows about what the other knows. These findings are of major importance for bargaining theory.

A further set of bargaining experiments carried out by Roth and various associates used ternary lottery games. These involve three prizes for each player: large and small prizes obtained from the lottery mechanism when agreement is reached, and a disagreement prize obtained when no agreement is reached in the allotted time. Let me denote these by x_2, x_1 and x_0 for player 1, and by y_2, y_1 and y_0 for player 2. As before $x_2 > x_1$ and $y_2 > y_1$, but the relative values of x_1 and x_0 and of y_1 and y_0 depend upon the particular bargaining problem under consideration. If x_1 exceeds x_0 and y_1 exceeds y_0 then any agreement is preferable to no agreement, but if x_0 exceeds x_1 and y_0 exceeds y_1 then a sufficiently risk-averse player might prefer the certain disagreement outcome to the random lottery.

Clearly in such ternary lottery games risk aversion is relevant to the Nash bargaining solution, so before carrying out any experiments involving such games it is necessary to discover the subjects' risk attitudes with respect to the three outcomes. For player 1, for example, we can put $u(x_1) = 0$ and $u(x_2) = 1$, so it remains to find $u(x_0) = u$. This can be discovered (in an incentive-compatible fashion) using the techniques discussed in part II of this book. Note that if the prizes are equal across players ($x_2 = y_2$, $x_1 = y_1$, $x_0 = y_0$) then player 2 will be more risk averse than player 1 if $v > u$ when $x_0 > x_1$ and if $v < u$ when $x_0 < x_1$ (where $v \equiv v(x_0)$). Nash bargaining theory comes up with some strong predictions under these circumstances. Suppose player 2 is more risk averse than player 1. Then if $x_0 > x_1$ (i.e. the disagreement prize is better than the losing prize on the lottery) $q > 0.5$ and $p < 0.5$, whereas if $x_0 < x_1$ (i.e. the disagreement prize is worse than the losing prize on the lottery) $q < 0.5$ and $p > 0.5$. These are clear predictions, which can be tested experimentally once the risk attitudes of the players have been ascertained.

Murnighan et al. (1988) tested such a symmetric game. Their conclusions were somewhat mixed as it was observed that when $x_0 < x_1$ a high percentage of games ended in a 50–50 split, whereas when $x_0 > x_1$ a high percentage of games ended in disagreement. There was a weak effect of risk aversion in the predicted direction, but it was not significant. It seems here that 'focal point effects' may have been overpowering any risk-aversion effects that were present. Experiments carried out with unequal prizes $(x_2 \neq y_2$ and/or $x_1 \neq y_1)$, which cannot test the risk-aversion hypothesis in the strong form stated above, indicated some considerable support for a rather weaker version of the risk-aversion hypothesis. Work is still ongoing.

In discussing these various experiments, and the methodological issues that emerge from them, Roth (1988) raises two points, at least one of which has implications beyond the particular context of the experiments. The first relates to a debate that has been ongoing between various experimental schools within the States (and between economists and psychologists) concerning the size of experimental payoffs. One argument is that certain effects (such as that of risk aversion) might be 'drowned out' in experiments with small monetary payoffs because of the influence of other factors: 'The effects are there, but too small to be observed.' Only repetition with larger payoffs can resolve this debate.

The other issue raised, but not solved, by Roth is that of 'deadline effects'. For practical reasons, most bargaining experiments have a fixed time limit. In computerized experiments, usually a clock comes onto the screen ticking off the final minutes and seconds. Roth notes (p. 983) that 'across all experiments, which varied considerably in the terms and distributions of agreements, the data reveal that a high proportion of agreements were reached in the very final seconds before the deadline'. Why? And what are the implications?

11.6 Conclusions

The experiments reported in this chapter are an excellent demonstration of the way that experimental economics has 'matured' over the past decade or so, and of the current power of experimental methods to test economic theories and to explore the implications of proposed economic policy measures. What is particularly satisfying is the way that the discipline has devised clever methods of controlling for certain irrelevant phenomena. The binary lottery method of Roth and Malouf is a very neat illustration of this: by restricting attention to just two prizes and by shifting the outcomes to probability points the problem of risk aversion can be bypassed. Of course, if the subjects are not expected utility maximizers (i.e. if their preference functionals are not linear in the probabilities) then this method does not work. A new solution would be necessary; I suspect the next few years will witness its introduction.

I also like the Partners and Strangers technique of Andreoni, which enables experimenters to distinguish between learning effects and strategic effects in repeated games and bargains. A further refinement, which does not seem to be used as much as it could, is the employment of a computer program as one of the players in a game.

Computerization, however, is rife in the actual running of experiments, and this is to be welcomed for reasons already discussed. Clearly, in the running of games of various sorts, computerization is of immense value in enforcing a uniform experimenter style, in enforcing the correct rules of the game and in carrying out any calculations necessary. Often such calculations are quite extensive, and manual experimentation could lead to sizeable frustrating delays.

Nevertheless, I am increasingly concerned that computerization could lead to a breakdown of trust between the subjects and the experimenter. Obviously others are aware of such potential difficulties: witness, for example, the frequent use of a 'real' random device to play out random gambles rather than the use of a computerized random-number generator. But my fears are at a rather more mundane level: consider, for example, a computerized public good experiment. How do the subjects know that the figure communicated to them by the computer as the aggregate public good contribution is indeed the sum of the individual contributions? Given anonymity, and given universal communication through the computer, there is no way that they can know for certain: any message could be contaminated by the software/experimenter. In these situations, therefore, we need some other method: for example, hand-written records kept individually by the subjects themselves during the running of the experiment, which could (and publicly should) be checked against a comprehensive printout provided by the experimenter at the end of the experiment. Tedious, maybe; but with increasing sophistication, increasingly necessary, I feel.

Notes

1 Though you should keep in mind Harrison's warning about the magnitude of the motivation for 'correct' behaviour provided by the experiment.
2 You might also want the subjects to play several Prisoner's Dilemmas in order to counter arguments about learning effects.
3 Here (i, j) denotes player 1 choosing option i and player 2 choosing option j.
4 In some versions of the story, time passes between alternative offers and a discount factor is applied, but the essential point remains: the real value of the amount to be divided shrinks as time passes.
5 One wonders why.
6 Which, in this case, are quite innocent.
7 It is assumed here that both subjects prefer more money to less. The procedure can be modified if that is not the case.

12

The Economic Theories of Auctions and Markets

12.1 Introduction

As with the two topics in chapter 10, games and bargaining, the two topics of this chapter, auctions and markets, tend to blur into each other: it is not always easy to tell where one topic stops and the other begins. Nevertheless, there is a distinct literature (both theoretical and empirical) on the two topics, even though ultimately both are concerned with essentially the same economic problem: the determination of prices in different kinds of markets.

Microeconomics is often termed the 'theory of price'. It is rather ironic, therefore, that microeconomics very rarely provides a theory of what prices will actually emerge in particular situations. Consider the classic compartmentalization of markets: competitive, oligopolistic and monopolistic. The third of these is straightforward – there is a well-defined unique firm whose (institutional) function it is to set the price for its product – but in the other two cases the situation is not so clear cut. In competitive markets, the theory does not provide an account of what price (or prices) will actually emerge; rather, it provides a theory concerning the existence of an equilibrium price. In competitive markets, all agents are price-takers, and the equilibrium price is one which has the property that aggregate demand at that price equals aggregate supply at that price. The theory usually tells us the conditions under which an equilibrium price exists and under which it is unique; in the latter instance, it therefore tells us that, if this unique equilibrium price prevailed, and if all agents were price-takers, then everyone in the market would be happy in the sense of being able to sell or buy as much as they wanted at that price. But note what the theory does not tell us: it does not tell us whether or how this equilibrium price comes to prevail. Indeed, it cannot, because there is no-one in the market whose job it is to set the price – all agents are price-takers! Usually, some fictitious additional agent – the Walrasian auctioneer – is involved to tell us the latter story.

This is all rather unsatisfactory, if only for the rather obvious reason that in virtually no real markets in the real world does the Walrasian auctioneer exist. This is where auctions and other bidding processes come into the picture, as ways of telling us whether (and how) the equilibrium price will actually be attained. This is the theoretical concern of section 12.3 and the experimental concern of section 13.3.

First, however, I consider the rather simpler auction material of section 12.2. This is largely confined to one-sided markets, where one side of the market plays a largely passive role. Indeed, this is what most people think of when auctions are being discussed. However, as we shall see in section 12.3, they can be extended to double-sided markets. I begin with the simpler case.

12.2   Auctions

An extremely readable introduction to auction theory can be found in the entry[1] under 'Auctions' in the *New Palgrave Dictionary* (and reprinted in Eatwell et al. (1989, pp. 39–53)). Rather interestingly, this entry is written by Vernon Smith, one of the earliest and most distinguished experimental economists, who has himself carried out numerous auction and market experiments. We shall be hearing more of Smith's experiments in chapter 13.

For simplicity, begin by considering auctions for single items; the extension to multiple units is often straightforward. So we envisage some item being offered for sale with several potential buyers interested in purchasing it. Of crucial importance are the institutional arrangements concerning the auction. Let me follow Smith in distinguishing the following broad categories.

English auction

Potential buyers announce successively higher bids for the item in question until no further bids are forthcoming. Bids, once made, cannot be withdrawn, and can only be replaced by higher bids. The person making the highest bid gets the item, as long as the bid exceeds the seller's reservation price, and pays this highest bid as the price.

Dutch auction

This works in the reverse direction. The easiest way to picture it is to imagine a clock, calibrated not in time but in prices, and going backwards from high prices to low prices. The clock is started at an excessively high price, and it runs backwards until some buyer stops it by offering to buy the item at the price indicated on the clock.

First-price auction

This is a written bid auction in which potential buyers make sealed bids. All the bids are opened and the item is sold to the highest bidder at the price of the highest bid.

Second-price auction

Again this is a sealed bid written auction. Again the item goes to the highest bidder, but now at a price equal to the second highest bid.

Smith also includes *tâtonnement* as an auction mechanism, though he does note that there are very few real-life instances of such a mechanism.

Tâtonnement is the embodiment of the Walrasian auctioneer process; it is more appropriately discussed in section 12.3.

The theory of auctions tells us something about the outcomes of these various auction processes, but first we need some assumptions. I deliberately start with a simple set. There is a single item for sale. There are I potential buyers, $i = 1, \ldots, I$. Each of them puts a maximum cash value v_i on the object; this v_i is i's maximum willingness to pay. It is the price at which individual i's consumer surplus for the object dwindles to zero. The value v_i is assumed to be independent of all v_j ($j \neq i$); in other words, individual i would not change his or her valuation of the object in the light of anyone else's valuation of the object. This rules out certain forms of uncertainty. However, there is uncertainty in the sense that, whereas i knows his v_i, he does not know any v_j ($j \neq i$). Finally, I assume that transactions costs, including the cost of thinking, calculating, deciding and bidding, are zero. Let me number bidders so that $v_1 > v_2 > \ldots > v_I$.[2]

These assumptions make the analysis of certain auction institutions rather simple. Consider first the English auction. Clearly it is not in a bidder's own interests to raise his or her own bid, but it is always preferable to bid more than a rival whenever that bid is less than or equal to one's own valuation. It immediately follows that individual 1 (the bidder with the highest valuation) will win the item, paying a price fractionally higher than the second highest valuation (that is, $p = v_2 + \varepsilon$, where ε is a small positive number). This, of course, is a Pareto-efficient outcome, though rather uninteresting.

The second-price auction, as we shall see, is similar in some ways to the English auction, though the mechanism itself, and the analysis, is rather different. Suppose i is the winner and j makes the second highest bid. Then individual i gets surplus $v_i - b_j$ where b_j is the bid made by individual j; all other individuals get zero surplus. Since the surplus i gets (whether he or she wins or not) is independent of the bid that i makes, then the optimal bid is simply that which maximizes the probability of winning, as long as $v_i - b_j$ is positive. This occurs only if each i bids v_i: to bid less than v_i is to reduce the chance of being the highest bidder (without any offsetting benefit); to bid more than v_i is to risk (without any offsetting benefit) winning at price b_j which exceeds v_i, which would yield a negative surplus. If everyone reasons in this fashion then $b_i = v_i$ for all i. Once again, agent 1 wins, now paying a price $p = v_2$, and again the outcome is Pareto efficient. Note that the price paid under the second-price auction differs only by ε from that paid under the English auction. It is for this reason that the two mechanisms are regarded as being essentially isomorphic.

The analysis of the first-price auction is rather more complicated. Here, resort has been made by some theorists to the Nash equilibrium solution concept. Under risk neutrality it can be shown[3] that the Nash equilibrium is given by

$$b_i = \left(\frac{I-1}{I}\right)v_i \tag{12.1}$$

and so, if there are a large number of bidders, the bids are almost equal to the private valuations. However, as risk enters the picture, so may risk aversion. If it does, it is possible that bids may exceed private valuations. Furthermore, if risk aversion varies amongst the bidders it may no longer be the case that bids are ranked in the same order as valuations: for example, b_1 may be lower than b_2 if individual 1 is sufficiently less risk averse than individual 2.

The analysis of the Dutch auction is even more complicated, though here it has been shown that, like the English auction and the second-price auction, the Dutch auction and the first-price auction are isomorphic. So, under essentially the same assumptions, the results from the theory of the first-price auction carry over to the Dutch auction.

Unfortunately, the assumptions used above are rather restrictive. One particularly suspicious assumption is that of certain and independent private valuations: many would argue that valuations are uncertain and positively associated. In English auctions, for example, it seems more reasonable to assume that bids made by some participants affect the valuations of others. An assumption possibly at the opposite end of the spectrum to that used above is one used in what are known as common value auctions. In these, bidders are bidding for some item with a given common monetary value to all. If this common value was known to all, there would be little further to discuss. However, if the common value is uncertain (as is usually the case) then the problem becomes more interesting. Once again, though, assumptions are crucial: here they concern the nature of the relationship between different bidders' estimates of the common value and the common value itself. One particular assumption which has been used in many experimental studies is the following: the common value v_0 is drawn from some known uniform distribution, and the private information signal v_i given to bidder i is a random drawing from a uniform distribution on $[v_0 - \varepsilon, v_0 + \varepsilon]$ for known ε. Crucial to the story is that the winning bidder, paying a price b, gets a surplus $v_0 - b$ equal to the difference between the actual common value and the price paid.

An implication of this assumption set is that those individuals with high private signals (large v_i) are likely to have signals that exceed the value of the object. In theory, this implication should be taken into account when determining the optimal strategy; in practice, however, as we shall see in the next chapter, people frequently fall prey to what is known as the winner's curse in such auctions – namely, winning but by bidding more than the object is worth, and hence ending up with a negative surplus.

There are, additionally, various intermediate cases. The value could be partly common and partly private. Information could be multi-dimensional with, for example, some public information and some purely private. Indirect information about others' valuations and others' information signals could emerge as the bidding process continued. And so on. A useful discussion can be found in Wilson's piece on 'Bidding' in Eatwell et al. (1989, pp. 54–63).

Wilson puts the general problem rather neatly: he characterizes a trading rule (an auction mechanism) as a specification of each agent's feasible actions and the prices and trades resulting from their joint actions; a model is a specification of each trader's information and preferences. It is typically specified that each agent i knows privately some observation s_i affecting his or her preferences, 'and the restrictive assumption is adopted that the joint probability distribution of these observations and any salient unobserved random variable v is common knowledge among the participants'. This is a key assumption; without it, the search for solutions would be more difficult. Yet it is of dubious validity.

Given the above general specification, one can now proceed to a specification of an agent's strategy, which is a mapping from an agent's observation and any further observations (such as others' bids) into an action. The main difficulty with deriving an optimal strategy is that this crucially depends on what the other agents do. The usual way round this difficulty is to assume that all agents reason similarly and that they will therefore all use the same strategy: this is the assumption of symmetry. Thus, for example, in a sealed bid auction the optimal (symmetric) strategy will specify a bid as an (increasing) function of the private observation. Given the joint distribution of the private observations and the assumption of symmetry it is a relatively straightforward matter to compute this function. The unresolved problem – which will necessarily remain unresolved in a one-off auction – is whether in fact the other agents did actually use the same strategy. Unlike the Nash equilibria discussed in chapter 10, there may be no scope for *ex post* verification of the optimality of a particular player's strategy. Things become more complicated still if it is not possible to verify *ex post* that the auction mechanism functioned as it was intended to do – ask any Scotsman whether the winning bid for a house was (a) in fact the highest or (b) submitted before the other bids were opened! (The first price sealed bid mechanism is used in Scotland for house purchases and sales.)

12.3   Markets

The discussion above has been largely confined to one-sided markets: to be specific, markets in which the seller has played an essentially passive role, being prepared to sell the item as long as the price was above some reservation price. But not all markets are so organized; in some markets both sides want to play an active role. Such markets are the concern of this section.

Consider again the perfectly competitive markets of the textbook, as discussed in section 12.1. In the textbook model, all agents on both sides of the market are price-takers, and the equilibrium is a hypothetical one in the following sense: at the equilibrium price, aggregate supply equals aggregate demand so that all agents are able to trade as much as they want at that price. Although some textbooks suggest that the equilibrium (and its properties) are the consequence of large numbers of agents on each side of the market, it is actually the assumption of price-taking behaviour on both sides that drives the results. It is for this reason that theorists are somewhat concerned about the translation of this model from the world of theory into the real world – for someone has to take over the price-making role.

One possibility, as I have already remarked, is to import the largely fictitious Walrasian auctioneer as the embodiment of some kind of *tâtonnement* process. This auctioneer announces a price and the buyers and sellers respond by announcing demands and supplies at that price. If the total of the demands equals the total of the supplies, all well and good; if the demand exceeds (falls short of) the supplies, then the auctioneer suggests a higher (lower) price and the process repeats itself. It is usually assumed that no strategic behaviour happens (although it is not obvious why it should not: there are clear incentives for agents to lie – they might end up buying or selling less than they would ideally like at that price, but they might end up with a sufficiently better price).

There are other possibilities. One which has received extensive experimental investigation and which preserves the symmetry between the two sides of the market is the oral double auction. This envisages the market participants to be either physically present in the same location or telephonically linked so that they can all communicate with each other. There is an auctioneer who administers the auction process but who otherwise takes a passive role. The active role is taken by the agents themselves, who are free to call out bids (offers to buy) or asks (offers to sell) depending upon whether they are potential buyers or potential sellers. If we confine attention to a good which is traded in discrete units – for simplicity one at a time – then, at any one time, there is at most one bid and one ask outstanding. Agents can either accept the bid or ask or can make their own bid or ask. A new bid must exceed any outstanding old bid, although it could fall short of previously accepted bids; similarly a new ask must be less than any outstanding old ask, although it could be greater than previously accepted asks. The process of calling out, and accepting, bids or asks continues until no new bids or asks are forthcoming and trade has ceased.

It will readily be appreciated that this is a rather unstructured market mechanism: as Wilson (Eatwell et al., 1989, p. 60) remarks, this kind of mechanism is 'the most challenging theoretically', which is a euphemism for 'extremely difficult'. He remarks that 'since trades are consummated in process at differing prices, "market clearing" is dynamic, and, for example, traders with extra-marginal valuations in the static sense can obtain gains from trade early on. Since traders are continually motivated to estimate the distribution of subsequent bids and offers [asks], the learning process is a key feature.' He gives some references to some of the theoretical literature, but it is clear that the theoretical treatment still has some way to go. In a sense this is unfortunate since much experimental experience has been accumulated in this area; but perhaps this can be used to advance the theory.

Double auctions preserve the symmetry between the two sides in the market. Other market mechanisms do not. In the latter category there are posted price auctions in which one or other side of the market posts prices at which they are individually prepared to buy or sell. The other side reacts passively. For example, consider a sellers posted price auction. Each seller announces a price at which he or she is willing to sell (one unit of) the good. Potential buyers either accept (buy at) or reject (not buy at) the posted prices. Dynamic elements may be involved if the sellers are allowed to change their posted prices.

There are also other mechanisms: in some markets, buyers and sellers meet in a series of changing one-on-one bargaining situations; in others, buyers and sellers notify some central clearing house of their reservation prices, and the clearing house then joins together suitable buyers and sellers so that trade can be consummated. This can be done in a variety of ways, depending upon which buyers are matched with which sellers and upon the rules determining the price at which trade takes place. The obvious symmetric rule is to let the price be halfway between the seller's reservation price and the buyer's reservation price (assuming that the former is lower than the latter) so that buyer and seller share the available surplus in an obvious sense. The matching process is rather less obvious: suppose there are three buyers with reservation prices 1, 2 and 3, and three sellers also with reservation prices 1, 2 and 3. One could match buyer 1 with seller 1, buyer 2 with seller 2 and buyer 3 with seller 3 at prices 1, 2 and 3 respectively. This set of matches would generate no surplus. Alternatively, one could match seller 1 with buyer 2, seller 2 with buyer 3, at prices $1\frac{1}{2}$ and $2\frac{1}{2}$ respectively, and leave seller 3 and buyer 1 out in the cold. There are other possibilities. Quite clearly the outcome (and hence the submission of the reservation prices) will be sensitive to the matching process used.

There is some theory on some of these market processes, though not as much as one would like to see. One message that does seem to emerge from the little theory that there is, however, is that the outcome does depend quite crucially on the precise market trading mechanism. For example, within almost exactly the same market structure, different trading mechanisms can push the market to the perfectly competitive outcome or the monopoly outcome. Such differences are not trivial. It is therefore important to discover whether the experimental evidence supports the few theoretical findings. This we shall examine in chapter 13.

12.4　Conclusions

I remarked at the end of chapter 10 that that chapter had been a rather frustrating one. This chapter has turned out to be even more frustrating. The main problem is the same – namely, the question of strategic interaction between the various economic agents – but the intensity of the problem has been compounded. First, we have been dealing with many more agents in this chapter, though some of the complexity resulting from this has apparently been dispelled by the use of a symmetry argument. Second, we have been dealing with situations where the agents cannot necessarily confirm that the other agents have been behaving as had been assumed, though this complication has been somewhat side-stepped by the use of the symmetry assumption and by implicit trust in the 'rules of the game'. Third, and perhaps most important, we have been analysing some situations in this chapter, most crucially that of the oral double auction, where the 'rules of the game' themselves begin to become blurred. At times (witness an oral auction in progress!) one is verging on sociological phenomena. What a thought! In this respect it is interesting to note, as we shall see in the next chapter, that experimental economists have been at great pains to remove any possible sociological interactions from their experiments.

But there is an even deeper problem, of which we have seen only a glimpse (because I have been economical with theoretical detail): namely an implicit assumption, throughout most of these models, to the effect that the agents know the appropriate joint probability distribution of any relevant random variables in the model (though not the values of the random variables themselves) and know how to react optimally to such knowledge. The experimental evidence of the early parts of this book make one entitled to be somewhat sceptical about such an assumption. In chapter 13 we shall see whether such scepticism is warranted.

Notes

1 There is also an entry by Robert Wilson on 'Bidding' in the same volume which usefully supplements the auction entry.
2 Certain inessential complications result if some of these strict inequalities are replaced by weak inequalities.
3 On the assumption that private values are identically and independently distributed uniformly over the range $[0, \bar{v}]$. For more on this, see section 13.2.

13

Experiments on Auctions and Markets

13.1 Introduction

As I remarked in chapter 12, the division of the material (between auctions and markets) in both that chapter and this is rather arbitrary, since in a motivational sense the whole of both chapters is concerned with a single issue: the determination of prices in various kinds of markets. In general, this determination is affected by both demand and supply considerations, though in certain markets either the demand or the supply is exogenously fixed – in which case the analysis of market equilibrium is somewhat simplified. This motivates the distinction made in this chapter and chapter 12: the material on auctions is concerned with markets in which either the demand or supply is exogenously fixed (a simple example being a single-good English auction, in which the supply of the good is exogenously fixed at 1 – above the seller's reservation price, of course); the material on markets is concerned with markets in which both demand and supply depend upon price. In this case, there is a further distinction which we shall have to consider in due course: whether particular buyers and sellers play an active or a passive role in the price-setting process. This distinction does not arise in the auctions material since, with one side of the market definitionally passive (the exogenously fixed side), all the agents on the other side must be active, for otherwise they would not be market participants. Note, however, that taking an 'active role in the price-setting process' is not synonymous with 'price-setting', nor indeed with taking an 'active role in trading'; these distinctions will become clear later. Finally, I should remark that some of the trading processes used in the markets material are of an auction form: this emphasizes that it is not the trading process that determines the distinction, but the exogeneity of one side of the market.

Experiments on auctions and markets were amongst the earliest experiments conducted, going back to the 1960s and earlier. There is therefore a wealth of material available, and it would be impossible to survey and summarize it adequately in just one chapter of this book. There are good surveys elsewhere; the two papers by Plott (1982, 1989) that I have already mentioned, and numerous papers by the doyen of experimental market studies, Vernon Smith – a useful starting point is probably Smith (1989) which contains a useful overview and some key references. In Kagel and Roth's *Handbook of Experimental Economics* (forthcoming), there are chapters on auctions by Kagel and on asset markets by Sunder, in addition to Holt's chapter on industrial organization, which overlaps in coverage with the two Plott surveys cited above. Roth's (1989) survey also contains some useful introductory material.

Although some of the early experiments were not financially motivated, virtually all the recent ones have been. Induced value theory (see Smith, 1976) plays a key role in indicating the appropriate motivatory procedures. As this lies at the heart of all the experiments discussed in this chapter, it is worth spending a little time describing it. I restrict attention to goods which are available only in discrete integer amounts: 0, 1, 2, ... Further, let me initially restrict attention to situations where each demander demands at most one unit of the good. Consider first the buyers: according to conventional demand theory, there will be, all other things being equal of course, a unique reservation price for each demander for his or her one demanded unit. Denote this by P_i^d for demander i ($i = 1, \ldots, I$). The interpretation of this is as follows. Demander i will be willing to pay up to and including an amount P_i^d for one unit of the good: at price P_i^d his consumer surplus becomes zero; at prices greater than P_i^d his surplus is negative, and so he will be unwilling to buy at such prices; and at prices less than P_i^d his surplus will be positive. In other words, the lower the price paid the greater the surplus. Individual i's demand curve for the good is the simple step function shown in figure 13.1(a).[1] Suppose now that there are I demanders ($i = 1, \ldots, I$) and for convenience suppose they are numbered so that[2] $P_1^d > P_2^d > P_3^d > \ldots > P_I^d$. Then the aggregate demand curve is the step function pictured in figure 13.1(b): at a price higher than the highest reservation price P_1^d no-one will want to buy a unit of the good, so demand is 0; at a price higher than P_2^d but less than or equal to P_1^d just individual 1 will want to buy one unit, so aggregate demand is 1; at a price higher than P_3^d but less than or equal to P_2^d just individuals 1 and 2 will want to buy one unit, so aggregate demand is 2; ...; at a price less than P_I^d, all demanders $i = 1, \ldots, I$ will want to buy one unit, so aggregate demand is I.

The individual demand curve illustrated in figure 13.1(a) (and hence the aggregate demand curve illustrated in figure 13.1(b)) is induced on the I subjects playing the role of demanders in a market experiment by telling demander-subject i ($i = 1, \ldots, I$) that the experimenter will buy one unit of the good that demander-subject i acquires during the running of the experiment at a price P_i^d. Thus, if demander-subject i acquires a unit for an amount $P < P_i^d$, he can resell it to the experimenter for the amount P_i^d and hence make a profit $P_i^d - P$. This profit is obviously monotonically related to the consumer surplus of the theory: the subject trying to maximize his or her profit, therefore, is precisely the same as the demander of the theory trying

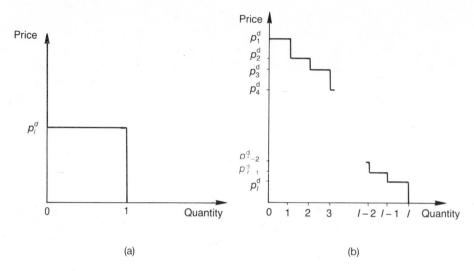

Figure 13.1   Demand: (a) i's demand; (b) aggregate demand.

to maximize his or her consumer surplus. The experiment is replicating the theory.[3]

Consider now the sellers. Again conventional theory suggests, for each supplier, that there is a unique reservation price P_j^s such that supplier j will supply one unit of the good at a price higher than P_j^s, but will not supply anything at a price less than P_j^s. Figure 13.2(a) illustrates. If we number the J suppliers ($j = 1, \ldots, J$) so that[4] $P_1^s < P_2^s < P_3^s < \ldots < P_J^s$, we can calculate the aggregate supply curve, as pictured in figure 13.2(b). The individual supply curve illustrated in figure 13.2(a) (and hence the aggregate supply curve illustrated in figure 13.2(b)) is induced on the J subjects playing the role of suppliers in a market experiment by telling supplier-subject $j(j = 1, \ldots, J)$ that the experimenter will sell one unit of the good that supplier-subject j has sold to another subject during the running of the experiment at a price P_j^s. Thus, if supplier-subject j sells a unit for an amount $P > P_j^s$, he or she can buy it off the experimenter for the amount P_j^s and hence make a profit $P - P_j^s$. As before, this profit is related to the (producer) surplus, providing the appropriate motivation. The experiment replicates the theory.

The extension, on both sides of the market, to multiple units is straightforward: the experimenter simply gives each supplier-subject a schedule specifying for how much he can resell each unit purchased back to the experimenter ('first unit 40p, second unit 35p, third unit 30p, . . .'); and the experimenter simply gives each supplier-subject a schedule specifying the cost of each unit bought from the experimenter ('first unit 35p, second unit 45p, third unit 60p, . . .'). The reader might like to explore the implications for the graphical analyses of figures 13.1 and 13.2.

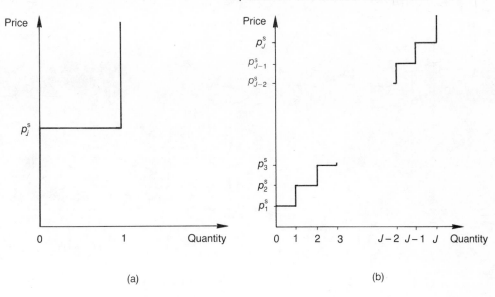

Figure 13.2   Supply: (a) j's supply; (b) aggregate supply.

The market as a whole is the combination of the demand and supply schedules. In an auction market (using my terminology) only one side of the market is induced in the manner described above – the other side is exogenous. An example is portrayed in figure 13.3(a); this is a single-unit supplied market. An example of a double-sided market is portrayed in figure 13.3(b). Note that the competitive equilibrium price in (a) is between P_{I-1}^d and P_I^d, and in (b) is between 3 and 4. (I ought to make one practical point at this stage concerning the equilibrium price in a double-sided market. As drawn in figure 13.3(b), there are several equilibrium prices – at any price between 3 and 4 there are three demanders willing to buy and three suppliers willing to sell. However, the demand and supply curves could intersect at a single price – in which case there would be a unique competitive equilibrium. A moment's reflection will show that in this case, at the point of intersection, either the demand curve is horizontal and the supply curve vertical, or vice versa. This means that one demander or one supplier (the one on the horizontal portion) is indifferent between participating (buying or selling) and not participating: the same profit (zero) results in either case. Early experiments, noting this problem, resolved it by rewarding subjects by a modest amount for participating in trade. However, more recently, the usual practice has been to arrange the demand and supply schedules so that they intersect as shown in figure 13.3(b); the resulting indeterminacy in the implied competitive equilibrium price is resolved by taking the mid-point. This procedure should be borne in mind when interpreting the results that follow.)

Having set the scene, let me now turn to one-sided – auction – markets.

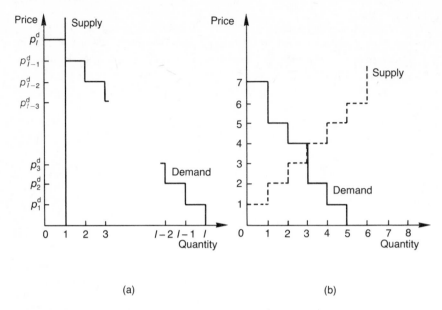

Figure 13.3 Demand and supply: (a) single-unit-supplied market; (b) double-sided market.

13.2 Auctions

Consider first the type of auction discussed in section 12.2: auctions for a single supplied good. In section 12.2 I used the notation v_i ($i = 1, \ldots, I$) to denote the maximum cash value that individual i would pay for the item in question. This v_i is simply the P_i^d of the discussion above – it is individual i's reservation value for the object in question.

In section 12.2 we explored two different scenarios with respect to the set $v_1, \ldots, v_I$ of valuations: independent private values and common values. The independent private values scenario assumes that each bidder i knows his or her own private value v_i, but does not know the values of the other v_k ($k \neq i$); in contrast, the common values scenario assumes that all bidders have the same value (if you like the 'resale value' of the item being auctioned) but none of the bidders knows this common value precisely. There are, additionally, intermediate scenarios, but I do not have the space to consider them here.

I begin with the independent private values scenario. The relevant theory was outlined in section 12.2. The theory suggested that the outcome was crucially dependent on the auction process. In section 12.2 four processes were described: the English auction, the Dutch auction, the first-price auction and the second-price auction. It will be recalled that the theory indicated that the English and the second-price auctions should be isomorphic, both leading to an outcome where the bidder with the highest private valuation, bidder 1 in our notation, won the auction, paying a price either equal to (second-price) or slightly higher than (English) the second highest valuation v_2; and that the Dutch and first-price auction should also be isomorphic, both leading to a price (under risk neutrality) of $[I - 1]/I]v_1$ paid by the winning bidder (bidder 1). There are complications in this story if risk neutrality does not hold; I shall discuss these later.

Two important early experimental investigations of these hypotheses, within the context of independent private values auctions, were conducted by Coppinger et al. (1980) and Cox et al. (1982), two of the many products of the Smith experimental organization. In these experiments, as in many subsequent experiments, the assumption – implicit in the analysis of section 12.2 – that subjects know their own values but not those of the other subjects, yet at the same time know the distribution of these other values (see my closing remarks in section 12.4) was operationalized by the experimenter drawing the I values independently from some given distribution, usually uniform over some specified range. I should also note that in many auction experiments subjects took part in several different auctions – sometimes against the same set of 'rivals', sometimes not. As far as I understand, all experimenters have interpreted such repetitions as being independent of each other, and considered as such by the subjects, there being no discussion of 'supergame' or 'repeated game' effects. This assumes, *inter alia*, that subjects did not attempt to operate a 'ring' against the experimenter!

The findings of the Cox et al. (1982) paper were that the theoretical hypotheses were not confirmed: they found higher prices (bids) in the first-price auction than in any of the others, all of which showed fairly similar prices. The English auction prices observed by Cox et al. were somewhat above those predicted by the theory (bidders bid their own private valuations) but this is largely accounted for by the fact that there were significant discrete gaps between the allowable bids. Implicit in the above is the implication that the first-price and Dutch auctions did not result in the same prices, contradicting the theoretical isomorphism noted above. One interesting result concerned the efficiency of the various processes, where efficiency is measured[5] in terms of the percentage of auctions where the high value bidder wins the item (this is the Pareto-efficient outcome). Cox et al. (1982) found the English auction the most efficient (97 per cent), followed by the second-price auction (95.7 per cent), the first-price auction (90.2 per cent) and the Dutch auction (80 per cent) respectively.

Coppinger et al. (1980) found similar results, although Cox et al. extended the analysis to explore the effect of the number of bidders on behaviour. (Recall from equation (12.1) that the (risk-neutral) Nash equilibrium strategy in the first-price auction is dependent on I, the number of bidders: as I increases then so should all bids.) Cox et al. (1982) observed the same phenomena as Coppinger et al. (1980): first-price auctions, though theoretically isomorphic to Dutch auctions, systematically produced higher prices. Moreover, the bids in the first-price auction were systematically higher than the risk-neutral Nash equilibrium (RNNE) (see equation (12.1)), except when $I = 3$ ('explained' by Cox et al. in terms of 'failure of the assumption of noncooperative behavior'). This systematic finding was the foundation for much subsequent experimental work and debate.

Much of the subsequent debate revolved around one possible explanation for these experimental observations (that bids in first-price auctions tend to be systematically above the RNNE) to the effect that bidders were not risk neutral. To illustrate this, let me extend the formula quoted in equation (12.1) to the case discussed above: here the bids b_i ($i = 1, \ldots, I$) are independently drawn from a uniform distribution over the range $[\underline{v}, \overline{v}]$. In this case (see, for example, Harrison, 1989a) the formula becomes

$$b_i = \underline{v} + \frac{I-1}{I}(v_i - \underline{v}) \qquad (13.1)$$

for a set of risk-neutral agents. Now suppose instead that subject i is constant relative risk averse with Arrow–Pratt relative-risk-aversion index $1 - r_i$, so that his or her utility function is

$$U_i(y) = y_i^{r_i} \qquad (13.2)$$

Further, suppose that the set $r_1, \ldots, r_I$ is independently drawn from the uniform distribution on $[0, 1]$. Then it can be shown that the Nash equilibrium bid function is given by

$$b_i = \underline{v} + \frac{I-1}{I-1+r_i}(v_i - \underline{v}) \qquad (13.3)$$

Note that equation (13.3) reduces to equation (13.1) when $r_i = 1$, that is, when subject i is risk neutral. Note also that, as r_i increases, the optimal bid b_i decreases: recalling that the risk-aversing index is $1 - r_i$, it follows that as risk aversion increases then so do bids. This is the 'risk aversion explanation' of the finding that bidding in first-price auctions tends to be above the RNNE.

Cox et al. (1982), in effect, tested whether their experimental data supported equation (13.1) (risk neutrality) or equation (13.3) (risk aversion). Given the experimenters' control over the distribution of the v_i, combined with the experimenters' assumption about the distribution of the r_i, this effectively reduces to a test of whether the distribution of bids coincides with that implied by equation (13.1) (a uniform distribution over $[\underline{v}, \{\underline{v} + (I-1)\overline{v}\}/I]$) or is a distribution shifted rightwards. For some values of I, the risk-neutrality hypothesis was accepted; for other values the risk-aversion hypothesis was accepted. Note, however, that these are very much indirect tests of the risk-attitude hypotheses, since no attempt was made in these experiments to measure subjects' attitude to risk. In a later paper, Cox et al. (1985) remark: 'the parameter r_i is not observable; it is a construct based on an interpretation of what is driving behavior, and other interpretations are potentially admissible' (p. 162). It is not clear to me what is meant by this: I see no reason why, in a prior experiment, the subjects' risk-aversion parameters could not be estimated using the methods discussed in part II of this book; these estimates could then be used to test directly the constant relative risk averse (CRRA) model of bidding behaviour.

Cox et al. (1985), however, persevered with indirect tests – which are of considerable interest in their own right, as they indicate how experimental methods can be used to distinguish carefully between competing models. First, they noted that, according to the CRRA model, if $\underline{v}$ is put equal to zero then the optimal bids (see equation (13.3)) are a linear function of the vs. Thus if $\bar{v}$ is doubled, then so should all the bids; if $\bar{v}$ is tripled, then so should all the bids. (This, of course, is an immediate consequence of constant relative risk aversion.) Second, they noted that if the payoff to the winning subject changes from $v_i - b_i$ to $a(v_i - b_i)^2$ then it is 'as if' the risk-aversion parameter in equation (13.3) changes from r_i to $2r_i$. As Cox et al. (1985) remark, this 'provides strong quantitative predictions of the effect of the transformation. A weaker qualitative prediction is that the individual will bid less under the transformation.' The experimental results did not, however, agree with this prediction. Third, they noted that if the payoff mechanism was changed so that the winning bidder, instead of receiving $v_i - b_i$ dollars, was 'paid' $v_i - b_i$ lottery tickets and then participated in a lottery in which he or she received $\$x_1$ with probability $(v_i - b_i)/\bar{v}$ and $\$x_2$ $(x_2 > x_1)$ with probability $1 - (v_i - b_i)/\bar{v}$ (the losers all received $\$x_2$) this should induce risk-neutral behaviour, and hence a predictable shift from the behaviour induced by the original payoff mechanism. This, of course, is the random lottery payoff mechanism, which was discussed in chapter 11. The experiment did not appear to induce risk-neutral behaviour when the random lottery payoff mechanism was used: only one out of 12 subjects displayed risk-neutral behaviour. Even more surprisingly, the qualitative prediction (that bidding should decrease with a switch to the random lottery payoff mechanism) was not supported by the experimental evidence.

Some considerable debate has taken place concerning the interpretation of these and other results in the auction literature. Let me focus attention on the repeated finding that bidders in first-price auctions tend to bid significantly higher than the RNNE prediction. This has been rationalized by some as clear evidence of (heterogeneous) risk-averse behaviour (see Cox et al. 1985 above); others have alternative explanations (such as perceptual errors). Others still regard the phenomena as evidence of lack of experimental control. A particularly clear statement of the latter point of view is in Harrison (1989a), a paper which has stirred the passions of the experimental community throughout America. Let me focus attention on his main point that, while the behaviour of subjects in first-price auctions appears to deviate significantly and systematically from that predicted by the RNNE when measured in terms of the bids themselves, the implications in terms of the departure of actual payoffs from optimal payoffs are by no means significant. This is the flat maximum critique which we discussed at some length in part III. The point is simple: the graph of the payoff to the subject as a function of the decision of the subject, in these and other experiments, is extremely flat-topped, so that sizeable departures from optimality in terms of the decision have relatively trivial implications for the departure from the maximum of the payoff. Given that it costs to think, it might therefore not be surprising if subjects' behaviour, in such circumstances, appears to depart 'significantly' from the optimal.

Harrison presents some revealing illustrations (of the costs to the subjects of departure from optimal behaviour) both in his experiments and in those of others. Generally he concludes that these costs are extremely small, so that what may appear significantly deviant behaviour when measured in decision-space is, in fact, insignificantly deviant when measured in payoff-space. This suggests that one should be careful when talking about 'significant' departures from theoretical predictions observed in experiments. In turn, it suggests that one ought to anticipate such considerations when devising one's experiments (and deciding on the magnitudes of the payoffs) in the first place. Of course, if Harrison's critique is correct it does suggest a testable hypothesis:[6] behaviour approaches the optimal as the magnitudes of the payoffs increase. It will be of interest to explore this hypothesis in future work.

I consider now the experimental literature on common value auctions; in one obvious sense they are at the opposite end of the spectrum to the independent private value auctions discussed above. Recall that in common value auctions there is a common but unknown value for the good being auctioned. In many experiments this is operationalized as follows: first, the common value is determined (by the experimenter) by a random draw from a uniform distribution $[\underline{v}, \bar{v}]$ (where $\underline{v}$ and $\bar{v}$ are known). Denote this common value by v_0. Subjects are not told this. Instead, they are each given a private information signal (v_i for subject i, $i = 1, \ldots, I$) drawn independently from the uniform distribution $[v_0 - \varepsilon, v_0 + \varepsilon]$ where ε is a known number. ε is, of course, subject to experimental control: a relatively small value indicates relatively accurate private information; a relatively large value indicates relatively inaccurate private information. Subjects are then asked to submit (written) bids for the item. After the bids are submitted, the highest bidder (bidding an amount b) gets paid $v_0 - b$; the other bidders get paid nothing. So the true value v_0 of the item being auctioned is revealed only after all the bids have been submitted. Note that the winning bid may exceed v_0, in which case the 'winning' bidder loses money as a result of his or her successful bid. This eventuality is known in the literature as the winner's curse; it has been the subject of much experimental investigation.

A particularly informative and systematic investigation of the winner's curse phenomenon (within the context of the first-price sealed bid common values auction scenario described above) can be found in Kagel and Levin (1986). This paper is of additional interest in that it relates the experimental findings to economic policy issues concerned with the US government's outer continental shelf lease sales. It accordingly provides policy-makers with useful information for correctly deciding the appropriate auction procedures for government assets. Kagel and Levin report on a series of eight auction experiments (each covering up to 32 market periods, that is, separate auctions) with experienced bidders. These are subjects who have survived earlier auction experiments without going bankrupt,[7] the idea being to counter suggestions that the winner's curse is found only with naive subjects, although Kagel and Levin's procedure does raise the possibility that their subjects were not only experienced but also risk averse. The basic scenario was as discussed above, with the basic hypothesis under test being that the bidders followed the RNNE strategy predicted by economic theory. For private values in the range[8] $[\underline{v} + \varepsilon, \bar{v} - \varepsilon]$ this can be shown to be given by (see Kagel and Levin, 1986, p. 899)

$$b_i = v_i - \varepsilon + Y \qquad (13.4)$$

where

$$Y = \frac{2\varepsilon}{I+1} \exp\left[-\frac{I}{2\varepsilon} (v_i - \underline{v} - \varepsilon) \right]$$

If bidders use this RNNE strategy, then the expected profits for the high bidder are $2\varepsilon/(I+1) - Y$; moreover the subject with the highest private value always bids the highest, and therefore always wins; this clearly follows from equation (13.4). It will be noted that the RNNE strategy discounts the private information signal by the amount $\varepsilon - Y$. This discounting is necessary since, although all private signals are unconditionally unbiased estimates of the true common value, the highest private value is an overestimate of the common value. More precisely (see Kagel and Levin, 1986, p. 900)

$$E(v_0 \mid V_i = v_1) = v_i - \frac{\varepsilon(I-1)}{I+1} \qquad (13.5)$$

If bidders do not take this overestimation (sufficiently) into account, then they might fall prey to the winner's curse.

Kagel and Levin's experimental results generally reject the RNNE prediction: bidding is consistently higher than the RNNE prediction. Nevertheless, they conclude that the actual outcomes 'come closer to the RNNE predictions than to the winner's curse in auctions with small numbers (3–4) of bidders'. They observe, however, despite some sizeable discounting with larger groups, that the discounting is not sufficiently high to avoid consistently negative profits with such larger groups. So the winner's curse is observed even with experienced subjects. Kagel and Levin explore a number of subsidiary hypotheses, some relating to the impact of an additional public information signal (either a further drawing from the uniform distribution on $[v_0 - \varepsilon, v_0 + \varepsilon]$ or the announcement of the lowest private information signal v_l) and others relating to strategic and learning effects in the data. This study is an excellent example of how experimental work should be performed.

Dyer et al. (1989) add a further twist to the 'inexperienced versus experienced' debate: they contrast the behaviour of 'experts' (experienced business executives in the construction contract industry) with 'naïve' student subjects. The 'experts' group consisted of four subjects, all but one of whom had had many years' experience in the actual bid preparation process; in contrast, the naive group of student subjects had had no prior laboratory (or presumably 'real-life') auction experience. Surprisingly, Dyer et al. found that the experts were just as prone to the winner's curse (and more generally to the overbidding observed by Kagel and Levin) as the naive subjects. Dyer et al. spend some time discussing this phenomenon, and relating it to the fact that the experts, who were highly successful in their work, were presumably not subject to the winner's curse in their professional life. Dyer et al. emphatically reject the criticism that the experts did not take the experiment seriously (*inter alia* pointing out that predicted profits under the RNNE approached $100 – not a trivial sum for a three-hour involvement), and conclude instead that 'the executives have learned a set of situation specific rules of thumb which permit them to avoid the winner's curse in the field but which could not be applied in the lab'. This is a very revealing statement, which all economists could fruitfully contemplate.

13.3   Markets

This is without doubt the single area in which most experimental work has been undertaken; a book could easily be written on this area alone. As a consequence, the treatment here can do little more than give a flavour of the experimental work that has been done and of the type of results that have emerged. The focus of the experimental work is largely on the convergence of 'competitive markets', with the key question relating to whether the competitive equilibrium is attained, and if so, how fast it is attained; and whether the nature of the trading process used in the market affects either the attainment itself or the speed of the attainment. At a fairly early stage in the experimental investigation of such issues it was repeatedly observed that one particular trading mechanism, the oral double auction, was especially efficient at attaining the competitive equilibrium, and attaining it fast. As a consequence, much of the experimental literature is concerned with studying this mechanism and in using it in various contexts.[9] I shall begin with a brief overview of this literature; my discussion will also include reference to other 'double' market mechanisms (such as the Walrasian *tâtonnement* process). I shall then examine various 'single' market mechanisms, both of an auction and of a posted type. I shall then return to the double auction mechanism and study its implications in various models of asset markets; these enable the economist, *inter alia*, to explore the effect of speculation on market behaviour, the influence of expectations and the possibility of experimentally generating real-life market phenomena such as bubbles and crashes. For completeness, the section will conclude with a brief examination of oligopolistic and monopolistic markets.

There are now several computerized implementations of the 'Oral' double auction mechanism (PLATO, MUODA and one by Harrison marketed alongside Varian's *Intermediate Microeconomics* text); these allow for trading in multiple units as well as in multiple markets. The term 'oral' with respect to these is somewhat of a misnomer as subjects communicate through the medium of the computer rather than orally, but the original experiments were conducted orally, as indeed are many still. In addition, of course, there are many real-life oral double auction markets, such as LIFFE in London.

Possibly the earliest oral double auction experiment was conducted by Smith (1962) and, although it was not financially motivated (as most of the present experiments are), it remains a model of its kind. Figures 13.4(a) and 13.4(b), reproduced from charts 1 and 2 of Smith (1962), capture the essence of the results reported in that paper. In both these figures the left-hand graph portrays the demand and supply schedules induced on the subjects by the mechanism described in section 13.1; these figures will bring to mind figure 13.3(b). In figure 13.4(a), for example, it can be seen that there were 11 supplier-subjects in that particular experiment, with valuations of $0.75, $1.00, $1.25, $1.50, $1.75, $2.00, $2.25, $2.50, $2.75, $3.00 and $3.25. (Recall that these are the amounts that the experimenter would charge to supply a unit of the good to the 11 suppliers.) Likewise, there were 11 demander-subjects with the same set of valuations. (Here they represent the prices at which the experimenter would buy a unit of the good from each of the 11 demanders.) The competitive equilibrium price is $2.00. At that price the supplier-subjects with valuations $0.75, $1.00, $1.25, $1.50, $1.75 and $2.00 would each supply a unit, making respective profits of $1.25, $1.00, $0.75, $0.50, $0.25 and $0.00; note that this final supplier, the marginal supplier, has no real incentive to trade. Further, at the equilibrium price of $2.00 the demander-subjects with valuations $2.00, $2.25, $2.50, $2.75, $3.00 and $3.25 would each buy a unit, making respective profits of $0.00, $0.25, $0.50, $0.75, $1.00 and $1.25; here the first of these is the marginal trader. Note that the competitive equilibrium price produces the largest aggregate monetary payoff/surplus.

In figures 13.4(a) and 13.4(b) the right-hand side graph portrays the results of the experiments carried out by Smith for these particular demand and supply schedules. In figure 13.4(a) there were five trading periods, in figure 13.4(b) three. The repetition is implemented simply by re-starting the trading process: in Smith's experiment each subject was given the same valuation in each of the trading periods. Within any trading period, the following auction rules were used: supplier-subjects could shout out an ask price, indicating the price at which he or she would be willing to sell his or her one unit, as long as this was less than any existing ask. Similarly, demander-subjects could shout out a bid price, indicating the price at which he or she would be willing to buy one unit, as long as this was more than any existing bid. At any time, a supplier could accept any bid on offer and a demander could accept any ask on offer; these would constitute trades and are indicated on the right-hand sides of figures 13.4(a) and 13.4(b) as a graph of the price accepted against the transaction number. The graph stops when trading ceases in that period. So, in figure 13.4(b) there were five transactions, at prices ranging from $1.70 to $1.90.

The immediate feature of these graphs, and indeed of many hundreds more produced by Smith and other experimenters, is the almost immediate convergence to a price very close to the competitive equilibrium price. The values of α given in the figures provide one measure of the 'speed' of convergence: α measures (100 times) the ratio of the standard deviation of prices at which trade took place to the competitive equilibrium price.

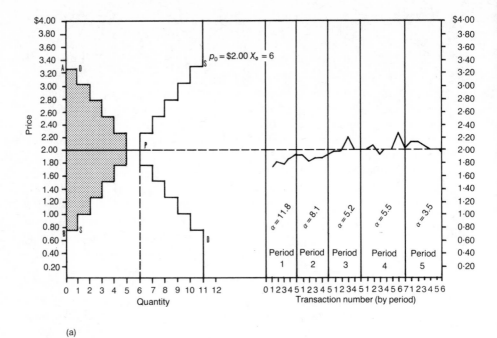

(a)

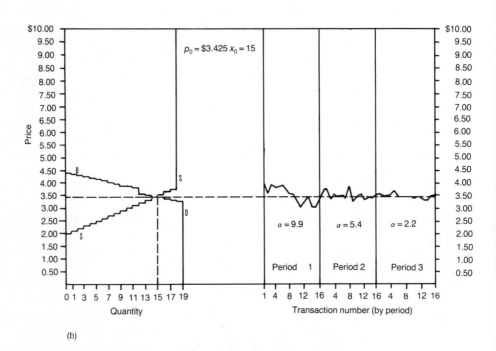

(b)

Figure 13.4 Smith's oral double auction experiments.
Sources: (a) Smith, 1962, chart 1, p. 113; (b) Smith, 1962, chart 2, p. 118

Generally, α decreases through the trading periods: thus not only do we get convergence but we get convergence which is increasingly rapid as experience is gained. An alternative way of indicating this is through the Pareto efficiency of the outcome: as Plott (1989, p. 1122) summarizes: 'Efficiency levels tend to converge to near 100 percent'.

Smith conducted a number of variations on this basic theme, investigating the robustness of these findings to a number of factors: the shape and relative position of the demand and supply schedules; a shift in one or other of the two schedules; and a restriction of bidding to one side of the market. Following Smith, numerous other experimentalists have replicated and extended his analyses. Generally the broad finding, that convergence to the competitive equilibrium is attained and is attained rapidly, is confirmed time and time again. A few refinements have been found: for example, that the path to equilibrium seems to be from above (below) if consumer's (producer's) surplus is greater than producer's (consumer's) surplus. Some authors have tried to characterize the nature of the dynamic adjustment path (see Plott, 1989, p. 1123) but with rather inconclusive results.

For anyone new to experimentation, the manual running of an oral double auction is a stimulating way to start: such an experiment is easy to run, is entertaining for both experimenter and subjects (it is also ideal as a teaching aid) and is instructive. Manual operation does require some strict control (a room full of people shouting out prices and acceptances can get rather chaotic) and strict enforcement of rules is necessary. The main disadvantage is that record-keeping is rather tedious; also it is difficult to control for 'sociological' factors. The running of a double auction on a computer therefore has certain advantages: the computer does all the accounting and record-keeping; it can enforce the rules strictly (so that the first person who accepts a bid or an ask is the one who carries out the trade); and it removes certain 'sociological' features that the typical economist might want to exclude. There are inevitably some disadvantages: some subjects may be 'allergic' to the computer; it may take them more time to learn; and it may remove certain features of real-life markets that are crucial. However, computerization in the area of market experiments does not seem to suffer from the problem identified in the public goods area – that subjects may not believe what is being told to them; there is no reason why that should be the case.

The double auction process has been used in many experiments. One experiment of particular interest is that reported by Isaac and Plott (1981) which examines the effect of price controls on market outcomes. The price controls being studied were a series of price ceilings and price floors. The implementation of, say, a price ceiling in an experiment is straightforward. Isaac and Plott informed their subjects: 'During this experiment, no bids or offers may be made or accepted at a price greater than ____ cents. Of course, you may still make or accept bids or offers at a price less than or equal to this amount.' Isaac and Plott investigated the effect of binding controls (when the ceiling (floor) was strictly below (above) the competitive equilibrium price) and non-binding controls. Interestingly, they found that convergence to the competitive equilibrium (when the control was non-binding) and to the control (when it was binding) occurred regularly; convergence was particularly rapid in the latter case. However, they found also that non-binding controls seemed to affect the average level of prices: furthermore, price levels and efficiency could be influenced by removing non-binding controls. These and other results have important implications for governments' regulatory practices.

Other double-sided, but not auction, mechanisms have been investigated experimentally. Two are of interest: one by Joyce (1984), which was effectively a *tâtonnement* mechanism, and one by Smith et al. (1982) which was a sealed bid–offer mechanism. The former was an implementation of the Walrasian auctioneer device discussed in chapter 12: an auctioneer would start with an arbitrary price and subjects would indicate how many units of the hypothetical good they would like to trade at that price. The experimenter would then calculate the excess demand, and the auctioneer's price would change according to a simple linear rule. This would continue until the market cleared exactly. Joyce found that trading in all markets was near the competitive equilibrium, though prices did not settle down to the competitive equilibrium price; strategic elements might have been an influential factor in producing this result. Smith et al. (1982) studied sealed bid–offer mechanisms: subjects submitted written and sealed bids and asks. The experimenter arranged these respectively in order to produce a market demand and supply curve like that of figure 13.3(b). The price was determined as the intersection of these two curves (if it was not unique, the mid-point of the intersection set was chosen). Smith et al.'s main concern was in comparing the efficiency of this process with the (oral) double auction process discussed above. It was found that the latter was more efficient. Again this has important implications for public policy.

Similar exercises have been conducted comparing the outcome and efficiency of various double-sided market mechanisms with various single-sided market mechanisms. The latter are ones in which the price announcements (either oral or posted) are made solely by one side of the market, with the other side essentially reacting passively, either accepting or rejecting the announced bids or asks. Plott and Smith (1978) made a systematic study of two such one-sided trading mechanisms: an oral auction in which buyers (sellers) make repeated oral price bids (offers) for the exchange of many units, one unit at a time; and a posted-price institution in which price quotations cannot be altered during the exchange period. Their conclusions were that both mechanisms revealed high efficiencies, with oral markets consistently close to 100 per cent. Plott and Smith also tentatively concluded that price convergence was rather different from that in the double mechanisms, but subsequent research has indicated that this is not in fact the case. The effect of price controls in markets with single-sided mechanisms was investigated by Coursey and Smith (1983); they concluded that the results of Isaac and Plott with respect to price controls and double-sided mechanisms carried over to single-sided mechanisms.

The distinction between oral mechanisms (in which prices can be changed by the traders during the trading process) and posted-price mechanisms (in which prices are fixed throughout a particular market period) merits some further discussion. Intuition would suggest that oral mechanisms are more flexible, enabling traders to respond to information revealed during the trading process. Indeed, this is the argument 'explaining' the rather surprising results of an experiment by Williams (1987) which explored not only the convergence properties of a market, over a sequence of market periods, but also the accuracy of traders' forecasts of future prices. Williams found that forecasts, which were made before trading began, were not as efficient as the markets themselves – possibly because the latter uses information revealed during the trading process.[10] In posted-price processes such information is not available. Plott (1989, p. 1140) reports on some experiments designed to shed light on the implications. He concludes that the posted-price mechanism does lead to market prices close to the equilibrium prices, with efficiencies approaching the 90–100 per cent range. Prices tend to be higher in posted-price markets than in oral double auctions, and efficiencies are lower. Other experiments confirm Plott's basic conclusion: 'The posted-price institution induces an upward pressure on prices ... and a downward pressure on efficiency.' One explanation may revolve around risk aversion.

One final market mechanism that ought to be mentioned is bilateral negotiation: buyers and sellers meet in pairs and negotiate individual contracts; if agreement is not reached, discussion is adjourned and the buyer and seller attempt to find another seller and buyer respectively with whom to negotiate. This is a rather difficult mechanism to study experimentally, since the question of experimental control is rather tricky. Clearly the experimenter needs to exclude certain undesirable features of person-to-person bargaining, such as threats of physical violence (which in real-life would be excluded by law), whilst at the same time permitting the full exploitation of all bargaining possibilities. Face-to-face bargaining introduces further complications that some economists might want to exclude (sociological and even psychological factors), though it is clear from experimental studies that such complications are important. The experiment could be designed so that all communication is made with (experimenter-censored) text messages sent through a net-worked computer system (though this has several disadvantages) or telephones could be used (thereby removing some of the sociological features). Possibly the earliest market experiments, reported in Chamberlin (1948), were conducted with all subjects in one room free to circulate and negotiate face to face with whom they pleased.

A study by Hong and Plott (1982) used telephone contacts: buyers and sellers could phone each other to negotiate and agree trades. This study revealed that, initially, traded prices were highly dispersed, though with time the price dispersion decreased. Much depends, of course, on the 'rules of the game', and, particularly, on whether agreed trades are publicly revealed to the other traders. Hong and Plott found efficiencies in the 80–90 per cent range. (Efficiency here measures subjects' actual earnings as a percentage of the maximum possible earnings; it therefore measures the percentage of the potential surplus actually achieved through trade. The competitive equilibrium, of course, yields 100 per cent efficiency.) A further study by Grether and Plott (1984) revealed similar results. This was a rather sophisticated study in terms of the communication mechanism employed: both telephones and digital display devices were used; the latter were designed for price announcements. The experiment also had a rather lop-sided design (it was specifically intended to shed light on a particular problem in industrial organization policy), with two large sellers (each with 35 per cent of the market) and two small sellers (15 per cent each). So it is interesting that it yielded similar results to those of Hong and Plott (1982): with time, the spread of prices is reduced and the competitive equilibrium is approached. A further discussion of these and other studies can be found in Plott (1989, pp. 1136–40). The general conclusion that seems to emerge, not surprisingly, is that bilateral negotiation does lead to the competitive outcome, but much more slowly and with greater variance than the other mechanisms discussed above.

The above market studies have been effectively concerned with (single) commodity markets, with values induced by the mechanism discussed in section 13.1. I now turn to an important new branch of market experimental models: the study of asset markets. Here values are induced through dividends, as in the real world. However, in contrast with the real world, the various experimental asset markets discussed here have a finite life; this removes one potentially crucial 'real-life' factor.

The first question that any experimental study of an asset market needs to address is: why should the asset be traded? In the commodity market studies the answer is straightforward: different values (to different subjects) are induced by the experimenter giving subjects different reservation prices (valuations). Moreover, buyers and sellers quite clearly have different motivations. In the asset market context the answer is not so straightforward. One possibility is to let the value of dividends differ from subject to subject; another is to induce differing expectations about the future path of uncertain dividends (either objectively or subjectively[11]). One important early study which used the former technique is that of Forsythe et al. (1982); it may be helpful to spend a little time examining this in detail.

The basic structure is simple: the experiment lasted for several market years, separated from each other in a physical sense though not necessarily in a learning (or possibly strategic) sense. Within each year there were two periods A and B and one tradeable asset. This asset paid a dividend at the end of each of these periods proportional to the amount of the asset held. All subjects started out with the same initial holding of the asset and the same stock of experimental money.[12] The asset became worthless at the end of the year. In order to induce trade in the asset, Forsythe et al. specified different dividend payments for different types of subjects. Thus, for example, in their first experimental treatment, the nine subjects were randomly allocated to three types (three to each type) with dividend payments specified as in table 13.1. Trade is now beneficial. I should note that short sales were not permitted.

The oral double auction mechanism was employed. The purpose of the experiment was to test a number of hypotheses about market convergence:

Table 13.1 Dividend specifications in Forsythe et al.'s experiment

Type	Dividend at end of period A	Dividend at end of period B
I	300	50
II	50	300
III	150	250

first, concerning each market period considered in isolation; second, concerning the two market periods taken together. For market period B, things are relatively straightforward: the competitive equilibrium prediction is simply that the price of the asset in period B should equal the maximum of the period B dividends (300 in table 13.1). This, of course, is the capital loss incurred by those who hold it at the end of period B. For period A, things are rather more complicated. The 'naive expectations hypothesis', as termed by Forsythe et al., implies that the competitive equilibrium price in period A is the maximum of the sum of period A and period B dividends. (Table 13.1 shows that this maximum is 400; type III subjects would bid up to that amount.) This, however, assumes that the asset will be bought in period A and held to the end of the year, thus ignoring the possibility of trade in period B. If the possibility of trade in period B is taken into account, then the competitive equilibrium prediction is that the price in period A should equal the sum of the maximum dividend in period A plus the maximum dividend in period B – 600 in table 13.1. This prediction is termed the 'perfect foresight hypothesis' by Forsythe et al. They also test a number of subsidiary hypotheses.

The results, illustrated in figure 13.5 (taken from figure 2 of Forsythe et al.) are fascinating: in the A periods the traded prices start off around the naïve-expectations-hypothesis price, but they drift upwards towards the perfect-foresight-hypothesis price by the end of the eight year; the period B prices converge very rapidly to the predicted price. The convergence process, termed by the authors the 'swingback hypothesis', is reminiscent of an iterative dynamic programming algorithm: 'the last period converges first and the convergence works back from this to earlier periods [sic] as the years replicate.' The results provide good support for the rational expectations hypothesis, yet at the same time provide useful ammunition for those who argue that it takes time for rational expectations to work: the adjustment to the perfect foresight equilibrium is not instantaneous, and so if there were continuing exogenous shocks operating on the system, convergence might never be attained. These are important findings. Further work in this general area includes that of Forsythe et al. (1984), who consider further the impact of futures markets on convergence, and that of Friedman et al. (1983, 1984) who include stochastic dividend structures. All, however, are concerned with what Harrison (1989b) terms 'short-lived assets'.

Long-lived assets are studied in an important paper by Smith et al. (1988), which lays to rest the notion that one needs differential dividends or different objective distributions to induce asset trading. In this paper,

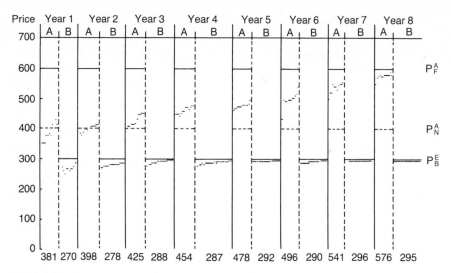

Figure 13.5   The asset experiment of Forsythe et al.
Source: Forsythe et al., 1982, figure 2, p. 550

the single asset with which subjects are (differentially) endowed has a life of 15 or 30 periods (depending upon the treatment). In each period it pays a dividend, which is *ex ante* risky. *Ex post* all subjects receive the same dividend rate (so that their dividend receipts are the same multiple of their holdings of the asset in that period); the actual dividend rate in any period is determined by a random draw from a known probability distribution – in all instances a four-point discrete distribution. Note that all subjects face the same objective distribution concerning dividends each period. Trading was carried out using the 'oral' double auction technique as computerized on PLATO.

Smith et al. (1988) report on 27 experiments carried out with this basic structure. The main hypothesis under test, of course, is that the mean price follows that predicted by rational expectations; for a risk-neutral subject this can easily be determined. Using backward induction it can be shown that the rational expectations price must equal the expected sum of the dividends remaining to the end of that repetition of the experiment – recall that the asset has a finite life (15 or 30 periods). For example, in design 1 the dividend distribution was uniform over the four values (0, 4, 8, 20), with mean 8, so the rational expectations price was 8 in the final period, 16 in the penultimate period, 24 in the period before that, and so on. Note crucially that the rational expectations price decreases towards zero as time passes, since the asset is ultimately worthless. Smith et al. found that this rarely happened: more common was a bubble followed by a crash. For example, the traded price, instead of falling through time, stayed approximately constant until almost the final period of the experiment, when its value crashed towards zero. This phenomenon was repeatedly observed, both with inexperienced subjects and experienced subjects – though it happened rather less with the latter group. Interestingly, when the same group returns for a third market, the bubble disappears, indicating that experience, of particular situations, does help. Perhaps generalized learning would occur after further experience? The Smith et al. paper lays the foundation for much fascinating experimental work.

I now conclude this section on market experiments with a return to commodity markets and a brief examination of experiments involving monopolists and oligopolists. In a sense one could argue that the latter have already been covered by the material above since in many of the experiments reported the number of subjects has often been very small. Indeed that was one of the surprising features of much of this work – that competitive outcomes would result even with small numbers of subjects. As Plott (1989, pp. 1149–53) remarks, this may well have been the consequence of the trading mechanism employed. For example, in a genuinely oral double auction market a subject who tries to exploit his or her oligopoly power, by suggesting 'outrageous' prices for trade, often provokes hostility and similarly outrageous responses from the other participants: subjects prefer not to trade rather than trade at unfair prices, even if it means harming themselves. This may be a rather sociological phenomenon (similar to ones encountered in chapter 11) which is peculiar to that particular market mechanism. Nevertheless, Plott (1989, section 4.2) reports numerous oligopolistic experiments, of a double-sided nature, which converge to the competitive equilibrium. He also (section 4.3) reports on one-sided markets where this convergence is not so pronounced. In such one-sided markets the demand side is effectively suppressed so that attention focuses on the supply side. For example, in a number of studies of duopoly using just two subjects (one for each duopoly and no demanders), the two subjects were simply given a profit table showing their profit as a function of their decision and their rival's decision; this can simply be expressed in matrix form. This type of experiment is rather far removed from the other market experiments reported in this section, and is more akin to the game experiments of chapter 11. It is perhaps not surprising, therefore, that the results of such experiments are also reminiscent of the results of the experiments of chapter 11.

A small number of monopoly experiments reveal that the market outcome is sensitive to the trading mechanism. When a single-unit oral double auction mechanism is used (see Smith, 1981; Plott, 1989) the traded price tends to oscillate between the competitive price and the monopoly price; when a posted-ask mechanism is used, convergence to the monopoly price is rapid. Perhaps this is not surprising, though it does underline the point that market institutions affect market outcomes, and these may be better regulatory devices than direct market regulation. Arguments along similar lines suggest that contestability is a desirable property which should be fostered by governments, since it apparently keeps pricing close to the competitive equilibrium even in the presence of a monopoly. Such arguments have been investigated experimentally by Coursey et al. (1984). Using the PLATO posted-offer mechanism with five buyers and two sellers, one an incumbent and one a potential entrant, Coursey et al. explored a number of hypotheses concerning contestability. Their results were mixed, though some broad conclusions could be drawn: first, in the absence of contestability, prices tended to converge to the monopoly price; second, with contestability and with zero entry costs prices were nearer to the competitive equilibrium outcome, and nearer to those observed when entry costs were not zero. Some instabilities were observed, and generally the results were not as clear cut as one might have hoped. There is obviously great potential for further work in this area.

13.4 Conclusions

Although covering a lot of material in this chapter, we have really only skimmed the surface of what is available: in the area of markets[13] in general more experimental work has been done than in any other area. The results that have emerged are important for a number of reasons: first, they have indicated which theoretical results seem to be robust to experimental investigation and which results are sensitive to changes in institutional detail; second, they have indicated potentially fruitful lines of theoretical inquiry in areas in which existing theory is inadequate or non-existent; third, they have indicated important policy implications which are potentially of considerable value for governmental regulatory practice; fourth, they have confirmed the strength and power of experimental methodology.

A number of existing avenues for further experimental work are now open. In my opinion, the most exciting are those concerned with asset markets. Already, further work to that discussed above has been done and more is under way: clear extensions to forward, futures and option markets are open for experimental investigation. These seem to have enormous potential. If experimentalists can get a firmer handle on the behaviour of financial markets than that currently provided by theory then the implications, and potential benefits, for financial regulatory practice would be enormous. If experimentalists can help capitalist economies to avoid stock market crashes, the rewards would be great. The ability of experimental economics to create bubbles and crashes within the laboratory is encouraging – if rather depressing – and if we can learn further why such bubbles and crashes occur even in simple experimental markets, then knowledge would be greatly advanced. My own feeling is that the main change in experimental practice that needs to be implemented is the abandonment of the finite known life for experimental assets. The introduction instead of random-horizon models appears to be the appropriate response; here the lessons learnt from the experiment of chapter 8 would be valuable. At EXEC, we are exploring the possibility of implementing a real-time experimental stock market on an ongoing basis. Entry and/or exit could be on a random basis and entrants could be endowed with certain assets. Traded prices could be published daily, and the whole operation could be administered through the University's mainframe. This kind of experiment would seem to have great potential.

Notes

1 The horizontal portion at P_i^d should be interpreted as implying that the individual is indifferent between buying no units and buying one unit (and, though rather meaninglessly, buying any amount in between) at price P_i^d.

2 I have used strict inequalities purely to keep the discussion simple; equalities can be introduced without altering the argument.

3 Note that demander-subject i should never pay more than P_i^d for the unit, for thereby he or she makes a loss (of $P_i^d - P$) from participating in the experiment. So demand is 1 at a price less than P_i^d and 0 at a price greater than P_i^d – as the theory requires.

4 See note 2 above.

5 Alternative definitions are, of course, possible.

6 Obviously this hypothesis needs a certain amount of qualification before it correctly captures the essence of the Harrison argument.

7 Bankruptcy occurs when the subject has accumulated losses on bidding in excess of an initial endowment (of $8 or $10) given to him or her at the beginning of the experiment.

8 For $v_i < \underline{v} + \varepsilon$ the function is $b_i = \underline{v} + (v_i + \varepsilon - \underline{v})/(I + 1)$, whereas for $v_i > \underline{v} - \varepsilon$ the function 'defies analytic solution'; see Kagel and Levin (1986, p. 899, footnote 8).

9 Once its properties were accepted, experimentalists felt able to adopt it as a maintained hypothesis in experiments where other hypotheses were under test.

10 There may, however, have been problems with the incentive mechanism for getting subjects to state their forecasts.

11 Smith et al. (1988) manage to achieve the latter whilst keeping objective expectations undifferentiated. See later.

12 Forsythe et al. (1987) denominated everything in francs, which had a pre-specified exchange rate with the dollar. It is not obvious why the use of such francs is superior to the use of real money.

13 Here I am using the word markets to include all the areas of coverage of this chapter.

Part V

Concluding Remarks

14

Other Experimental Work

14.1 Introduction

This brief chapter is not designed to fill in the gaps that have been bequeathed by the earlier chapters in this book; that would be impossible. Rather, its purpose is to illustrate somewhat selectively the potential of experimental methods in directions other than those considered in detail earlier. I shall begin within the general area of economics as implicitly defined by the contents of the book and look briefly at a number of experiments that go beyond what has been treated before; this will be the concern of section 14.2. I shall then explore the interface between economics and other disciplines in section 14.3, though this may take us somewhat outwith the boundaries of economics as we conventionally recognize it. In section 14.4 we then examine a number of experiments that have used rather unconventional subjects. I then go outside the traditional laboratory experiment in section 14.5 to comment briefly on field experiments and other 'experiments' (such as 'Mrs Thatcher's economic experiment') and to relate these, and other ways of collecting economic data and testing economic hypotheses, to the experiments that have been the subject of study in this book. In section 14.6 I discuss experiments that have specifically policy objectives (rather than 'theory-testing' objectives), while in section 14.7 I shall explain the difference between experiments and simulations (often confused by some as experiments). Section 14.8 briefly concludes.

14.2 Other Experiments in Economics

This section alone could be larger than the rest of the book taken together, so I need to be selective. I shall focus attention on two main sub-topics: first, the experimental investigation of specific models which have, in a sense, already been investigated but at a general level; second, the experimental investigation of the interaction of two or more phenomena, each of which have been studied at an individual level. For some economists, the prior investigation of the general components would render pointless such further experiments. I, and others, disagree, for reasons already partly expressed; I shall expand on these reasons in chapter 15.

I begin here with specific applications of general phenomena already investigated. In particular, I look at the outcome of certain specific market models, involving insurance, borrowing and product quality. The experiments to be discussed build upon the robust finding reported in chapter 13 that (oral) double auction markets converge rapidly to the competitive equilibrium outcome. Taking this as given enables experimental economists to investigate and test other hypotheses of interest. An excellent example can be found in the bizarrely proof-read[1] but otherwise splendid paper on experimental markets in insurance by Camerer and Kunreuther (1989). This study employs the double auction technique and takes as given the competitive equilibrium convergence property: the authors state (p. 266) 'consumers are assumed to be price-takers . . . firms are price- takers . . .'. The innovative feature of this paper is that the subjects are endowed with, and trade in, hazards that produce only losses; earlier work, as should be apparent from the discussion of chapter 13, used endowments which were economic goods rather than bads.

Of course, endowing subjects with losses raises a number of ethical problems, to which we have briefly alluded in earlier chapters. Camerer and Kunreuther have particular problems (see p. 274) in that the committee which oversees their experiments (with human subjects) will not allow subjects to lose their own money.[2] Accordingly, Camerer and Kunreuther had to use the usual technique of giving all subjects $5 (or more, depending on the experiment and on the subject's role) at the start of the experiment. If a subject lost more than the $5 during the running of the experiment, he or she was declared bankrupt and excluded from the proceedings until the next market.

Markets had between three and six buyers and between three and eight sellers. At the beginning of each market period each seller was endowed with one (lottery) ticket, and at the beginning of each market (lasting for five market periods) each was endowed with 5000 francs (worth $5). All trading was carried out in francs, which had a given exchange rate with the dollar. The lottery ticket with which each seller was endowed could lead to a loss to the person who owned it at the end of the period of either nothing or 2000 francs;[3] the probabilities of these two outcomes were known to all subjects. The buyers were endowed with 100,000 francs (worth $100) at the start of each market. The double auction was then carried out; at the end of each market period all the lottery tickets were played out, and the subjects' accounts were updated accordingly.

The experimental design enabled Camerer and Kunreuther to test several hypotheses and, in particular, to investigate whether a prospect-theory-based explanation of behaviour performed better than a SEUT-based explanation. As it happened, 'market prices were close to expected values in all experiments', which is consistent with SEUT with risk-neutral subjects. Unfortunately, the authors did not carry out an independent test of whether the subjects did obey SEUT and whether they were risk neutral, so it cannot be concluded definitively that that was the case; but it appears plausible. A rather contrasting conclusion emerges from a study I carried out, again using the oral double auction technique,[4] into Galiani's theory of interest (Hey, 1989). Galiani was a famous Italian economist, who died in 1787, who proposed, *inter alia*, that interest was a reward for risk taking. I can do no better than to quote him:

> It was understood that intrinsic value always varies according to the degrees of probability which might or might not be enjoyed from a thing. It was understood, moreover, that 100 future ducats with 90 degrees of probability of not being lost and 10 degrees of being lost, become 90 present ducats and should be valued as 90 ducats for any contract, game or exchange.
>
> (Galiani, 1977, p. 261)

I implemented this experimentally through a double auction involving trade between black and red tokens, each of which had a non-linear exchange rate with money. To implement the probability 'of being lost' I randomly selected certain subject(s) whose holdings of red tokens were declared valueless after trade. According to Galiani's theory this should create a specific rate of exchange between black and red tokens, the precise value depending upon initial endowments and the probability 'of being lost'. My experiments showed that the exchange rate moved in the right direction when the probability changed, though it did not agree precisely with the risk-neutral prediction.

This experiment was similar in flavour to a number of experiments discussed in section 5 of Plott (1989) on product quality. Here the outcomes after trade are probabilistic, as the essence of the product quality literature (see, in particular, Akerlof's lemons story and subsequent literature) is that the buyer is unaware of the quality of the good that is being traded.

If the quality is known, however, then goods of differing qualities trade in different markets. So, instead of getting the kind of problem discussed in the three examples described above (insurance, rate of interest and product quality), we get a multi-market problem. Experiments of this type are now being conducted: both PLATO and MUODA, as well as other experimental software packages, allow for trading in several markets simultaneously. They enable an investigation of the robustness of the competitive equilibrium convergence properties to be carried out. A rather simple example of this type of experiment, with serial rather than parallel markets, can be found in Goodfellow and Plott (1989). They explore an input market and an output market, both implemented as a double auction, linked through firms' production functions. Although an exploratory study, it shows that convergence still occurs, though not as quickly and not as positively as in single markets. This is a fascinating finding, suggesting that as complexity increases then convergence is less strong, and hence, perhaps, that once some complexity threshold is breached then convergence to the competitive equilibrium disappears. We await the results of further studies.

14.3 Experiments on the Interface Between Economics and Other Disciplines

In Hoffman's invaluable bibliography of the experimental economics literature, there are several references to experimental investigations on the
interface between economics and other disciplines: in particular, there is
experimental work in accounting (including auditing), education, history,
law, politics, psychology (naturally), public choice and sociology. It should go
without saying that the psychology–economics interface is the one that is
most developed – here a useful reference is Thaler (1987). Of course, the
economist as imperialist regards most, if not all, of these disciplines as
sub-disciplines of Greater Economics; indeed, I suspect it will be from this
perspective that most of the readers of this book will approach this rather
diverse literature.

Let me give a little flavour of this type of work. I shall give two examples,
one from the law–economics interface and the other from the political
science–economics interface. I begin with politics and economics and a paper
by Collier et al. (1988) which follows on from an earlier study by the same
authors. They examine the outcome of voting procedures and, in particular,
investigate the role of information in the voting process. The experimental
set-up is straightforward: there are two candidates, one the incumbent and
the other the challenging candidate. There are five voters, making a total of
seven subjects, two of whom (the candidates) are stooges[5] of the experimenters. The experiment lasts for 35 periods, in each of which each voter casts a
vote for one or other candidate. The candidate with the most votes wins and
is incumbent in the following period. Now some economic incentives are
introduced into the story: each candidate in each period chooses a 'policy' –
a number between 0 and 999. The incumbent's policy is translated into a
monetary payoff to each subject by the following formula:

$$W_i = a - b \mid p - p_i^* \mid \qquad (14.1)$$

where W_i is voter-subject i's payment, a and b are parameters and p and p_i^*
are the incumbent's policy and subject i's ideal policy respectively. So each
subject has the incentive of trying to get the candidate elected whose policy
is closest to his or her ideal policy. The authors are interested in observing
the outcome of the voting process both without and with the possibility of
information purchase concerning the challenger's intentions. Not surprisingly, their results are very unstable, and much depends on whether the two
candidates keep their pre-electoral policy promises. As the authors comment,
'individual decisions also appear to be idiosyncratic'.

A paper on the law and economics boundary, published in the *Journal of
Legal Studies* by Hoffman and Spitzer (1985), explores subjects' concepts of
distributive justice. This uses essentially the same framework as the
bargaining/cake-eating problems discussed in chapter 11, but there is a twist
to the story. This arises as a consequence of the fact that the authors are
trying to test three hypotheses about the outcome of the bargaining process,
only one of which is the 'economic' hypothesis that was the concern of

chapter 11. Before stating these three hypotheses, let me first give an example of the bargaining problem given to the subjects. There are two subjects A and B, one of whom is designated the controller (see later). The controller, once designated, can choose any number from a table such as table 14.1. Any such choice would be binding.

However, the other player may attempt to persuade the controller to choose some other number and to enter into a written and signed agreement to that effect; such an agreement would also specify any side payment that is to be made under the agreement. Thus, for example, if A is designated the controller he or she could unilaterally choose number 2 (thereby getting $5 and giving B $2), or A and B could sign an agreement to choose number 3 and for B to give A $2.50 (thereby ending up with $5.50 and $2.50 respectively). The three hypotheses under test were all concerned with the nature of the agreement reached. They were as follows: (a) utilitarian; (b) egalitarian; (c) natural law/desert. The third of these is a Lockean concept. Crucial to it is the notion that property rights that are earned are 'better' than those that are randomly acquired. To test this, Hoffman and Spitzer adopted a 2 × 2 treatment structure relating to the choice of controller: in two of the treatments the position of controller is earned through some prior task, whilst in the other two the controller is chosen at random; in two of the treatments the phraseology 'earns the right' is used with reference to the controller, whilst in the other two the phraseology 'is designated' is used. These are subtle distinctions. The conclusion that the authors draw is that the Lockean approach explains the outcomes best; this has important implications for subjects' concepts of distributive justice.

14.4   Experiments with Other Types of Subjects

In most of the experiments reported in this book the subjects used were typically students at the researchers' University. In some cases, school pupils were used. The main advantage of using such subjects is that they are relatively cheap to motivate. However, some experiments require other types of subjects – experts in particular fields or just ordinary human beings. My feeling is that experimental economics is now getting to the stage where it needs to think more carefully about the type of subjects that are being used, particularly if the experiments are meant to be representative in some sense. In such experiments, one needs to try to obtain a representative set of subjects.

Table 14.1   An example of a payoff matrix in the Hoffman and Spicer experiment

Number	A's payoff	B's payoff
1	$4	$1
2	$5	$2
3	$3	$5

However, there are other experiments where one specifically does not want a representative set, but rather a particular set. In this section, I shall briefly describe two such experiments. The first is one which Roth (1989) describes as a natural experiment, and which therefore overlaps somewhat with those which are the concern of the next section. Roth's natural experiment concerns the market for newly graduated medical students as they seek their first hospital positions in different regions in the United Kingdom. This natural experiment arises because there are different market organizations in the different regions within the United Kingdom; these differences enable the economist to study how market behaviour is influenced by market organization. In one obvious sense, this returns us to the concerns of chapter 13, but here the experiment is done outside the laboratory. However, the key element required for experimentation is still there: as one goes from regional market to regional market, the market organization changes but other features stay unchanged (at least in broad terms) and so we have the 'control' necessary to observe the effects of organizational change.

Battalio et al. (1977) report on two other natural experiments outside the laboratory. These were concerned with income distributions in 'experimental economies': the first was in a female ward for chronic psychotics at the Central Islip State Hospital in New York, and the second was in the Addiction Research Foundation in Ontario. Both these 'experimental economies' could be considered as microcosms of real economies: in each, income could be earned and the income expended. Battalio et al.'s interest was in examining the resulting income distribution and comparing it with income distributions in real economies. A close correspondence was found. These were experiments in the sense that the microcosms were separate from, and hence independent of, the outside world; in this sense, therefore, experimental control was exercised. It is not clear, however, whether there is further potential in using these types of experimental economies and in using these kinds of subjects.

14.5   Other Kinds of Experiments

The natural experiments discussed above are somewhat different from the laboratory experiments which have been the main focus of interest in this book. As my remarks should make clear, some experimental control is exercised, though perhaps not as much as one would like. However, such natural experiments have the advantage that they are closer to the real world than those conducted in the laboratory.[6] Even closer to the real world, perhaps, are those experiments which are termed field experiments; a useful introduction and critique can be found in Neuberg (1989). The most famous such field experiments in economics are the four American income-maintenance experiments carried out over the period 1968–1980. These experiments were originally motivated by agricultural and biomedical experiments, the essence of which was random assignment of subjects between a treatment group and a control group. The same idea was employed in the income-maintenance experiments: a randomly selected group of households was given/offered a new negative income tax schedule, and a control group was not. In this way, experimental control could be obtained over the key element of interest: the effect on household behaviour, particularly labour supply behaviour, of a change in the income tax system from the old schedule to some new schedule. To a limited extent these experiments were successful, though probably not as successful as had been hoped. Neuberg (1989) identifies two major problems: first, that the subjects were volunteers so that those subjects who were offered and accepted the new schedule were different from those who were offered but did not accept the new schedule; second, that the subjects had a natural incentive to distort their behaviour and hence influence the policy outcome of the experiments. Both these factors are likely to bias the observations.

Nevertheless, such field experiments remain of considerable potential value, particularly in conjunction with laboratory experiments. I make no comment about other types of experiment, such as 'Mrs Thatcher's economic experiment', where, I suspect, the word 'experiment' is being used in a rather different sense from that employed in this book!

14.6   Experiments with Other Objectives

The majority of experiments discussed in this book have been theory-testing experiments; some have been theory-suggesting experiments; a few have been policy-testing and policy-suggesting experiments. The distinction is not clear cut, but it is worth making. As Plott in particular (Plott, 1987, and elsewhere) has observed, experimental methods have considerable potential for resolving policy disputes: the use of such methods enables proposed policies to be tried out relatively costlessly in the laboratory before being implemented, possibly at great cost, in the real world. Plott (1987) cites a number of examples, ranging from agenda design at a small flying club, through landing slot allocations at major airports and regulation of the inland waterways barge industry, to the allocation of space in NASA's space station. Let me present one example, to give a flavour of this type of work. This is Plott's 'Ethyl Case', reported in Grether and Plott (1984), which revolved around a lawsuit brought by the Federal Trade Commission (FTC) against the major US manufacturers of tetraethyl and tetramethyl lead (the lead-based gasoline additives that increase octane levels). The FTC's case was that industrial practices were 'anticompetitive': the defendants' response was that the practices had no effect on industry performance because the industry was an oligopoly which 'implied' that there was no room for such an effect. The FTC employed Grether and Plott to conduct experiments to rebut this defence position. The experiments were highly specific: matching the industry in terms of the numbers of suppliers and demanders, concentration ratios, demand elasticities, excess capacity and so on. Subjects were carefully chosen, and were not students! The results of the experiment were clear cut – it showed without doubt that the industrial practices did have a major impact on the industry. The FTC was correct in bringing the lawsuit. Unfortunately, for experimental economics at least, the experimental testimony was not entered by the FTC. Nevertheless, this example does demonstrate its potential in this respect.

14.7 Experiments and Simulations

Before concluding, mention must be made of simulation, which some people confuse with experimentation but which is, in fact, completely different. Simulation is used, usually with a computer, to explore the properties of theoretical models, typically when such models are too complex to solve analytically. In contrast, experimentation is used to observe behaviour. The two can be used together to good effect, however, with experimentation used to discover how economic agents behave, and then simulation used to explore the implications of that behaviour. Some very interesting studies are under way at the moment to try to discover good and/or robust behavioural rules to use: one such study is a 'Double auction market for computerized traders' which is being run at the Santa Fe Institute; another is a computerized duopoly simulation (IDEAS) being run under Selten at the University of Bonn. It will be intriguing to see which strategies perform best in these simulations, and whether, indeed, these are the strategies to which behaviour in the corresponding experiments converges after many repetitions.

14.8 Conclusions

The main thrust of this chapter has been to illustrate the range of applications of experimental methods outwith the confines of the examples presented earlier in the book. I hope that I have given a flavour of what can be achieved with such methods. Of course, it should be noted that, when moving from the narrow confines of the laboratory to these other applications, one is moving to 'more realistic' applications. At the same time, one is usually losing control, and moving away from experimentation proper towards applied econometrics. This is not necessarily bad, although it does change the nature of the inferences one can draw. This should not necessarily be a deterrent.

Notes

1 For example (see page 272): 'Instructions were read aloud to inexperienced objects. Experienced subjects read their instructions silently.'
2 This restriction implies a rather odd valuation by the committee of the subjects' time input.
3 In one experiment the loss was 4000 francs, and in another 10,000.
4 I have a short edited video-recording of the experiment, which may be of interest.
5 The American word for 'stooge' appears to be 'shill'.

6 One needs to be careful here: experimentalists are often accused of doing something artificial in their laboratory experiments. But this is wrong: we use real people tackling real problems (usually) for real money. There is nothing artificial about this, so those who use this objection must have something else in mind.

15

Conclusions and Suggestions for Future Research

15.1 Introduction

This concluding chapter attempts to provide an appraisal of what experimental economics has achieved to date, an assessment of its strengths and weaknesses, its good points and its bad, and a vision of what it might achieve in the future. Despite the rapid growth of experimental economics over the past two decades, particularly in America, there are still vast areas of ignorance concerning what experimental economics is and what it does. Accompanying such ignorance is often a bemused hostility, based on the natural fear that experimental economics is, in some sense, threatening. So I begin my assessment by overviewing, in section 15.2, what experimental economics has achieved so far, concentrating on its main strength – the ability to provide reliable data under controlled conditions. In section 15.3 I shall examine a number of methodological considerations which are currently under debate amongst experimentalists and which need to be solved in order to allow further progress. Then, in section 15.4, I shall look to the future, indicating what developments are likely to be made and what developments should be made, in my opinion. Section 15.5 concludes.

15.2 Progress to Date

Let me recall the prime motivation for experimental economics: the ability to collect economic data under controlled conditions, and hence to test economic theory under the same conditions as those under which it was formulated. The conventional alternative, of course, is the use of data that have generally been collected by others for other purposes and which were not generated under the *ceteris paribus* conditions of the theory. Inevitably, there may be a trade-off problem to consider: experimentally generated data, although hopefully of better quality, might be more expensive to obtain than conventional data; but this is not necessarily so. On the face of it, data generated under the controlled conditions of the theory that they are designed to test would appear to be better suited to that test than data generated under other conditions. There are those in the mainstream of the profession who would disagree. They would argue that experiments are artificial and that the data generated by them are less reliable than 'real-life' data. I suspect there are two strands to this argument: the first is essentially more a comment on the nature of the theory that is being tested (that it is 'artificial' or too far removed from the real world) than a comment on the methods used to test that theory. Experimentalists can legitimately claim that this is not their problem, and pass it on to the theorists (though I will comment on this in section 15.4). The second strand relates to the 'artificiality' of the laboratory environment: 'the subjects, who are not "real" decision-makers, are not taking "real" decisions for "real" rewards'. The hard line response to this argument, of course, is simply to retort that economic theories do not specify when a decision-maker becomes 'real', nor when the decisions are 'real', nor when the rewards are 'real'. A more mature response would be to recognize that the criticism may have force, and that experimentalists should counter it by (a) carrying out replicative experiments with experienced decision-makers, thus testing the hypothesis that they take decisions better than naive subjects; (b) carrying out experiments that are closer in structure to the type of decision problems that such experienced decision-makers face in their real life, thus testing the hypothesis that such decision-makers tackle familiar problems in an optimal fashion; and (c) carrying out replicative experiments involving larger payments – adding a zero, or two zeros, to the ends of all payoffs, thus testing the hypothesis that subjects perform better when the rewards are greater.

Some such experiments have been, and are being, performed; many more will be performed in the future. Preliminary findings are mixed: they suggest that experts might be no better than naive subjects in taking the kinds of decisions that are normally subjected to test in the laboratory, although it is clear that experience with such tasks improves performance (this could, simply be a reflection on hypothesis (b) above); and some (particularly psychologists carrying out economic experiments) conclude that the magnitudes of the rewards, possibly above some threshold, do not matter. Indeed, some would argue that the actual payment of monetary rewards is unimportant, though the neoclassical economist might be well advised not to make too much of this!

I suspect that experimental economics has had its greatest impact (both on theorists and policy-makers) in those areas of economics where theory has shed relatively little light. I think it is no coincidence that experiments on the dynamic and equilibrium behaviour of markets under different forms of market organization have been the most successful in influencing the profession, for in these areas there is virtually no worthwhile theory. The same is true, though to a lesser extent and for different reasons, with respect to experiments on auctions and bargaining behaviour; here, in a sense, there is too much theory – with, consequently, indeterminate theoretical predictions. Experiments in both these areas have led to some new theory, though not to a new paradigm, largely because the experiments have been theory-suggesting rather than theory-testing. However, it is gratifying to see experimental methods contributing to a genuinely scientific approach to economics in the field of basic decision-making under risk and uncertainty. Here, experimental evidence has contributed to the near-overthrow of one paradigm in economics – subject expected utility theory. Here the power of experimental methods for testing old theories and suggesting new ones is very evident: even the diehard neoclassicists in the profession recognize that.

15.3   Methodological Considerations

Experimental economics, though a relatively young discipline, is steadily building up a stock of expertise concerning 'best practice' experimental procedures. Some of this expertise has been acquired from psychology, where the tradition of experimental work is more firmly established. However, there are important differences between the two disciplines, which mean that one cannot import the methodology of experimental psychology lock, stock and barrel into experimental economics. I have discussed these issues elsewhere (Hey, 1991), but I should note here some key differences. First and foremost is the fact that many economics experiments have been, and will increasingly be, theory-testing experiments – and of theories with a well-defined structure and a well-defined objective function for the subjects. This provides such economics experiments with well-defined incentive mechanisms; with appropriately large payments (see later) this avoids many of the difficulties encountered in psychology experiments. Second, economists' concerns are less fine-grained than psychologists'; this lessens many of the observational problems. Nevertheless, economists can fruitfully learn many lessons from psychologists concerning 'best practice' technique: the need to avoid experimenter bias in instructing subjects; the need to avoid influencing the subjects' behaviour implicitly or explicitly through the experimental design; the necessity of keeping detailed records of all procedures so that experiments can be replicated; the importance of preventing one set of subjects from influencing the behaviour of other subjects; and so on.

With experience, experimental economists are gaining knowledge about the efficacy of certain experimental techniques. Let me give two recent examples, one relating to the random-lottery incentive technique and the other to the Becker–DeGroot–Marschak elicitation technique (a further example is the binary lottery technique). The first of these is used repeatedly in many types of experiments, especially those concerning individual decision-making discussed in part II of this book. For example, the technique was used in the experiment reported in chapter 5 where subjects had to answer a set of pairwise preference questions, one of which was selected at random at the end of the experiment to be played out. If subjects obey SEUT then this elicits true preferences; if subjects do not obey SEUT it might not. This is Holt's conjecture (see Holt, 1986); if it is correct it has potentially worrying implications for experimental design. Starmer and Sugden (1990) provide a very clever experimental test of Holt's conjecture: they were looking for evidence of a 'contamination effect' – 'that is, some tendency for the preferences elicited in random-lottery experiments to be influenced by the nature of the experiment as a whole, and thus to differ from true preferences'. They concluded that their evidence was mixed, though the experiment did suggest a method for controlling for such contamination effects if indeed they did exist. This new method adds further ammunition to the experimenter's armoury. Safra et al. (1990) examine another elicitation technique used by experimentalists: the Becker–DeGroot–Marschak mechanism for eliciting a subject's certainty equivalent of some risky prospect. As originally proposed it was implicitly set within an expected utility framework; with non-expected-utility-maximizing subjects, the mechanism could apparently imply preference reversals (see chapter 6). What Safra et al. (1990) provide is a sequence of testable hypotheses concerning the announced 'certainty equivalent', one of which can be used to find the utility and probability transformation functions of an anticipated utility maximizer. This extension of a familiar technique has considerable potential.

In looking towards the future, there seem to me to be three major methodological issues that experimental economists will need to confront as an increasing matter of urgency. The first concerns computerization, the second representativeness and the third the size and sign of monetary payoffs. Until a few years ago, the bulk of experiments were carried out by hand. Now, with the advent of modern, cheap and relatively reliable computing power in the form of networkable PCs, more and more experiments are being computerized. I have discussed the advantages and disadvantages of this trend earlier in the book; not least amongst the former is the ability to replicate experiments exactly, with different subjects and different payoffs etc., thereby testing for certain effects. But there are offsetting disadvantages; one that is increasingly concerning me is the question of trust. Does the computerization itself destroy the trust that the subject should have in the experiment and the experimenter? As I have argued before, it seems to me particularly crucial that experiments in economics remain 'whiter than white', and are seen to be so by subjects. Unfortunately, computerization offers the experimenter the possibility of 'cheating' on the subjects in a number of ways, most crucially by passing on incorrect information about the decisions of other subjects and fiddling the outcome of allegedly random processes. Many experimentalists use physical random devices to get round the latter problem. The first is more subtle, however, as there are experiments where the experimenter has a natural incentive to pass incorrect information, thereby saving money. In these cases, and indeed in all cases, a practice should be adopted whereby subjects can verify that correct information has been passed. This is relatively simple to do (after the experiment, if necessary), but I suspect it is not done as often as it should be.

Representativeness (of the subjects), strangely enough, is not an issue that seems to have worried many experimentalists, nor indeed many journal editors. This may reflect the nature of the experimental tests that have been carried out. For example, those who wish to discredit SEUT seem to be content with observing some violation of SEUT amongst the subject pool. Indeed, the fact that some people violate SEUT is of interest. But we are now getting to the stage of needing to know what proportion of people out there obey SEUT, what proportion obey regret and so on. I suppose that in principle it is possible to infer the information using conventional econometric methods – once the various types of behaviour have been observed, possibly by experimental methods – but I see no reason why experiments could not be used to detect not only different types of behaviour but also the prevalence of the different types in the population at large. This would require representative subject pools.

Finally, and without apology, I raise again the issue of the size and sign of monetary payoffs. Recall Harrison's argument that departures from optimality may be caused by insufficiently peaked objective functions. To shed light on whether this is indeed the case, we need to increase the magnitude of payoffs as well as introducing sizeable potential real losses into experiments. I appreciate that this introduces a serious moral hazard problem and that some experimentalists are forbidden to carry out experiments with losses. (I do not think that giving subjects an initial endowment which they might subsequently lose is the same as giving them sizeable potential real losses.) But the moral hazards can be avoided, at least in certain types of experiments, and I think it important that such experiments are carried out. We can then test Harrison's hypothesis.

15.4   Experiments in the Future

During the course of this book, I have noted a number of areas which are ripe for experimental investigation (such as modern industrial organization theory). In addition, we have encountered several areas in which experimental work is under way but only partly completed; in these areas, the way forward is usually clear. In principle, the research agenda for experimental economics coincides with that for economics as a whole: there appear to be few areas where experiments cannot be performed. But, given the existence of scarce experimental resources, it is clear that some areas will pay greater dividends in a shorter period of time than others; let me list my own perceived order of priorities. I begin with 'small' plans and work up to grandiose ones.

In the immediate future, I think one major priority in all areas where experimental work is theory-testing is to develop a theory of errors. Now let me be careful about this, as I have been chastised more than once by referees and been accused of being ignorant of the literature. Let me take as an example the theories of decision-making under risk and uncertainty discussed in part II. Those theories were deterministic theories: they predicted particular deterministic choices (except in the trivial case of indifference). I appreciate that there are also stochastic theories of decision-making under risk (so that in a pairwise choice between A and B, A is chosen x per cent of the time and B $(100 - x)$ per cent of the time) but if you are testing one or other of the deterministic theories then you are forced to conclude on the basis of the experimental evidence that either the theories are wrong (because no subject's behaviour fits them exactly) or the subjects make decisions with error. I think most economists would prefer the latter; but this means that we need to append a theory of errors to the original decision theory – not in any *ad hoc* way but in a manner which is consistent in some sense with the original theory. That has not yet been done to everyone's satisfaction, but it needs to be done as a matter of urgency. One useful recent attempt is that by Smith and Walker (1990).

Experimental economists may also find it helpful to change the focus of their theory-testing hypotheses away from tests of the absolute correctness of the theory to tests of the comparative statics predictions of the theory. Clearly the latter are weaker tests, and the experimental evidence is more likely to satisfy them, but this change of focus would bring experimental applied work more into line with conventional econometric applied work, which almost exclusively focuses on comparative statics tests of theories.

My main suggestion for change in the future is a plea for experimental economists to 'occupy the middle ground'. At present, most experimental work is done towards the ends of a spectrum ranging from individual decision-making at the one end to market models at the other. The historical reasons are clear: much work has been done at the markets end of the spectrum because that is where theory sheds least practical light; much work has been done at the individual decision-making end because that is the foundation stone of the whole of economics. Many economists would argue that, once you get the foundations right, then all the rest will follow. As a consequence, much of economics is serial. This type of argument is the basis of that used to suggest that experiments in 'the middle ground', like those discussed in part III of this book, are misdirected. When presenting seminars on search, consumption, the firm and so on, I have frequently been told that I should concentrate on the foundations: if SEUT works as a description of individual decision-making under risk then *a fortiori* it will work when it forms the foundation of a theory of search, or a theory of consumption, or a theory of the firm. I call this the 'stripped-down' argument: it is also used in areas of economics which build on the foundation of game theory. Thus, for example, it is misdirected to investigate experimentally the Fudenberg et al. (1983) patent race (discussed in chapters 10 and 11) because it is essentially an application of game theory. What one should do is test game theory itself. Indeed, some proponents of this line of argument would take it to its limits, completely stripping down game theory, for example, to its barest essentials. Some experimentalists are now doing this. Let me give one example. It is, admittedly, a parody, but one not too far removed from the truth. There are two players; each, independently of but simultaneously with the other, selects and announces a point in a square. If both players select the same point then they both get a prize; otherwise not. Note that there are an infinite number of Nash equilibria in this game, none of which dominates any other. Let me conjecture what experimental scrutiny reveals: that players tend to choose one of the four corners and that top-left is more frequently chosen than any of the other three corners.[1]

That seems to me to be a sociological or psychological experiment rather than an economic one. This 'stripped-down' argument takes us away from our genuine concerns. What we should be doing, following the development of economic theory if you like, is experimentally investigating more and more complex models of decision-making, rather than simpler and simpler models. This reflects my belief that it is not the foundation stones of economics that are 'wrong'; rather, it is the weight of the building we erect on top of those foundation stones that causes them to crack under the weight. Recall that SEUT is developed initially in an extremely simple static world; it is then extended to dynamic and adaptive worlds. My belief is that focusing on the initial development is misguided: what we should be doing is examining the extension to more and more complex (dynamic and adaptive) worlds and discovering where it breaks down. Implicit in this is the belief that SEUT 'works' in its initial simple static world, but breaks down (at different points for different people) in the extension to complex dynamic worlds. Let me give you Hey's conjecture: if you present subjects with the types of tests (of SEUT) discussed in part II sufficiently often, and if you put enough zeros on the ends of the payoffs and a minus sign in front of a few of them, you will observe SEU behaviour. This is simply because those decision problems are essentially trivial – all except the dimmest subjects will eventually discover what is sensible behaviour. Not so, however, with complex problems. This is where I think we should be heading.

I base this line of argument on casual observation: I observe that some people are better decision-makers than others and that some people can solve complicated decision problems while others have difficulties with relatively simple ones. So, I observe different degrees of decision-solving abilities and differing degrees of complexity of decision problems. If we focus all our experimental energy on studying essentially trivial problems we are not going to make any headway in beginning to understand complexity, and human beings' methods of handling it. But this is crucial, I believe, to a full understanding of economic behaviour.

So I think we need to move to more complex decision problems. Also, at some stage, we need to cast ourselves adrift from neoclassical economics and take the plunge into the sea of ill-defined experiments. I talked about such experiments briefly in part I, but we encountered relatively few examples on our journey through the book. The reasons are simple: well-defined experiments are much easier to do; moreover, they usually involve a well-defined hypothesis that can be tested. This pleases journal editors. Well-defined experiments, however, constrain economics to operate within the straitjacket of well-defined worlds, in which the only admissible reason for suboptimal behaviour is poor decision-making ability on the part of the economic agents. But this misses the point on two counts. Consider the game of chess. This is a well-defined problem: do economists really think it helpful for understanding the outcome of chess games to assume that all players are perfectly good at solving that decision problem? Now consider how much less well defined is the economic world. What then do we gain and lose by assuming that it *is* well defined *and* that agents can solve the resulting decision problems perfectly?

Unfortunately, ill-defined experiments are difficult to construct and implement. Almost definitionally, they need to be both ill defined as far as the subjects are concerned and well structured as far as the experimenter is concerned: he or she needs to retain control over the experiment. The problem then is to control how much and what part of the structure is to be hidden from the subjects; how questions from them about the 'rules of the game' are to be handled; and how the experimenter can control for the prior knowledge (about the hidden aspects of the experiment) that is brought to the experiment by the subjects. These are not easy questions. Nor are they insoluble.

15.5   Conclusions

Experimental economics is still a relatively young discipline, but it is becoming established. There are pockets of ignorance about what it has done and what it can do even in America, where it is strongest. Outside America, the pockets are frighteningly large. I hope that this book helps to spread the word about what experiments can do and that it will encourage other economists to try some experiments of their own. If sufficient numbers do, then economics must surely benefit.

Note

1 Except amongst Chinese subjects, when bottom-right is chosen more frequently.

References

Allais, M. and Hagen, O. (eds) (1979) *Expected Utility Hypothesis and the Allais Paradox: Contemporary Discussion of Decisions under Uncertainty with Allais' Rejoinder*, Reidel.

Andreoni, J. (1988) 'Why Free Ride?', *Journal of Public Economics*, 37, 291–304.

Ansic, D. (1990) 'An Experimental Investigation of the Miller–Orr Transactions Demand for Cash Model', mimeo, University of York.

— and Loomes, G. C. (1990) 'The Bond Model: A Laboratory Experiment into the Demand for Money', mimeo, University of York.

Appleby, L. and Starmer, C. (1987) 'Individual Choice Under Uncertainty: A Review of Experimental Evidence, Past and Present', in Hey, J. D. and Lambert, P. J. (eds), *Surveys in the Economics of Uncertainty*, Basil Blackwell.

Banks, J. S., Plott, C. R. and Porter, D. P. (1988) 'An Experimental Analysis of Unanimity in Public Goods Provision Mechanism', *Review of Economic Studies*, 55, 301–22.

Battalio, R. C., Kagel, J. H. and Reynolds, M. O. (1977) 'Income Distributions in Two Experimental Economies', *Journal of Political Economy*, 85, 1259–71.

—, — and Komain, J. (1988) 'Testing Between Alternative Models of Choice under Uncertainty: Some Initial Results', mimeo, Texas A & M University.

Bergman, B. R. (1988) 'An Experiment on the Formation of Expectation', *Journal of Economic Behavior and Organization*, 9, 137–51.

Bernasconi, M. and Loomes, G. C. (1990) 'Failures of the Reduction Principle in an Ellsberg-type Problem', mimeo, University of York.

Binmore, K. (1987) 'Modelling Rational Players. Part I', *Economics and Philosophy*, 3, 179–214.

— and Dasgupta, P. (eds) (1987) *The Economics of Bargaining*, Basil Blackwell.

—, Shaked, A. and Sutton, J. (1985) 'Testing Non Cooperative Bargaining Theory: A Preliminary Study', *American Economic Review*, 75, 1178–80.

Bolle, F. (1988) 'Learning to Make Good Predictions in Time Series', in Tietz, R., Albers, W. and Selten, R. (eds), *Bounded Rational Behaviour in Experimental Games and Markets*, Lecture Notes in Economics and Mathematical Systems 314, Springer-Verlag, 37–50.

Camerer, C. F. (1989) 'An Experimental Test of Several Generalized Utility Theories', *Journal of Risk and Uncertainty*, 2, 61–104.

— and Kunreuther, H. (1989) 'Experimental Markets for Insurance', *Journal of Risk and Uncertainty*, 2, 265–300.

Chamberlin, E. H. (1948) 'An Experimental Imperfect Market', *Journal of Political*

Economy, 56, 95–108.

Chew, S. H. and Waller, W. S. (1986) 'Empirical Tests of Weighted Utility Theory', *Journal of Mathematical Psychology*, 30, 55–72.

Collier, K., Ordeshook, P. C. and Williams, K. (1988) 'The Rationally Uninformed Electorate: Some Experimental Evidence', Caltech Social Science Working Paper 668.

Cooper, R. W., De Jong, D. V., Forsythe, R. and Ross, T. W. (1990) 'Selection Criteria in Coordination Games: Some Experimental Results', *American Economic Review*, 80, 218–33.

Coppinger, V. M., Smith, V. L. and Titus, J. A. (1980) 'Incentives and Behavior in English, Dutch and Sealed-Bid Auctions', *Economic Inquiry*, 43, 1–22.

Coursey, D. L. and Smith, V. L. (1983) 'Price Controls in a Posted Offer Market', *American Economic Review*, 73, 218–21.

——, Isaac, R. M., Luke, M. and Smith, V. L. (1984) 'Market Contestability in the Presence of Sunk (Entry) Costs', *Rand Journal of Economics*, 15, 69–84.

Cox, J. C. and Oaxaca, R. (1986) 'Laboratory Experiments with a Finite Job Search Model', Discussion Paper, University of Arizona.

——, Roberson, B. and Smith, V. L. (1982) 'Theory and Behavior of Single Object Auctions', in Smith, V. L. (ed.), *Research in Experimental Economics*, JAI Press.

——, Smith, V. L. and Walker, J. M. (1985) 'Experimental Development of Sealed-Bid Auction Theory; Calibrating Controls for Risk Aversion', *American Economic Review*, 75, 160–5.

Currim, I. S. and Sarin, R. K. (1986) 'Empirical Evaluation of Properties and Predictive Power of Prospect Theory', Working Paper, Graduate School of Management, UCLA.

Dekel, E. (1986) 'An Axiomatic Characterization of Preferences under Uncertainty: Weakening the Independence Axiom', *Journal of Economic Theory*, 40, 304–18.

Dwyer, G. P., Williams, A. W., Battalio, R. C. and Mason, T. I. (1989) 'Tests of Rational Expectations in a Stark Setting', Discussion Paper, Clemson University.

Dyer, D., Kagel, J. H. and Levin, D. (1989) 'A Comparison of Naive and Experienced Bidders in Common Value Offer Auctions: A Laboratory Analysis', *Economic Journal*, 99, 108–15.

Eatwell, J., Milgate, M. and Newman, P. (eds) (1989) *Allocation, Information and Markets*, Macmillan.

Ellsberg, D. (1961) 'Risk, Ambiguity and the Savage Axiom', *Quarterly Journal of Economics*, 75, 643–69.

Forsythe, R., Palfrey, T. R. and Plott, C. R. (1982) 'Asset Valuation in an Experimental Market', *Econometrica*, 50, 537–67.

——, —— and —— (1984) 'Futures Markets and Informational Efficiency: A Laboratory Examination', *Journal of Finance*, 39, 955–81.

Friedman, D., Harrison, G. W. and Salmon, J. W. (1983) 'The Informational Role of Futures Markets: Some Experimental Evidence', in Streit, M. D. (ed.), *Futures Markets: Modelling, Managing and Monitoring Futures Trading*, Basil Blackwell.

——, —— and —— (1984) 'The Informational Efficiency of Experimental Asset Markets', *Journal of Political Economy*, 92, 349–408.

Fudenberg, D., Gilbert, R., Stiglitz, J. and Tirole, J. (1983) 'Preemption, Leapfrogging and Competition in Patent Races', *European Economic Review*, 22, 3–31.

Galiani, F. (1977) *On Money* (English translation by P. Toscano), University Microfilms International.

Goodfellow, J. and Plott, C. R. (1989) 'An Experimental Examination of the Simultaneous Determination of Input Prices and Output Prices', Caltech Social

Science Working Paper 691.

Green, L. and Kagel, J. H. (eds) (1987) *Advances in Behavioral Economics*, vol. 1, Ablex.

Grether, D. M. and Plott, C. R. (1984) 'The Effects of Market Practices in Oligopolistic Markets: An Experimental Examination of the Ethyl Case', *Economic Inquiry*, 22, 479–507.

Gul, F. (1991) 'A Theory of Disappointment Aversion', *Econometrica*, forthcoming.

Guth, W. and Tietz, R. (1988) 'Ultimatum Bargaining for a Shrinking Cake – An Experimental Analysis', in Tietz, R., Albers, W. and Selten, R. (eds), *Bounded Rational Behavior in Experimental Games and Markets*, Springer Lecture Notes in Economics and Mathematical Systems 314, Springer-Verlag, 111–28.

—, Schmittberger, R. and Schwartz, B. (1982) 'An Experimental Analysis of Ultimatum Bargaining', *Journal of Economic Behaviour and Organisation*, 3, 367–88.

Hagen, O. (1979) 'Towards a Positive Theory of Preferences under Risk', in Allais, M. and Hagen, O. (eds) (1979) *Expected Utility Hypothesis and the Allais Paradox: Contemporary Discussion of Decisions under Uncertainty with Allais' Rejoinder*, Reidel, 271–302.

Hall, R. E. (1978) 'Stochastic Implications of the Life Cycle–Permanent Income Hypothesis: Theory and Evidence', *Journal of Political Economy*, 86, 971–87.

Hammond, P. J. (1988) 'Consequentialist Foundations for Expected Utility', *Theory and Decision*, 25, 25–78.

Harless, D. W. (1989) 'Actions versus Prospects: The Effect of Problem Representation on Regret', mimeo, Drexel University.

Harrison, G. W. (1989) 'Payoff Dominance in Experimental Economics', mimeo, University of Western Ontario.

— (1989) 'Theory and Misbehavior of First-price Auctions', *American Economic Review*, 79, 749–62.

— (1989) 'Rational Expectations and Experimental Methods', in Goss, B. A. (ed.), *Rational Expectations and Efficiency in Futures Markets*, Routledge.

— and Morgan, P. B. (1990) 'Search Intensity in Experiments', *Economic Journal*, 100, 478–86.

Hey, J. D. (1980) 'Optimal Consumption under Income Uncertainty: An Example and a Conjecture', *Economics Letters*, 5, 129–33.

— (1982) 'Search for Rules for Search', *Journal of Economic Behavior and Organization*, 3, 65–81.

— (1985a) 'The Possibility of Possibility', *Journal of Economic Studies*, 12, 70–88. (Reprinted in Frowen, S. F. (ed.) (1990) *Unknowledge and Choice in Economics*, Macmillan.)

— (1985b) 'A Dynamic Theory of the Competitive Firm with a Forward Market', *Journal of Economic Studies*, 12, 21–35.

— (1987) 'A Pilot Experimental Investigation into Optimal Consumption under Uncertainty', in Maital, S. (ed.), *Applied Behavioural Economics*, 11, 653–67, Wheatsheaf.

— (1989) 'Il Prezzo del Batticuore: The Price of Heartbeats', in Palmerio, G. and Ruggeri, V. (eds), *Proceedings of the Galiani Bicentennial Memorial Conference*, Fabriano.

— (1990a) 'Dynamic Decision Making under Uncertainty: An Experimental Study of the Dynamic Competitive Firm', mimeo, University of York.

— (1990b) 'Expectations Formation: Rational or Adaptive or ...?', mimeo, University of York.

—— (1990c) 'A Pilot Experimental Study of the Dynamic Competitive Firm under Spot Price Uncertainty', *Journal of Behavioral Economics*, 19, 1–22.

—— (1991) 'Experiments in Economics – and Psychology', in Lea, S. E. G., Webley, P. and Young, B. M. (eds), *New Directions in Economic Psychology: Theory, Experiment and Application*, Edward Elgar.

—— and Dardanoni, V. (1988a) 'A Large-Scale Experimental Investigation into Optimal Consumption under Uncertainty', *Economic Journal*, 98, 105–16.

—— and —— (1988b) 'A Preliminary Analysis of a Large-Scale Experimental Investigation into Consumption under Uncertainty', in Tietz, R., Albers, W. and Selten, R. (eds), *Bounded Rational Behavior in Experimental Games and Markets*, Springer Lecture Notes in Economics and Mathematical Systems 314, Springer-Verlag, 51–65.

—— and Di Cagno, D. (1990) 'Circles and Triangles: an Experimental Estimation of Indifference Lines in the Marschak–Machina Triangle', *Journal of Behavioral Decision-Making*, 3, 279–306.

—— and Strazzera, E. (1989) 'Estimation of Indifference Curves in the Marschak–Machina Triangle', *Journal of Behavioral Decision Making*, 2, 239–60.

Hoffman, E. and Spitzer, M. L. (1985) 'Entitlements, Rights, and Fairness: An Experimental Examination of Subjects' Concepts of Distributive Justice', *Journal of Legal Studies*, 14, 259–97.

Holt, C. A. (1986) 'Preference Reversals and the Independence Axiom', *American Economic Review*, 76, 508–15.

Hong, J. T. and Plott, C. R. (1982) 'Rate Filing Policies for Inland Water Transportation: An Experimental Approach', *Bell Journal of Economics*, 13, 11–19.

Isaac, R. M. and Plott, C. R. (1981) 'Price Controls and the Behavior of Auction Markets: An Experimental Examination', *American Economic Review*, 71, 448–59.

—— and Reynolds, S. S. (1988) 'Appropriability and Market Structure in a Stochastic Invention Model', *Quarterly Journal of Economics*, 103, 647–71.

——, Walker, J. M. and Thomas, S. H. (1984) 'Divergent Evidence on Free Riding: An Experimental Examination of Possible Explanations', *Public Choice*, 43, 113–49.

——, McCue, K. F. and Plott, C. R. (1985) 'Public Goods Provision in an Experimental Environment', *Journal of Public Economics*, 26, 51–74.

Joyce, P. (1984) 'The Walrasian Tatonnement Mechanism and Information', *Rand Journal of Economics*, 15, 416–25.

Judge, G. G., Griffiths, W. E., Hill, R. C. and Lee, T.-C. (1980) *The Theory and Practice of Econometrics*, Wiley.

Kagel, J. H. (1987) 'Economics According to the Rats (and Pigeons too)', in Roth, A. E. (ed.) (1987) *Laboratory Experimentation in Economics: Six Points of View*, Cambridge University Press, 155–92.

—— and Levin, D. (1986) 'The Winner's Curse and Public Information in Common Value Auctions', *American Economic Review*, 76, 894–920.

—— and Roth, A.E. (forthcoming) *Handbook of Experimental Economics*, Princeton University Press.

Kahneman, D. and Tversky, A. (1979) 'Prospect Theory: An Analysis of Decision under Risk', *Econometrica*, 47, 263–91.

Karni, E. and Safra, Z. (1987) 'Preference Reversal and the Observability of Preferences by Experimental Methods', *Econometrica*, 55, 675–85.

Kim, O. and Walker, M. (1984) 'The Free Rider Problem: Experimental Evidence', *Public Choice*, 43, 3–24.

Kogut, C. A. (1988) 'Consumer Search Behavior and Sunk Costs', Discussion Paper, University of South Florida.

Lave, L. B. (1962) 'An Empirical Approach to the Prisoner's Dilemma Game', *Quarterly Journal of Economics*, 76, 424–36.

— (1965) 'Factors Affecting Co-operation in the Prisoner's Dilemma', *Behavioral Science*, 10, 26–38.

Loomes, G. C. (1989) 'Predicted Violations of the Invariance Principles in Choice under Uncertainty', *Annals of Operations Research*, 19, 103–13.

— (1991) 'Evidence of a New Violation of the Independence Axiom', *Journal of Risk and Uncertainty*, 4, 91–108.

— and Sugden, R. (1982) 'Regret Theory: An Alternative Theory of Rational Choice under Uncertainty', *Economic Journal*, 92, 805–24.

— and — (1987) 'Some Implications of a More General Form of Regret Theory', *Journal of Economic Theory*, 41, 270–87.

—, Starmer, C. and Sugden, R. (1990) 'Observing Violations of Transitivity by Experimental Methods', *Econometrica*, forthcoming.

MacCrimmon, K. R. and Larsson, S. (1979) 'Utility Theory: Axioms Versus "Paradoxes"', in Allais, M. and Hagen, O. (eds) (1979) *Expected Utility Hypothesis and the Allais Paradox: Contemporary Discussion of Decisions under Uncertainty with Allais' Rejoinder*, Reidel, 333–409.

Machina, M. J. (1982) 'Expected Utility Analysis Without the Independence Axiom', *Econometrica*, 50, 277–323.

— (1989) 'Choice under Uncertainty: Problems Solved and Unsolved', in Hey, J. D. (ed.), *Current Issues in Microeconomics*, Macmillian.

Marschak, J. (1950) 'Rational Behaviour, Uncertain Prospects, and Measurable Utility', *Econometrica*, 18, 111–41.

Marwell, G. and Ames, R. E. (1979) 'Experiments on the Provision of Public Goods. I. Resources, Interest, Group Size and the Free-Rider Problem', *American Journal of Sociology*, 84, 1335–60.

— and — (1980) 'Experiments on the Provision of Public Goods. II. Provision Points, Stakes, Experience, and the Free-Rider Problem', *American Journal of Sociology*, 85, 926–37.

— and — (1981) 'Economists Free Ride, Does Anyone Else?', *Journal of Public Economics*, 15, 295–310.

Moon, P. and Keasey, K. (1989) 'Information Search and Competitive Tendering: An Exploratory Study', mimeo, University of Warwick.

— and Martin, A. (1989) 'Better Heuristics for Economic Search – Experimental and Simulation Evidence', *Journal of Behavioral Decision Making*, 3, 175–94.

Murnighan, J. K., Roth, A. E. and Schoumaker, F. (1988) 'Risk Aversion in Bargaining: An Experimental Study', *Journal of Risk and Uncertainty*, 1, 101–24.

Neelin, J., Sonnenschein, H. and Spiegel, M. (1988) 'A Further Test of Noncooperative Bargaining Theory', *American Economic Review*, 78, 824–36.

Neuberg, L. G. (1989) *Conceptual Anomalies in Economics and Statistics: Lessons for the Social Experiment*, Cambridge University Press.

Neumann, J. and Morgenstern, O. (1944) *Theory of Games and Economic Behavior*, Princeton University Press.

Ochs, J. and Roth, A. E. (1989) 'An Experimental Study of Sequential Bargaining', *American Economic Review*, 79, 355–84.

Plott, C. R. (1982) 'Industrial Organization Theory and Experimental Economics', *Journal of Economic Literature*, 20, 1485–527.

— (1987) 'Dimensions of Parallelism: Some Policy Applications of Experimental Methods', in Roth, A. E. (ed.) (1987) *Laboratory Experimentation in Economics: Six Points of View*, Cambridge University Press, chapter 7.

—— (1989) 'An Updated Review of Industrial Organization Applications of Experimental Methods', in Schmalensee, R. and Willig, R. D. (ed), *Handbook of Industrial Organization*, Elsevier, vol. II, 1111–76.

—— and Smith, V. L. (1978) 'An Experimental Examination of Two Exchange Institutions', *Review of Economic Studies*, 45, 133–53.

Rapoport, A. and Chammah, A. M. (1965) *Prisoner's Dilemma: A Study in Conflict and Cooperation*, University of Michigan Press.

Roth, A. E. (ed.) (1987) *Laboratory Experimentation in Economics: Six Points of View*, Cambridge University Press.

—— (1988) 'Laboratory Experimentation in Economics: A Methodological Overview', *Economic Journal*, 98, 974–1031.

—— (1989) 'A Natural Experiment in the Organization of Entry Level Labor Markets: Regional Markets for New Physicians in the UK", University of Pittsburgh Working Paper 245.

—— and Malouf, M. W. K. (1979) 'Game-Theoretic Models and the Role of Information in Bargaining', *Psychological Review*, 86, 574–94.

—— and Murnighan, J. K. (1978) 'Equilibrium Behavior and Repeated Play of the Prisoner's Dilemma', *Journal of Mathematical Psychology*, 17, 189–98.

Safra, Z., Segal, U. and Spivak, A. (1990) 'The Becker–DeGroot–Marschak Mechanism and Non-Expected Utility', *Journal of Risk and Uncertainty*, 3, 177–90.

Schneider, F. and Pommerehne, W. W. (1981) 'Free Riding and Collective Action: An Experiment in Public Microeconomics', *Quarterly Journal of Economics*, 116, 689–704.

Schotter, A. and Braunstein, Y. M. (1981) 'Economic Search – An Experimental Study', *Economic Inquiry*, 19, 1–25.

Segal, U. (1987) 'The Ellsberg Paradox and Risk Aversion: An Anticipated Utility Approach', *International Economic Review*, 28, 175–202.

Selten, R. and Stoecker, R. (1986) 'End Behavior in Sequences of Finite Prisoner's Dilemma Supergames: A Learning Theory Approach', *Journal of Economic Behavior and Organization*, 7, 47–70.

Smith, V. L. (1962) 'An Experimental Study of Competitive Market Behavior', *Journal of Political Economy*, 70, 111–37.

—— (1976) 'Experimental Economics: Induced Value Theory', *American Economic Review*, 66, 274–9.

—— (1979) 'An Experimental Comparison of Three Public Good Decision Mechanisms', *Scandinavian Journal of Economics*, 81, 198–215.

—— (1980) 'Experiments with a Decentralised Mechanism for Public Good Decisions', *American Economic Review*, 70, 584–99.

—— (1981) 'An Empirical Study of Decentralized Institutions of Monopoly Restraint', in Horwich, G. and Quirk, J. P. (eds), *Essays in Contemporary Fields of Economics in Honor of Emanuel T. Weiler (1914–1979)*, Purdue University Press.

—— (1989) 'Theory, Experiment and Economics', *Journal of Economic Perspectives*, 3, 151–69.

—— (ed.) (1990) *Experimental Economics*, Edward Elgar.

—— and Walker, J. M. (1990) 'Monetary Rewards and Decision Cost in Experimental Economics', Paper presented to the FUR-V Conference, Duke, Durham, NC, June.

—— Williams, A. W., Bratton, W. K. and Vannoni, M. G. (1982) 'Competitive Market Institutions: Double Auctions vs Sealed Bid-Offer Auctions', *American Economic Review*, 72, 58–77.

——, Suchanek, G. L. and Williams, A. W. (1988) 'Bubbles, Crashes and Endogenous Expectations in Experimental Spot Asset Markets', *Econometrica*, 56, 1119–52.

Starmer, C. and Sugden, R. (1989) 'Probability and Juxtaposition Effects: An Experimental Investigation of the Common Ratio Effect', *Journal of Risk and Uncertainty*, 2, 159–78.

—— and —— (1990) 'Does the Random-Lottery Incentive System Elicit True Preferences?', Discussion Paper, University of East Anglia.

Sugden, R. (1987) 'New Developments in the Theory of Choice under Uncertainty', in Hey, J. D. and Lambert, P. J. (eds), *Surveys in the Economics of Uncertainty*, Basil Blackwell, 1–24.

Thaler, R. (1987) 'The Psychology of Choice and the Assumptions of Economics', in Roth, A. E. (ed.) (1987) *Laboratory Experimentation in Economics: Six Points of View*, Cambridge University Press, chapter 4.

Tirole, J. (1988) *The Theory of Industrial Organization*, MIT Press.

Weber, M. and Camerer, C. (1987) 'Recent Developments in Modelling Preferences under Risk', *OR Spectrum*, 9, 129–51.

Wilde, L. L. (1986) 'Consumer Behavior under Imperfect Information: A Review of Psychological and Marketing Research as it Relates to Economic Theory', in Green, L. and Kagel, J. H. (eds), *Advances in Behavioral Economics*, vol. 1, Ablex.

Williams, A. W. (1987) 'The Formation of Price Forecasts in Experimental Markets', *Journal of Money, Credit and Banking*, 19, 1–18.

Name Index

Allais, M. 41, 71, 72–5
Ames, R. E. *see* Marwell, G.
Andreoni, J. 174, 178
Ansic, D. 129, 139–41
Appleby, L. 84

Banks, J. S. 174
Battalio, R. C. 89, 91–2, 93, 143, 218
Bergman, B. R. 129
Bernasconi, M. 83–4
Binmore, K. 153–4, 158–9, 161, 166–7
Bolle, F. 129
Braunstein, Y. M. 100, 110

Camerer, C. F. 48, 57, 82, 86, 87, 89–91, 93, 214
Chamberlin, E. H. 203
Chammah, A. M. 162
Chew, S. H. 87
Collier, K. 216
Cooper, R. W. 164–6
Coppinger, V. M. 193
Coursey, D. L. 207–8
Cox, J. C. 110, 193–5
Currim, I. S. 87

Dardanoni, V. 121, 126
Dasgupta, P. 158–9
de Finetti, B. 72–5
Dekel, E. 42
Di Cagno, D. 55, 57, 59
Dwyer, G. P. 129, 143
Dyer, D. 197

Ellsberg, D. 82
EXEC 20, 21, 93, 139, 171, 208

Forsythe, R. 204–5, 209 n.
Friedman, D. 205

Fudenberg, D. 156, 171, 227

Galiani, F. 215
Goodfellow, J. 215
Green, L. 143–4
Grether, D. M. 203–4, 219
Gul, F. 47, 70
Guth, W. 166, 167

Hagen, O. 72, 76–7
Hall, R. E. 112–13, 116, 120
Hammond, P. J. 52
Harless, D. W. 88–9, 90
Harrison, G. W. 110, 129, 141, 145–6, 179 n., 195–6, 198, 205, 209 n., 226
Hey, J. D. 56, 57, 59, 98, 100, 110, 116, 118, 121, 126, 130, 133, 134, 137, 224, 228
Hoffman, E. 216–17
Holt, C. A. 85–6, 189, 224
Hong, J. T. 203–4

Isaac, R. M. 168–71, 173–4, 201

Joyce, P. 202
Judge, G. G. 7, 13

Kagel, J. H. 143–5, 189, 196–8, 209 n.
Kahneman, D. 47–8, 71, 78–82
Karni, E. 51, 85
Keasey, K. 27, 143
Kim, O. 172–3
Kogut, C. A. 110
Kunreuther, H. 214

Larsson, S. 77–8, 82–3
Lave, L. B. 162
Levin, D. 196–8, 209 n.

237

Subject Index